AMERICAN PREJUDICE

With Liberty and Justice for Some

AMERICAN PREJUDICE

With Liberty and Justice for Some

RICHARD H. ROPERS, Ph. D.
AND
DAN J. PENCE, Ph. D.

 INSIGHT BOOKS

PLENUM PRESS • NEW YORK AND LONDON

Library of Congress Cataloging-in-Publication Data

Ropers, Richard H.
    American prejudice : with liberty and justice for some / Richard
H. Ropers and Dan J. Pence.
        p.   cm.
    Includes bibliographical references and index.
    ISBN 0-306-44946-3
    1. Racism--United States. 2. Prejudices--United States.
3. United States--Race relations.   I. Pence, Dan J. II. Title.
E184.A1R67 1995
305.8'00973--dc20   95-5887
                                                            CIP

ISBN 0-306-44946-3

© 1995 Plenum Press
A Division of Plenum Publishing Corporation
233 Spring Street, New York, N.Y. 10013-1578

10 9 8 7 6 5 4 3 2 1

An Insight Book

Printed in the United States of America

Foreword

American Prejudice exposes the rationalizations for racism and other forms of prejudice and bias in American society. But before discussing racial prejudices or biases, the initial questions should be: How is the term *race* being used and what is meant by its use? Also, how impartial is the reference to *race*? Is there a negative attitude implied concerning other abilities or does *race* refer only to external physical appearances? Frequently, *race* is used in context with social problems created by one or another group of people, as when the news media discuss "race riots." In this situation there is often a negative implication in the reference to race, which involves such qualitative aspects as mental and/or physical abilities. The more impartial use of *race* is the separation of world populations into three or more groupings usually based on skin color, hair and eye color, and sometimes eye shape. This latter use of *race* is most often encountered on application forms. There, a person chooses from a list of categories and places himself or herself in that race.

Physical anthropologists have described and divided the world's populations into races since the 1800s, although humans have grouped each other for centuries as part of an "in-group" or "out-group" recognition. There are physical, genetic differences between peoples today, but here *race* describes the physical appearances of people based on their external traits. Color is the major dividing characteristic used in describing races, as well as the colors of hair and eyes, which are directly related to the amount of melanin in the layers beneath the outer protective surface of the skin, hair, or eyes. Other genetic modifying factors are also present and can interact with melanin.

Determining race is difficult because of the long years of ongoing genetic admixture. Assessing race or ethnic group in skeletal remains poses even more problems. Nasal bone measurements differentiate between whites and blacks or between Native Americans and whites. These measurements cannot, however, separate one group of Europeans from another, or Native Americans from blacks, or Chinese from Indonesians.

A new technique theoretically differentiates black from white skeletal remains by the measurement of the midshaft of the thighbone. The statement "Race is only skin deep" is true, at least for present researchers in the field of skeletal identification.

Today, skin color ranges from "white" or flesh-colored (notice that white skin is named *flesh-colored*) through light brown or tan, to darker browns, the darkest brown being "black." The peoples of Africa south of the Sahara and those of Melanesia in the Pacific Islands generally have dark brown skin colors, while the Bushmen and Hottentots in southwest Africa have light brown skin color. Australian aborigines, while frequently described as "black," have a broad range of skin tones.

The rest of the world's populations vary in skin color. Eastern Indians have darker to lighter brown colors; those of a higher caste may have lighter colored skin, but not always. Native Americans in both North and South America generally have brown skin, but not "red" skin. Europeans tend to have the lightest skin colors, but they also range from light to dark skin depending on the country and its history of invasions and conquests.

If skin color creates problems in differentiating living races, so does hair color. Hair color ranges from red or auburn shades, through blond, to brown and black. Most of the world's people have dark brown or black hair with the exception of Australian aborigines and Euro-Americans, or Europeans, among whom blond or red hair occurs.

Hair shape and amount are also used to classify people. Head hair can be straight, wavy, curly, frizzy (tightly curled), or peppercorn. The latter is so tightly curled or coiled that the scalp shown in the spaces between the curls is head or body hair.

Body hair can be profuse or almost absent. Europeans, or those with European genes, also have more body hair, as do the Australian aborigines and the indigenous inhabitants of Japan. Asians and Africans have almost no body hair, and the peoples of India and the Pacific Islands vary, but both have some beard and/or body hair.

Minor traits, such as fullness or thinness of lips, are used to separate peoples into races. Africans have the fullest lips; Europeans and Native Americans the thinnest. The rest of the world's populations show neither extreme. Eyelids that are smoother appearing are seen among Asians and some Native Americans, giving their eyes a somewhat slanted look. The Mongoloid spot, a small, irregular cluster of melanin at the base of the spine, about the size of a quarter, is a trait seen only in Asian or Native American newborns; it disappears around age three to five. The Mongoloid spot is under genetic control and is a "marker trait" that indicates Asian or Native American genetic influence.

What is important about all of these similarities and differences is that the physical or genetically controlled differences in peoples are actually rather small, except for those of color and hair distribution. The color traits, especially skin color and hair color, as well as hair shape and its distribution, are the characteristics that biased individuals use in their description of races. Of course, these are the most obvious, visible, and easily used means to differentiate groups. It is unlikely that racial prejudice could develop based on such traits as a higher frequency of eyefolds, nose form, or shovel-shaped incisors. Color, especially skin color, is immediately recognizable and has been used for years to denigrate those with darker skins.

As an aside, the melanin in individuals with darker skin protects them, as they are less likely to develop skin cancers than individuals with light skin and are less bothered by insect bites, according to dermatologists. Some light-skinned persons purposely darken their skin by "tanning" through sun exposure. This is puzzling. Why darken your skin if lighter skin color gives higher status?

Biases occur among all humans. What one group considers beauty another group does not. These biases are learned from childhood, are difficult to "unlearn," and are carried from the mild to the extreme by peoples in some cultures who give higher status to those with particular bodily traits. Some people alter the head shapes of their children, since flattened backs or fronts of the head are considered elegant in some cultures. Tattooing or scarification, both of which give higher status to individuals who have endured the pain of acquiring these "improvements," is also practiced. There are also the "beauty contests" that occur in many towns in the United States, as well as elsewhere in European admixed (culturally not physically) areas. A number of years ago in the *Singapore Times* an article said that Euro-American women always won the contests because they had long legs. Asian women never won because they had short legs, the result of working in the rice paddies!

The problems concerning race are not the concept itself, the way different peoples appear, or the number of different races into which humans can be divided. They are rather what individuals of a particular race consider themselves, and the way they view their neighbors or peoples of a different race. Hitler and his colleagues proclaimed the Germans, especially the Nazis, the "Master Race," which was characterized by blond hair, blue eyes, and light skin. How could anyone believe Hitler would view himself in the mirror and accept such a fiction? There is no factual basis to the assumptions of many Germans prior to and even after World War II that these so-called racial traits have any value. Unfortunately, when people discuss race they seem to accept completely the beliefs that were firmly instilled in childhood—many of which are mythical.

Racial prejudice, especially in the United States, is directed toward Africans, Asians, or others such as Mexicans. Most people denigrated by prejudicial viewpoints are actually admixtures of at least two or more "races." A biased racial attitude seems to arise most often among Euro-Americans. Such biases are not uncommon when people talk about the indigenous inhabitants of the Americas, the Native Americans, whose lands Europeans invaded, but prejudices of this type also occur outside the United States. They occur among Europeans with regard to Asians, Africans, and Southeast Asians, who, for example, were the indigenous inhabitants of the countries the Europeans "conquered" and colonized.

Prejudice is not limited to race; it also occurs when one group differs from another in religious or political views. This is currently happening in the country once known as Yugoslavia. Sarajevo is a prime example of the barbarous treatment of humans by humans—and yet these are all the same people, their differences being religious or linguistic, not racial. There are no observable physical changes between Bosnians and Serbians, so how does one tell an enemy from a friend?

People in particular countries that are delineated by national borders and are relatively stable over time will appear more physically similar than groups that have more outside contact through immigration. This physical similarity can be seen in such self-isolated religious communities as the Mennonites, where the women can only marry within the group. The men may, in addition to their official wife, have another "wife" outside the group. These other women are not acknowledged, of course, within the group, nor are their children accepted within the religious community.

Physical similarities help define "racial classifications" and range from those seen on forms for admission to a university to the more complex ones for government jobs, or on those used by physical anthropologists. The choices at one university are black, white, Asian, Native American, and Mexican. What do people from India mark down, or Polynesians from Easter Island? Many forms use the term *Caucasoid*, instead of white, meaning people whose parents or ancestors, or themselves, immigrated from Europe (including western Russia), North Africa, and, today, the

United States and Canada (for the most part). These racial selections usually do not include terms for Pygmies (not that very many of these are registering at that university), Bushmen-Hottentots, or even Australian aborigines (many of whom attend universities), let alone differentiating between the dark-skinned people of New Guinea and adjacent islands in Melanesia, and the Africans. Black is black, whether the individual is an admixed African American, an Australian aborigine, or a Melanesian.

As one professor stated bluntly, the major problem in attempting to classify humans is that it involves "a discussion of man, embracing women." This is more truth than fiction, especially considering the ongoing exploration and trade conducted by various peoples throughout recorded history. Today there are no "pure races." People talk about being Italian or Spanish, English or Irish, but these are political nationalities and ignore the worldwide genetic admixture that has occurred. People forget their own history and the movements of armies and ships.

Let us briefly examine the impact ships and armies directed by men had on "races." Presumably, ships sailed from Europe and other places to every part of the Old World; for Europeans, lastly the New World. Some of the results of that travel were the Egyptians and "black" pharaohs because of their contacts with African groups to the south. The Arabs traveled into Southeast Asia and persuaded some Malaysians to move to Madagascar; their admixed descendants are called the Malagasy. The Arabs traded with India and Southeast Asia, including the islands of Borneo, Sumatra, Celebes, and the Philippines. Arab influence can be seen in the prevalence of the Muslim religion in these areas.

Then there were the various Crusades through Europe to save the Holy Land. Marco Polo visited China and Columbus discovered the West Indies, and as a result Europeans, Asians, and Africans eventually occupied the "New World." The implications of exploration, or of armies moving through a land in conquest, or even of casual contacts with neighboring peoples result in admixture. There are no "pure" races, and humans today are the evidence of innumerable genetic exchanges, which are still ongoing.

So why this quick summary of peoples exploring and traveling? To demonstrate that the admixture considered unique from World War II, the Korean, and the Vietnam wars is actually a continuation of contacts that have occurred historically, through trading expeditions, warfare, and conquests. Some people worry about the racial admixture resulting from these recent wars, but this type of exchange, as just discussed briefly, has been a factor among human groups for centuries. American and European males have fought in the South Pacific, Japan, Korea, and Vietnam, among other places. Their resulting offspring defy simple racial classification. For example, an anthropology student doing research found several children in Las Vegas schools whose mothers were Japanese and whose fathers were "blacks" who had been stationed in Japan. Into what racial classification do they fall?

Another intent of the previous discussion on racial contacts and exploration is to demonstrate that there are no so-called pure races. Hitler assumed and stated there were in the 1930s and 1940s—and many Europeans and Euro-Americans believe this today. There were some more isolated groups, such as the Australian aborigines, but even they traded with New Guinea peoples, who traded with other Melanesians. Also, the Native Americans, through the Aleutians (originally inhabitants of Japan) and the Inuit, had contact with the peoples of Siberia.

Admixture also occurs when armies enter and dominate a state or country. After the Germans invaded adjacent countries, some European women were impregnated by rape or an affair. One European woman in a classroom assured students that women deliberately aborted the fetuses. She also claimed the same for European women who were impregnated by the invading Mongol armies, which reached the gates of Paris and dominated eastern Europe. Regarding the Germans, there is no evidence, but the relative frequency of Mongoloid spots, a small cluster of melanin at the base of the spine, among some Europeans is evidence that not all women killed the children conceived with the Mongols.

This introduces a more significant question: What is a human race to the average individual? Certainly not the descriptions and delineations presented in this Foreword. Are human races, as in dog breeding, only maintained by mating individuals within the same race or "breed"? Human races *may* have developed much earlier in history, when groups were smaller and more isolated. Limiting the size of a people can lead to inbreeding, as will cultural marriage patterns. In many groups, for example, a man married his father's sister's daughter, or his mother's brother's daughter. The key word is *marry*, which has reference to an official ceremony but may or may not have relevance to reproductive activities leading to the birth of offspring.

Unfortunately, eliminating racial terms or leaving out questions of race on various forms is not going to eliminate prejudice. Educating people about the absurdity of using the term *race*, especially in a world with ongoing genetic admixtures, may help. We must also teach that there is no base for prejudice related to skin, hair, or eye color. Today, skin can be lightened or darkened; hair can be dyed and straightened; and colored lenses can be used to alter eye color. However, perhaps the past, present, and future admixing and the education about the similarities between peoples may help understanding. Meeting and working with individuals from various countries through exchange programs, for example, can also help create understanding that the colors of skin, hair, or eyes and the shape of the hair or the lack of it and the many other physical traits discussed here have nothing to do with the quality of the individuals who may, or may not, have these characteristics.

Sheilagh Brooks, Ph.D.

Professor Emeritus
Department of Anthropology
University of Nevada
Las Vegas, Nevada

Acknowledgments

This book is an attempt to alert Americans to the pervasiveness and destructiveness of prejudice in American society. In trying to show broader connections to what often seem to be isolated acts of discrimination and hate, we hope to add a small part to the struggle to make this a more equal and just world.

Several students at Southern Utah University provided invaluable research and logistical support. Chief among these were Suzanne Taunton and Kisha Gill, who cheerfully did some of our work before they did their own. Their intelligence and wit were greatly appreciated. Others providing help were Leigh Ann Oman, Susan Berge, Darcy Osborn, and Maretta Brown.

The Department of Social Sciences, Southern Utah University, provided facilities and additional logistical support. The department staff also provided continual and cheerful support, particularly Debbie Robinson, Dianne Werber, and Sharrisa Turnbaugh, and a degree of tolerance that made our year easier.

Professors Eleanor Hubbard and Donald Yates contributed substantively: Chapter 8 was written by Dr. Hubbard and Chapters 7 and 10 were contributed by Dr. Yates. Sage Publications gladly allowed us to reprint part of the article "Eight Bullets: A Survivor's Story."

Each of us has our own personal acknowledgment to make. First, Richard Ropers would like to thank Frank Darmstadt, editor

of Insight Books, for suggesting the idea for this book and inviting
Dan and me to write it. My son, Ryan, endured me once again
through one of my projects, and others dear to my heart, especially Brenda Benally, helped me along.

—R.R.

The writing and production of this book would not have been
possible without the efforts, interest, support, and contributions
of my longtime companion and lover, Jennifer Geerlings. She
endured my tantrums, bad jokes, and touchiness. She also served
as lead copyeditor for several chapters of this book and was a
constant sounding board for most of my ideas and directions. She
is a better sociologist than I.

Not only did my parents, Margaret and Bob Pence, offer
continuous support, but my mother even spotted some of the
newspaper articles used in this book. I offer a special thanks for
the love of my best friend, Steve Susoeff, and the friendship of
Curtis Loyd, who helped bring some color to southern Utah. And
finally, I need to acknowledge the birth of our child midway
through this project. I dedicate this work to you, Dylan Rose
Pence-Geerlings, in the hope that when you are old enough to
read, this will seem like ancient and outdated history.

—D.P.

Contents

Introduction

As we were completing this book in April 1994, terrorists in South Africa killed 19 people in two bomb explosions on the eve of that country's first multiracial democratic elections. In Rwanda, Africa, as many as 500,000 people were murdered in a national genocide between majority Hutu and minority Tutsi ethnic groups. In Bosnia, Christian Serbs continued their "ethnic cleansing" by bombing and slaughtering Muslim civilians in the town of Gorazde despite UN and U.S. threats to intervene.

These foreign events may seem distant and alien to most Americans, but U.S. history is also bloodstained from racial, ethnic, social-class, and cultural conflicts. It is critical not only to compare U.S. history with the events in other nations; it is also imperative that Americans see how their past and present are inextricably entwined.

When Europeans arrived to stay in North America in the fifteenth century, there were literally thousands of different native tribes and millions of Native Americans who had lived on the continent for perhaps as long as forty thousand years. Yet, by the start of the twentieth century, there were only approximately 250,000 Native Americans left alive. America was "ethnically cleansed."

Political scientist Andrew Bell-Fialkoff (1993) defined *ethnic cleansing* as the "expulsion of an 'undesirable' population from a

1

given territory due to religious or ethnic discrimination, political or strategic considerations, or a combination of these." He argues, "Under this definition, then, the slow dispersal and annihilation of North America's indigenous population was indeed ethnic cleansing" (p. 110).

Though stretching Bell-Fialkoff's definition, America's treatment of African Americans could also be examined as ethnic cleansing. Millions were dispersed, not out of a territory but into one, and then isolated and segregated. Millions more were annihilated, either in transport from Africa, as slaves in the South, or today, as continuing victims of prejudice and discrimination. For example, the current mortality rates for young African-American males are higher than in many third-world countries. African Americans and other minorities are overrepresented among America's crime victims, poor, and unemployed. An estimated two million Americans are homeless, the majority of them African American, Latino, and Native American.

Racial and ethnic prejudice and discrimination exist. They are tangible realities that have a tremendous impact on entire groups of people. Their existence and consequences cannot be dismissed; to a large degree they can be described, counted, and measured. But the targets of prejudice and the ideas that justify a system of inequality are something different.

In the Foreword, Sheilagh Brooks asks the rhetorical question: What are races? This and similar questions such as "What are social classes?" point at one of this book's intellectual underpinnings. Part of the book's conceptual glue is that the answer to these sorts of questions is social in nature. By this we mean that exactly who is classified as "African American" or "Latino" or what standards describe someone as "middle class" are determined, or "constructed," by each particular society. We tend to see "race" and "class" as fixed—unchanging and objective—but when examining U.S. history and making contemporary international comparisons, we find that answers to these questions are very fluid. There are *enormous* differences in how terms such as *race* and *social class* are defined or constructed.

Though the groups themselves change, what does not change, either historically or internationally, is that *some* groups are targets of prejudice and hatred and are subjected to discrimination and violence. Also unchanging is that *some* groups have an excessive amount of power and resources, though, again, *which* groups have power changes. A final aspect that does not change is that groups with power and wealth continually try to legitimize their own control and influence. In the United States the currently dominant WASP (white, Anglo-Saxon, Protestant) group maintains power because it has successfully established a belief that the unequal distribution of power, wealth, and prestige is "natural" and "morally correct."

Through vigilance and constant struggle, what can be changed is both a culture's ideology *and* the inequality it justifies. For example, in 1994, Nelson Mandela and the African National Congress took political control in South Africa, demonstrating that once-oppressed groups can gain power.

ORIENTATION OF THIS BOOK

Part of this book's orientation can be described as a social constructionist perspective. We believe that a society's belief system has an enormous impact and influence on how a society divides itself into groups and how it distributes important resources. Who constitutes social groups, such as social class, race, gender, and sexual orientation, and what are the consequences of being categorized into these groups have been "constructed" within America's ideology. Those with economic, political, and social power invariably have the influence to establish social definitions. They not only have a huge interest in maintaining inequalities within the status quo, and thus keeping their power, but also need to maintain the belief system that allows inequality, prejudice, and discrimination to appear "just" and "fair."

One particular strategy used by those with extensive economic, political, and social power is referred to as *blaming the victim.* For example, blaming those who are poor, homeless, or on public assistance for their circumstances promotes the myth that the U.S. economic system is based on a process of individual merit, where jobs and promotions are "earned" and where a person's individual talents and abilities are "rewarded." Thus, by social definition, anyone who is poor or homeless lacks the talents and abilities necessary to succeed. Failure to be economically successful becomes the "fault" of the poor or those on welfare. They have been socially defined as lacking the qualities, such as intelligence, ambition, and desire, that "successful" people possess; prejudice and discrimination play no role. In America's economic arena, this ideological justification hides job discrimination against *groups* of people, such as those identified by class, race, gender, or sexual orientation, and keeps alive destructive social stereotypes.

We could apply the blame-the-victim scenario to other groups who experience widespread prejudice and discrimination and the stereotypes that accompany their victimization: African Americans are lazy and want to live on welfare; women who have been raped or sexually harassed have, in some ways, "asked for it"; gays and lesbians should simply stop choosing to be homosexual. What is important to realize is that a vicious circle emerges: Groups are denied equal access to social rewards, even to the point of being without food and shelter; those with power and wealth define this unequal system as "morally right"; and continued discrimination appears justified based on the ability of powerful groups to manipulate and control the definitions of what is "natural" and "morally right."

The second major orientation we use is a conflict perspective. There is constant struggle and competition for the things that sustain life, both materially, such as food and shelter, and nonmaterially, such as power and prestige. And these conflicts divide people and often generate many types of conflict, including social, political, religious, racial, ethnic, generational, gender, and cultural forms of conflict.

This book does not cover the standard issue of race or other group relations. We do not necessarily think race relations, for example, will get better or that prejudice, discrimination, hatred, and violence are going away soon in the United States or anywhere else. We cannot and do not offer a grand plan for harmony and social stability. However, we believe that as long as some children go to bed hungry, as long as some do not have a place to sleep at night, and as long as some cop or other representative of the power elite and status quo abuses their authority, people will struggle and fight for a better world. Justice is not simply an end result; it is a process, a movement, a way of living every day. We, the authors, hope this book will contribute to this process.

Although we are professional social scientists and we refer to many formal research studies, including our own, this book is written in a more popular style than that required of social science textbooks and incorporates what some might consider less-than-traditional types of data. Consequently, the "methodology" of this book offers a wide range, including standard survey techniques and statistical analyses, unobtrusive measures and participant observation, case studies, personal interviews, and content analysis.

For us, social science is not just what we do for a living; it is, in the tradition of C. Wright Mills, a vision—a way of comprehending the world around us. Social science exists to solve social problems, to help make the world a better place. Social science does not exist just for intellectual titillation or to fulfill career goals. Its primary mission has been and should continue to be to help establish a world of greater social well-being. We firmly believe that a solid foundation for this greater well-being will come through social justice and human equality.

Mills (1959) felt that to understand human behavior and the world around us, we need to understand the constant interplay between "personal troubles" and "public issues." Prejudice and discrimination are felt at intensely personal levels. They are also powerful and perplexing social issues. In this book, we move between the broad public dilemmas of racism and sexism, for example, and at the same time highlight the more personal consequences of these major themes in American society.

Chapter 1 introduces four social groups that are major targets of prejudice, based on social class, race, gender, and sexual orientation. We focus on race and racial groups also because racism is the defining example of prejudice in the United States, past and present.

Chapter 2 addresses the question of why prejudice is so widespread, both in the United States and around the world. We also explore the interrelationships of three levels of prejudice: cultural, institutional, and personal. Chapter 3 examines the intellectual roots of racism and prejudice. Unfortunately, the racist and prejudicial beliefs of many ordinary citizens are derived from the theories of university intellectuals.

The social and economic foundations of racial and cultural conflict are exposed in Chapter 4. Focusing on the family and the school, Chapter 5 describes how American children and students are *taught* to be prejudiced and *learn* how to discriminate against groups of fellow citizens. This chapter on socialization also documents how children who are targets of prejudice often come to believe destructive messages about their own group.

Chapter 6 offers a more intimate look at prejudice. With very little commentary on our part, people speak about their own experiences of prejudice.

Moving from individual stories to societal issues, Chapter 7, contributed by Donald Yates, illustrates how the U.S. criminal justice system reflects prejudice against the country's most vulnerable groups. Examining crime, delinquency, and drugs, this chapter shows how historical prejudices continue to operate in today's system.

Contributed by Eleanor Hubbard, Chapter 8 looks at prejudice and discrimination against women and girls in contemporary America. Repeating Mills's theme of the interplay between the personal and the public, this chapter connects the public issue of sexism with the personal trouble of intimate violence.

Shifting again to a broader perspective, Chapter 9, also contributed by Donald Yates, reviews the persistence of racism and prejudice in the 1990s. Chapter 10 traces the historical influences of prejudice on the contemporary political scene, contrasting the Reagan–Bush era with the start of the Clinton years.

Chapter 11 talks about the realities of America's changing face. Shortly after moving into the twenty-first century, the United States will cease to be an Anglo-majority nation. We also discuss some of the limits and possibilities in our approach to combating American prejudice and discrimination.

Chapter 1

Prejudice and Discrimination

We have all been burned by the torch of prejudice, such as school-yard taunts about our hair, skin, teeth, clothes, or father's occupation, or the status of our family. No one has escaped this prejudice. But the depressing reality is that some people suffer a lifetime of prejudice and hostility simply because the *groups* to which they belong are different from what is considered "normal." The following four stories are presented as a graphic illustration of what prejudice *means* on a personal, individual level.

The common thread that binds these four stories is horror, stemming from the humiliation and pain that some inflict on others. But throughout this book, we show that there is a more profound theme—prejudice—that motivates such horrendous and desperate situations. We also show that the prejudice that creates these despicable experiences is *not* limited to perverse or "sick" individuals. Rather, the prejudices are rooted in the fundamental ways American society is structured, that is, in the inequities found in all its institutions and its belief system that justify such widespread discrimination.

The targets of prejudice and hate are not randomly selected. The four stories that follow illustrate a very disturbing aspect of prejudice and hate: It is often *groups* of people who are the targets and victims of hate. This book focuses on four groups in American society often targeted by acts of prejudice and discrimination: groups based on social class, race, gender, and sexual orientation.

EIGHT BULLETS: A SURVIVOR'S STORY

The first bullet: When the first bullet hit me, my arm exploded. My brain could not make the connections fast enough to realize I had been shot. I saw a lot of blood on the green tarp on which we lay and thought for a split second about earthquakes and volcanoes. But they don't make you bleed. Rebecca knew. She asked me where I had been shot.

The second bullet: When the second bullet hit my neck I started to scream with all my strength. Somehow the second bullet was even more unbelievable than the first.

The third bullet: The third bullet came and I now know hit the other side of my neck. By then I had lost track of what was happening or where we were except that I was in great danger and it was not stopping.

The fourth bullet: I now know a fourth bullet hit me in the face. Rebecca told me to get down, close to the ground.

The fifth bullet: The fifth bullet hit the top of my head. Rebecca saw that even lying flat I was vulnerable and told me to run behind a tree.

The sixth bullet: The sixth bullet hit Rebecca in the back of her head as she rose to run for the tree.

The seventh bullet: The seventh bullet hit Rebecca's back as she ran. It exploded her liver and caused her to die.

The eighth bullet missed.

He shot us because he identified us as lesbians. He was a stranger with whom we had no connection.

He shot us and left us for dead. (Brenner, 1992, p. 11)

HEALTH-CARE STRUGGLE SEEN FROM THE FRONT

At 10:30 A.M., the emergency room waiting area at Harbor-UCLA Medical Center is full. Signs on the wall warn:

"Patients are seen according to the severity of illness or injury and not necessarily in the order of arrival."

Six hours will pass before many see a doctor. They're lucky. Had they come at 10 P.M., the sun would be up before they'd get past the bullet-proof registration area.

Earaches, alcohol withdrawal and assorted pains brought them here. One in five doesn't require emergency care, but knows of nowhere else to go. Welcome to the front lines of the health care crisis.

In this room, where sick kids doze in their parents' laps and adults wince with pain as they squirm in hard plastic chairs under a silent TV, is a microcosm of what's ailing the nation's health-care system:

Uninsured patients and a lack of preventative care that result in expensive, can't-wait treatments and hospitalization for conditions that could have been handled earlier on a cheaper outpatient basis. (Keen, 1993, pp. A1, A2)

TOURIST SET ABLAZE IN NEW YEAR'S DAY ATTACK

Set ablaze with gasoline in a vicious racial attack, Christopher Wilson stumbled along a country road screaming for help. Omer and Kathy Surface were sitting down to breakfast when they heard his cries New Year's Day.

"It was a shock that one human would do that to another," recalls Kathy Surface, who called for help while her husband soothed the scalded black man with a garden hose. "He was waving his arms and yelling, 'Help me. Help me. I'm burned.' "

Burned over 40% of his body, Wilson underwent a three-hour skin graft this week—the first of several likely operations.

Said Enid Plummer, Wilson's mother: "I want a picture taken so people can see his pain. I want people to see how ugly racism is." (Sharp, 1993a, p. A6)

Christopher Wilson, abducted and set on fire with gasoline, was in pain so great he begged a rescuer to shoot him. Taunted with "Die, nigger, die," Wilson survived. A note found nearby read "one les (*sic*) nigger more to go" and is signed "KKK."

Charged with attempted murder, robbery, and kidnapping:

- Mark Kohut, 26, who has a swastika tattooed on his hand.
- Charles Roark, 33. Police found a cache of guns and a Confederate flag in his trailer. (Sharp, 1993b, p. A5)

THE "SHE ASKED FOR IT" DEFENSE

On March 1, 1989, a retarded young woman followed a high school football star to the basement of a Glen Ridge [New Jersey] house with the promise of a date. There, 13 high school athletes gathered. Six left.

Seven others stayed, and while the 17-year-old, who has an I.Q. of 64 and is described as operating on the mental level of an eight-year-old, lay on a couch, they told her to disrobe. What followed was an afternoon of sexual activity that ended after she was told to spread her legs so that several of them could penetrate her vagina with a baseball bat, a stick, and a broom as others urged "go further."
... The case has bitterly divided the community of Glen Ridge. . . . Many see the case as a morality play pitting high school heroes against a social outcast. Some blame the heroes. Some blame the outcast.

Stopping just short of depicting the young men themselves as victims, [defense lawyer Michael Querques] drew a picture of a dangerous seductress.

"She is a full-breasted young lady, a full-blown young lady." Boys, he argued, "will be boys. Pranksters. Foolarounds. . . . Are men going to forget, 'Hey, I got a girl who is loose, do you want to join me?' "

"She did it." Mr. Querques told the judge. . . . "She knew what she was doing. She did it with a smile on her face." (Manegold, 1993, p. B1)

Virtually every known society, past and present, makes distinctions among its members; that is, every society arbitrarily creates ways to classify its members into groups, for example, according to sex (female/male), status (high/low), and age (young/old). Cultures also universally make distinctions between their members and those of other societies. For example, the Navajo refer to themselves as the Din'e, which loosely means "the people." A rough translation of the name *Kiowa* is "real or principal people." The Jews are the "chosen people," and they and the Mormons divide all humankind into themselves and "gentiles."

"Culture" creates an enormous number of human groups. It is conservatively estimated, for example, that at the time of European "discovery," the North American continent alone contained over seven hundred different languages, and most represented a separate and distinct culture. Even in 1994, after many indigenous cultures had been extinguished by white "civilization," 541 *different* American Indian tribes were represented at a meeting with President Clinton.

In addition to culture, we group people according to social class, race and ethnicity, gender, sexual orientation, age, religion, and geographical location, to mention only a few such classifications. By any measure, we are enormously diverse from each other.

Rather than celebrate this phenomenal diversity as a source of strength and potential knowledge, human societies too frequently use physical, sexual, cultural, and even geographical differences to separate and value unequally groups of people who share certain characteristics "socially defined" as "different." We know that these characteristics are socially defined because every culture has different ways not only of dividing its members, but also of valuing its different groupings. The unequal social value of these groups and their differences have led to fear, hostility, prejudice, discrimination, hatred, and outright violence against them.

WHAT ARE PREJUDICE AND DISCRIMINATION?

American society shares this dismal human trait of valuing groups of people unequally. According to research, the American group most highly valued is traditionally defined as white, straight, upper-middle-class, college-educated Protestant males, generally referred to as WASPs, that is, white, Anglo-Saxon Protestants (Rokeach, 1968; Rossides, 1976). Indeed, much of the fear and hatred in contemporary American society is aimed at *groups* of people who have been socially defined as "different" from the majority of Americans. Social scientists describe these attitudes of bias, bigotry, and hatred as *prejudice,* that is, irrational, negative feelings about *groups of people and their members* based on social stereotypes.

Crimes and violence against groups are examples of *discrimination,* which is generally defined as unequal and unfair treatment of group members. While *prejudice* refers to attitudes, *discrimination* is a behavior, or an action.

As a nation of immigrants, the United States has always been marked by phenomenal diversity, a land of strangers who are different because they do not share a common culture. Lacking a common heritage or background, we are more at the mercy of the prejudices and fears that class, racial, and cultural differences seem to provoke. Prejudice and discrimination threaten our tolerance of diversity, which is the very fabric of America's pluralist society. According to Jess Hordes of the Anti-Defamation League, "Crimes of hate tear at the fragile bonds that hold together America's diverse society" (Mauro, 1993, p. 7A).

"Hate crimes"—that is, attacks on Americans because of their social class, race, ethnic origin, or sexual orientation—have increased at such a rate that even the federal government, historically a poor protector of those with little power or influence, has been moved to respond. According to Representative John Conyers (Michigan), who in 1988 introduced the Hate Crimes Statistics Act, "[Hate crimes] are intended to harm their victims and to also to send a message of intimidation and fear to entire communities of people. . . . Hate crimes are extraordinary in nature and require a special governmental response" (Herek and Berrill, 1992, pp. xiii–xiv). The Hate Crimes Act directed the FBI to begin compiling national figures, as shown in Figure 1.1. Though barely 15

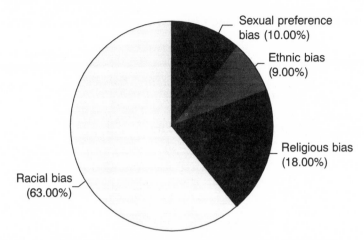

Figure 1.1. Prejudice behind hate crimes, 1992. Source: Federal Bureau of Investigation.

percent of all law enforcement agencies supplied information in 1991, then-FBI Director William Sessions commented, "They give us our first assessment of the nature of crimes motivated by bias in our society" (U.S. Department of Justice, 1993, p. 1).

PREJUDICE AND HATE

There are many ways in which our culture divides its members into groups that are then treated unequally. The most common way of examining this separation in the United States is along the lines of social class, race and ethnicity, and gender. We add sexual orientation because issues of hetero- or homosexuality inflame and provoke an enormous amount of prejudice and violence.

Prejudice Based on Social Class

Most Americans dislike thinking or talking about "social class." Although most realize that class biases exist, an open admission of this could shatter romanticized ideals embedded in the "American dream." One such cherished historical ideal is that "all men are created equal." These magnificent words hide a disturbing reality. Until 1815, only those white males who owned property or paid taxes could vote; *not allowed to vote* were white males who did *not own property; all* women; *all* African Americans, including nonslaves; and *all* Native Americans. In some southern states, the vote was restricted to white males who owned at least one hundred acres of land. The property requirements for those running for elected office were even greater. Thus a social class bias against those Americans without property was applied to one of our most cherished rights: the right to vote. Obviously some men were more equal than others. And social class discrimination is as pervasive today as it was two hundred years ago.

In the early 1800s, noted French social observer Alexis de Tocqueville remarked that Americans were forever bragging about absolute equality in the United States, but in traveling across the nation he found a far different reality. He wrote, "Men living in [America] have many passions, but most of their passions either end in the love of riches or proceed from it. . . . When . . . birth, condition, and profession no longer distinguish men . . . hardly anything but money remains to create strongly marked differences between them" (Nisbet, 1966, p. 187).

If Tocqueville noticed social class differences nearly two hundred years ago, today's United States would be depressingly familiar to him. Most social scientists agree that class biases continue in contemporary U.S. society. Although social class remains difficult to define, personal and family income are usually included.

Income distribution for Americans *appears* constant in Table 1.1, even showing greater income equality developing between

1945 and 1970. However, from 1970 on, the richest 20 percent *increased* their percentage of all income, a fact that the trend is toward greater *inequality*.

This challenges another American ideal, that society provides equal opportunities for all citizens. The working class and the poor continue to receive the least while paying the most—the price they pay for prejudice and discrimination based on their social class. They receive the least health care, have the fewest educational opportunities, and die disproportionately earlier. They are overrepresented in prison populations, among abused children, and as victims of violent crime.

Examples of discrimination based on social class are too easy to find. Poor people with no medical insurance are more likely to suffer from inferior treatment than privately insured patients, and uninsured patients have more than twice the risk of substandard care than privately insured patients (Snider, 1992). And because

Table 1.1. Percent Distribution of Income in the United States, from Highest to Lowest Income Group

Year	Lowest 5th	Second Lowest 5th	Middle		Highest 5th
			5th	5th	
1990	4.6	10.6	16.5	23.7	44.6
1985	4.7	10.9	16.9	24.2	43.3
1980	5.1	11.6	17.5	24.3	41.6
1975	5.4	11.8	17.6	24.1	41.1
1970	5.4	12.2	17.6	23.8	40.9
1965	5.2	12.2	17.8	23.9	40.9
1960	4.8	12.2	17.8	24.0	41.3
1955	4.8	12.2	17.7	23.7	41.6
1950	4.5	12.0	17.4	23.5	42.6
1945	4.6	10.9	16.9	24.2	43.5

Source: *Statistical Abstract of the United States*, 1991, p. 455.

many poor people cannot afford medical insurance, as shown in Figure 1.2, they rarely see a doctor. Consequently, it is estimated that "nearly half the patients waiting in hospital emergency rooms don't need urgent care, but that is the only place they can get treated because they lack health insurance" (Keen, 1993, p. A1).

And while the lower class receive the least, they pay pro-

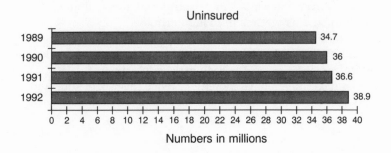

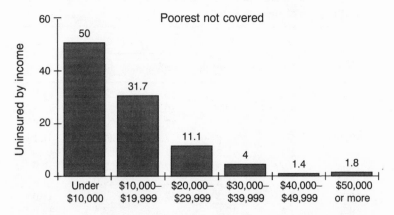

Figure 1.2. Americans without health insurance and those who are uninsured, by income. Copyright 1993, *USA Today*. Reprinted with permission.

portionately more. According to the Federal Reserve's Survey of Consumer Finances, the economic boom of the Reagan years benefited primarily the richest Americans, shown in Figure 1.3. In 1983, the richest *1 percent of all Americans accounted for 31 percent of all private net worth* in the United States; by 1989, that appalling figure had ballooned to 37 percent, a 20 percent increase. According to Harvard economic historian Claudia Goldin,

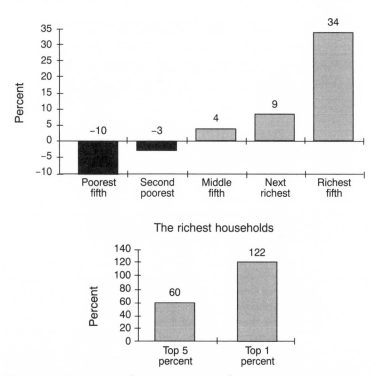

Figure 1.3. Percentage change in average after-tax income, 1977–1988. Source: Congressional Budget Office.

"Inequality is at its highest since the great leveling of wages and wealth during the New Deal and World War II" (Nasar, 1992a, p. 10).

While inequality and discrimination among social classes has remained constant, prejudicial attitudes against poorer Americans have also remained steady. National surveys about U.S. attitudes consistently show the public to be very skeptical of, even hostile toward, those receiving public assistance. According to a 1994 *New York Times*/CBS news poll, 48 percent of Americans felt that most people who receive welfare could get along without it if they tried; 63 percent felt that most welfare recipients did not want to work ("Crime Rivals Economy," 1994, p. A4).

This prejudice bears no relationship to reality. An analysis of U.S. Department of Health and Human Services data revealed the following about those receiving public assistance:

Children, under 14	34.4 percent
Elderly, over 65	18.2
Ill and disabled	4.7
In school, 14 and over	6.6
Total	63.9 percent

Virtually 64 percent of all those on public assistance were unable to work. Of the remaining 36.1 percent, 23.8 already had jobs but were not earning enough to rise above the official poverty level. Of the 12.3 percent who did not work, 10.9 percent were women, the overwhelming majority of whom were at home caring for small children. Thus, approximately 2 percent of all those receiving public assistance were physically or circumstantially able to work (Robertson, 1987, p. 272).

Prejudice Based on Race and Ethnicity

Historically ideas of race and ethnicity hold a central place in prejudices leading to inequality, hostility, and violence. The potential list is endless, but a few examples make the point. In third-century B.C. China, a historian of the Han dynasty described Europeans as barbarians "who greatly resemble monkeys from whom they are descended" (Gossett, 1963, p. 4). A Japanese lawmaker commented in 1993 that Japanese feel "tainted" when they shake hands with an African-American person. Recognizing this was an irrational prejudice, Masao Kokubo admitted, "When you shake hands with someone who is completely black, you feel your hand getting black" ("Blacks Make Japanese," 1993, p. 36). Prejudice based on skin color is irrational and noxious, but such attitudes and treatment are frightening when they turn violent. Again, a few examples highlight what is unspeakable but all too frequent.

Nazi Germany established the prototypical national policy aimed at racial, ethnic, and cultural genocide in its attempt to exterminate world Jewry and other "impure" groups, such as Gypsies, homosexuals, and the handicapped. Not only were Jews made to wear the yellow Star of David during the Holocaust, making them easy public targets of ethnic attack, but special insignia were also attached to some stars signifying "Race Defiler," for those Jews who had had sex with an Aryan (*Pink Triangles,* 1985).

Between 1992 and 1994 the world was horrified by the claims of "ethnic cleansing" that emerged in the Bosnian civil war. While such horror was immensely justified, we Americans need to be reminded of our own history, lest we become too arrogant and self-righteous. After all, how many members remain of the Narraganset, Panamint, Piegan, Micmac, Miami, Mandan, or Omaha tribes? When Columbus "discovered" North America, native peoples had had tens of thousands of years of history, and had a staggering diversity in language, culture, custom, and tribal organization. Yet few comtemporary Americans have ever heard of the above-named tribes because they were either destroyed or remain in such few numbers as to have faded from our collective memory.

Throughout North America, British, Spanish, French, Portuguese, and American policies toward American Indians also reflected a desire for ethnic cleansing and often bordered on genocide as a means of ensuring ethnic and racial purity (Riga, 1993). In 1755 the following proclamation was issued in Boston regarding the Penobscot Indians:

> (At the desire of) the House of Representatives . . . I (do hereby) require his majesty's subjects of the Province to embrace all opportunities of pursuing, captivating, killing, and destroying all and every of the aforesaid Indians. . . . (The General Court of this Province have voted that a bounty . . . be granted:) For the capture of every male Penobscot Indian above the age of twelve and brought to Boston, fifty pounds. For every scalp of a male Indian above the age aforesaid, brought in as evidence of their being killed as aforesaid, forty pounds. . . . For every scalp of such female Indian or male Indian under the age of twelve years that shall be killed and brought in as evidence of their being killed as aforesaid, twenty pounds. (Robertson, 1987, p. 303)

Examples of American ethnic cleansing are certainly not limited to Anglo treatment of Native Americans. Thousands of Africans were forcibly abducted and enslaved *legally* for 250 years in North America. The consequences of defining this group of people as inherently subhuman continue to plague the United States as we approach the twenty-first century.

A consequence of continuing racial prejudice is the location of minority-owned businesses. The federal government's flagship program for minority businesses awarded $19 billion in contracts from 1988 to 1994, with the overwhelming majority going to firms whose headquarters were located in well-to-do white neighborhoods. One construction company owner reluctantly moved from Benton Harbor, Michigan, where 90 percent of the residents are African American, because the "Small Business Association was reluctant to give me jobs." Now he does business from Northville, a Detroit suburb where half the households make more than $160,000 and 90 percent of the residents are white ("Minorities Get Short End," 1994).

Less obvious consequences are that 56 percent of all African-American babies are born to single mothers; nearly 50 percent of these children are *born into poverty* (DeParle, 1994). Perhaps even more ominous for these babies are results from a study of prenatal care. Among the women studied, African-American women were 20 percent more likely than whites to report *not* being told to quit smoking, and 30 percent were more likely *not* to be told to quit drinking during pregnancy ("Does Prenatal-Care," 1994).

We are also seeing the reemergence of school segregation, a situation described by former Chief Justice Earl Warren as "inherently unequal." According to the Harvard Project on School Desegregation, 66 percent of African-American students were enrolled in predominantly non-Anglo schools in 1991–1992. This segregation rate is the highest since the late 1960s, when busing first began, and is concentrated in northern states such as New York, Illinois, Michigan, and New Jersey (Henry, 1993).

While the treatment of Native and African Americans often offers the most powerful examples, the history of our republic is littered with gross examples of racial and ethnic prejudice and discrimination. For example, in an attempt to halt immigration of Asians, Slavs, Jews, and other non-Aryans, the 1880s saw the rise of the American Nativist movement, which warned against "mongrelizing" the white race. Specific groups within this movement had their own particular prejudices. The Know-Nothing Party, for example, was instrumental in establishing English literacy tests and poll taxes as requirements for voting. The vicious and violent Ku Klux Klan remains the defining symbol of this movement and of hatred of all non-Anglo groups. During World War II, though white German Americans were not harassed as a group, tens of thousands of Japanese Americans were imprisoned in concentration camps (American history books still call this *internment*), and their property was lost.

Currently, overt racial prejudice and hatred appear to be increasing. For example, anti-Semitic violence has shown a disturbing rise, now accounting for over 15 percent of all hate crimes. In addition, the leadership of the white supremacy movement is now the Church of Jesus Christ Christian, also referred to as the Christian Identity Church. Once dominated by isolated hate groups such as the KKK, American Nazi Party, and Aryan Nations, the white supremacy movement now has a broader, more coherent, Bible-based explanation for its racial hate (Cochran, 1994). An Aryan Nations flyer, shown in Figure 1.4, offers a flavor of its religious justification for racism.

No, the desire to keep one's group ethnically and racially "pure" is neither new nor behind us; it is ahead of us. According to New York Senator Daniel Patrick Moynihan, "The defining mode of conflict in the era ahead is ethnic conflict. It promises to be savage. Get ready for 50 new countries in the world in the next 50 years. Most of them will be born in bloodshed" (Binder and Crossette, 1993).

Moynihan was warning about ethnic conflict outside the United States, but he could be describing our own future as well. Some described the Los Angeles riots following the Rodney King verdict as the opening uprising in the upcoming race war. Consider that over 50 percent of all arrests during the LA violence were Latinos, not African Americans; consider the continuing widespread institutional racism directed at non-Anglos, such as through California's anti-Latino Proposition 187; consider the frustration and rage produced by hundreds of years of racial prejudice and discrimination. Without systemic change, Moynihan's words could describe a coming American nightmare.

Prejudice Based on Gender

Using sex or gender as the basis for prejudice and discrimination also has a remarkable legacy. Among writings influencing Western culture in general and U.S. culture in particular, those of the ancient Greeks and the Bible (both Old and New Testaments) offer some startling comments about the "proper" roles and power of women and men. These prejudicial attitudes have been used for three thousand years to justify continued discrimination

DID YOU KNOW THERE EXISTS A STATE OF WAR AGAINST YOU, WHITEMAN !

1 : : :   DID YOU KNOW THAT THE U.S. CONSTITUTION ESTABLISHED A NATIONAL STATE ONLY FOR THE WHITE RACE?

2 = = =   DID YOU KNOW THAT IN EVERY ONE OF THE SEVERAL STATES CITIZENSHIP APPLIED ONLY TO "FREE WHITES"?

3 = = =   DID YOU KNOW, WHITEMAN, THAT WHILE YOU SLEPT A "BILL OF ATTAINDER" WAS LEVELED AGAINST YOU BY AN OCCUPATIONAL GOVERNMENT?

4 = = =   DID YOU KNOW THAT SINCE 1979, AS A WHITE AMERICAN MALE, YOU ARE NO LONGER CONSIDERED ENTITLED TO THE FULL PRIVILEGES OF CITIZENSHIP?

5 = = =   DID YOU KNOW THAT A "BILL OF ATTAINDER" IS TREASON TO YOUR CONSTITUTION?

6 = = =   DID YOU KNOW THAT "AFFIRMATIVE ACTION GUIDELINES" WERE MADE BY A PANEL CONSISTING OF ONE BLACK FEMALE, ONE MEXICAN MALE, ONE BLACK MALE, ONE WHITE FEMALE, AND ONE WHITE MALE (WHO WAS NOT PRESENT)?

7 = = =   DID YOU KNOW THAT E.E.O.C. COMMISSIONERS STATE: "TAKING BLACKNESS INTO ACCOUNT...MUST MEAN DENYING OPPORTUNITIES TO (WHITE MALES) SOLELY BECAUSE THEY WERE BORN WHITE"?

8 = = =   DID YOU KNOW THAT THE ISRAELI JEWS BRAG THAT THEY OWN 75 U.S. SENATORS AND OVER 425 U.S. CONGRESSMEN?

9 = = =   DID YOU KNOW, WHITEMAN, THAT ONLY TWO PATHS LIE BEFORE YOU ?

SLAVERY AND DEATH OR LIBERTY AND LIFE

CONTACT:

ARYAN   NATIONS

CHURCH OF JESUS CHRIST CHRISTIAN
P.O. BOX 362
HAYDEN LAKE. IDAHO 83835

When the enemy shall come in like a flood, the Spirit of the Lord shall lift up a standard against him.

Isaiah 59:19

Figure 1.4. Aryan Nations flyer: Mixing religion and racism.

against and oppression of women, around the globe and within the United States.

It was Aristotle who claimed "We should regard the female nature as afflicted with a natural defectiveness" (Bem and Bem, 1991). Not long after the Greeks taught prejudice, the ancient Hebrews established their own litany of gender bias. Even today, male Orthodox Jews recite this bias in their daily morning prayer:

> Blessed art thou, oh Lord our God, King of the Universe, that I was not born a gentile. Blessed art thou, oh Lord our God, King of the Universe, that I was not born a slave. Blessed art thou, oh Lord our God, King of the Universe, that I was not born a woman.

This antifemale bias was transmitted to Christianity, not through the teachings of Jesus but from the later writings of Saint Paul and Saint Augustine. It was Saint Paul who proclaimed that women's inferior status was divinely ordained and a part of the "natural" order of things:

> A man . . . is the image of God and reflects God's glory; but woman is the reflection of man's glory . . . and man was not created for the sake of woman, but woman was created for the sake of man. (I Corinthians 1:7–9)

Saint Paul also wrote:

> Wives should regard their husbands as they regard the Lord . . . and as the Church submits to Christ, so should wives submit to their husbands, in everything. (Ephesians 5:22–23)

You might wonder how influential these sorts of writings are on contemporary American society. Aren't these a bit outdated in the sophisticated and politically correct 1990s?

Perhaps, but Pope John Paul II recently announced, "In the name of liberation from male 'domination,' women must not appropriate to themselves male characteristics contrary to their own feminine originality" (*Boulder Daily Camera*, 1988, p. D3). Elder

Boyd Packer, a leader of the Church of Jesus Christ of Latter-Day Saints, one of the fastest growing churches in the world, claimed, "Both the scriptures and the patterns of nature place man as the protector, the provider. By divine decree, men were given the responsibilities of the priesthood" (Scarlet and Stack, 1994, p. A1).

As we saw with racism, once attitudes of prejudice become institutionalized as discrimination, their effects become more damaging and harder to eradicate. For example, by keeping women in an inferior position, our society invites men to discriminate against, abuse, and even murder them at staggering rates. And perhaps most disturbing, this abuse does not wait until adulthood:

> The leers and lurid comments started as soon as Cheltzie Hentz left home in the morning—teasing, foul language, lewd remarks aimed at her and her friends. It continued throughout the day: jokes about her body parts, taunts and demands for sexual acts. It sounds like a textbook case of sexual harassment. But consider this: Cheltzie Hentz was 6 years old. (Lillard, 1993, p. A16)

According to a survey conducted by the American Association of University Women, 34 percent of girls report being sexually harassed before they reach the seventh grade (Manning, 1993, p. A1). Routinely dismissed as mere pranks and "boys-will-be-boys" behavior, this startling statistic gets translated into more deadly figures as girls and boys grow into adults.

Once every 15 seconds in the United States a woman is beaten by her husband or boyfriend. Approximately four million women are battered in the United States every year. One out of every eight women—at least twelve million—has been raped sometime during her life, according to a 1992 government-financed survey. More than 60 percent of these rapes took place before the woman was eighteen, almost one-third before the age of eleven. One in seven women who have been married have been raped by their husbands or ex-husbands. In one-third of these relationships, the rape has been repeated two to twenty times; in another third, the rape has been repeated over twenty times (Johnston, 1992). Even more chilling, if that is possible, the FBI reported that, from 1988 to 1990, 40 percent of all women murdered in the United States were murdered by their intimate partners ("Marriage and Murder," 1990).

There are numerous other, less deadly, examples of continuing sexist attitudes and discrimination against women. For example, women in top-level congressional staff positions earn less than men in the same position. On average, women employed as House of Representatives staffers earn eighty-two cents for every dollar men make; in the Senate, only about eighty cents. "It's a public shame that the Capitol dome operates as a glass ceiling," commented Judith Lichtman, president of the Women's Legal Defense Fund (Brogan, 1993, p. A4). *Glass ceiling* is a term used by the U.S. Department of Labor to describe a barrier that keeps women from advancing into salary brackets and positions usually occupied by men.

Our society considers women inferior to men, and this stance is often justified through "natural" or "moral-religious" excuses. It is not surprising when alarming numbers of women are murdered within the supposed security of intimate relationships. The causes of such astonishing behavior, according to Leslie Wolfe, director of the Center for Women's Policy Studies in Washington, D.C., lie at the core of our society: "It's the assumption that women are supposed to be men's possessions, that men are entitled to women sexually. . . . There's not a single person in this society who grows up without experiencing the notion that women aren't as important as men" (Maples, 1993, p. A1).

Prejudice Based on Sexual Orientation

"Queer bashing" and other forms of discrimination and violence against gays, lesbians, and bisexuals have long been a part of American culture. As with prejudicial attitudes toward women, prejudice and discrimination against gays, lesbians, and bisexuals also tries to locate its rationale in the Bible, though with precious few examples used to justify this prejudice. In the entire Bible, there are only two references that are generally interpreted as referring to homosexuals. The most direct is Leviticus 19:22: "You shall not lie with a male as with a woman; it is an abomination." It is important to see how irrational this sort of justification for hatred is. While the Bible devotes such limited attention to homosexuality, it lavishes four entire verses on the eating of shell fish as an "abomination" (Leviticus 11:9–12). Yet there are no attacks upon shrimp eaters as blasphemous, nor beatings of crab lovers for "violating God's laws."

Laws against sodomy in the American colonies mandated the penalty of death, castration, or mutilation as early as the 1600s (Katz, 1976). Over the years, private citizens have also engaged in antihomosexual discrimination and violence, acts that have often been ignored by police and other public officials. The celebrated Jeffrey Dahmer case illustrates this point. Police officers returned a naked, bloody thirteen-year-old to Dahmer because they thought the boy was gay, and that Dahmer and the boy were merely having a "lover's quarrel." This assumption that the boy was gay—and the horrifying prejudices that went with it—helped doom him to a gruesome and unnecessary death.

When violence is directed against those deemed "different" in American society, the victims are often blamed for their own victimization. For example, after the murder of a gay man in Miami, local newspapers "demanded that homosexuals be punished for tempting 'normals' to commit such deeds" (Taylor, 1982, p. 9). In this hostile and even violent environment, it is hardly surprising that many gays and lesbians choose to remain invisible.

From the Stonewall riots in New York City, which were provoked by a 1969 police raid on the Stonewall bar (a gay bar), emerged the gay liberation movement. Gay activism has increasingly put prejudice and violence against gays and lesbians on the front pages of American newspapers. Nearly 10 percent of hate crimes are committed against homosexuals, a crime that is perhaps as underreported as rape, often for similar reasons. Survey results report that between 60 and 70 percent of all gays and lesbians have been verbally harassed, and that between 12 and 25 percent have been physically assaulted (Berrill, 1992). According to the National Gay and Lesbian Task Force (NGLTF), antihomosexual hate crimes rose 172 percent between 1988 and 1993. According to NGLTF spokesperson Torie Osborn, "We see a direct correlation between right-wing intolerance against us and the rising violence" (Howlett, 1993a, p. 3A).

Although we will refer to various groupings of people throughout this book, "race" and "racism" occupy center stage in discussions of American prejudice and discrimination. Most of the descriptions of and writings about the debilitating "isms" that face our society, such as classism, sexism, and heterosexism, find their historical and intellectual roots in discussions about race and racism. In fact, *racism* is often used as a synonym for *prejudice.*

Because of the centrality of race and racism in considerations of American prejudice, we need to examine the idea of race in the United States.

RACE IN THE UNITED STATES

Because it is one of the most visible, powerful, and violent ways of dividing peoples, social scientists have long considered race one of the greatest concerns confronting the United States. In 1835, Tocqueville's classic *Democracy in America* described how appalled he was by the inequality of African Americans in U.S. society, both slave *and* free. While lauding the United States for its egalitarian sentiments and institutions, he noted that these attitudes were for white society alone. The same person "who is full of humanity toward his fellow creatures when they are at the same time his equals becomes insensible to their afflictions as soon as that equality ceases" (Nisbet, 1966, p. 193).

Ever since the British colonists purchased their first African slaves in 1619, African Americans have lived in a culture of oppression. While the Civil War "freed" the slaves, it did little to change the material conditions of most African Americans. By the 1890s, the acute antebellum image of African Americans' possessing a "gentle, childlike immaturity, clownishness, and laziness" (Turner, Singleton, and Musick, 1984, p. 23) had given way to an undisguised hatred of African Americans. They were vilified as "permanently inferior beings," completely disenfranchised, segregated through codified legal systems, and increasingly lynched and brutalized to be kept in their place (Turner et al., 1984, p. 27).

In 1903, nearly a century after Tocqueville's observations, American sociologist W. E. B. Du Bois again reminded American society of the task it faced. He told the white audience the importance of trying to understand the "strange meaning" of being African American in American society: "This meaning is not without interest to you, Gentle Reader; for the problem of the Twentieth Century is the problem of the color line" (Du Bois, 1961, p. 4).

Race has certainly played a major role in this century. Issues of color have dominated American society since the 1954 Supreme Court ruling *Brown v. Board of Education,* and since Rosa Parks refused to give her seat to a white man on a Birmingham bus in 1955: school integration in the 1950s and 1960s; busloads of Freedom Riders in the late 1950s; and civil rights and black power movements and urban riots in the 1960s and 1970s.

Yet it was at the close of this century that the specter of a racial war spotlighted the consequences of racial prejudice and hatred. Police violence against minorities, generally regarded by minority communities as a common occurrence, received enormous attention *not* because of complaints and charges by African American victims and leaders, but only because the savage beating of Rodney King was videotaped for the world to see. The eighty-one seconds of amateur video footage showed the rest of American society what minority community members have been saying for decades. The rage and violence in Los Angeles in May

1992 following the acquittal of four white police officers charged with brutality resulted in one of the most violent riots in the nation's history. More than fifty people died, and nearly $1 billion in property was damaged. American society approaches a new millennium that promises to bring *more*, not less, ethnic and racial diversity. Du Bois's prophetic words accurately describe the twentieth century, but they carry a more desperate tone as we approach the twenty-*first* century.

Obviously, all societies value groups of people unequally. What changes are the criteria used to establish who is different and the degree of inequality that those perceived differences produce. In the United States, race is a fundamental way to separate groups and produces enormous social inequality.

How Do We Define *Race*?

On the surface this seems to be an obvious, even silly, question. Everyone knows what "races" are—don't they? When we asked over 200 people this very question, more than 60 percent defined race in terms of physical appearance, which was usually specified as skin color. Perhaps the most descriptive comment was "Races are to humans what breeds are to dogs. We all have the same parts but look different." Over 40 percent of the comments also included notions of ethnicity and culture in their definitions of race, but as one remarked, "It is easier to define race in terms of skin color because it is something that stands out and is easy to see."

These comments and definitions probably represent a sizable section of the American public's perceptions and definitions of race, what social scientists refer to as *commonsense* or *taken-for-granted definitions*. But as Sheilagh Brooks pointed out in her foreword to this book, using "easy-to-see" skin color differences as a definition of race is questionable, confusing, and unreliable.

For example, poet and novelist Maya Angelou described how, one hundred years ago, some American churches had a pinewood slat with a fine-toothed comb hanging outside the door.

People could enter the church only if their skin color was not darker than the pinewood and if they could run the comb through their hair without it snagging (Finnigan, 1986).

An admissions clerk at an urban Colorado hospital was admitting a Saudi male for treatment. His skin color was quite dark. Her questions came quickly and automatically: "Name? Address? Race?" "White," he replied to the last question. She looked at him more closely, then scanned the categories under race on the admissions form: Caucasian (white), African American, Native American, Asian. She again looked at him: He did not fit anywhere. "Should I put what I think or what he said," she thought. A sociological dilemma. She left the answer blank.

These vignettes are used to demonstrate how confusing and *inaccurate* the term *race* is. Biologists and other natural scientists find the idea of race far too imprecise and unscientific to be useful. Social scientists use the term only because it has such important and far-reaching consequences.

The Importance of Race

Although the idea of race is essentially meaningless scientifically, race consciousness has emerged as a global phenomenon—and nowhere is it more important than in the United States. From the landing of Europeans in what became Virginia and New England until today, race has remained the cruelest, most divisive, and most prejudiced way of grouping peoples.

Ideas of race and racial prejudice were not unknown to sixteenth-century Europeans, but once the English came into contact with Native Americans and Africans in the New World, race as a way of classifying groups of people became critically important. Historically, slavery had usually been confined to conquered groups or to those who were in some form of debt, such as indentured servants. American slavery became the first instance of a *racist ideology* used to meet the greedy economic needs of white landowners in the Atlantic and southern states (Fredrickson, 1971).

Prejudice and discrimination based on "race" soon became embedded in the American self-concept. For example, all Native Americans and Africans, slave *or* free, were denied citizenship under the U.S. Constitution. Defining these two groups of people as inferior races is found in virtually all aspects of U.S. history. In one of his debates with Stephen Douglas, Abraham Lincoln claimed: "There is a physical difference between the white and black races which . . . forbid[s] the two races living together on terms of social and political equality . . . and I . . . am in favor of having the superior position assigned to the white race" (Gossett, 1963, p. 254).

Lincoln's opposition to interracial marriage reflects one of the most enduring ideas of racism, fears of "diluting" a superior race. Miscegenation laws prohibiting interracial marriages lasted one hundred years *after* the Civil War. These laws and attitudes led Malcolm X to declare, "White society has always considered that one drop of black blood makes you black. To me, if one drop can do this, it only shows the power of black blood" (Malcolm X, in Preston and Smith, 1989, p. 285).

An illustration of the limits and consequences of our commonsense definition of race is reflected in the U.S. Census Bureau's categorization of Latino Americans. When the 1990 census limited options for describing race as black, Asian–Pacific Islander, white, or American Indian, half of California's Americans who traced their biological and cultural ancestry from Mexico, Central and South America, and the Caribbean basin described themselves as "other" (Lewis, 1993, p. A16). It takes only a brief look at any gathering of Puerto Ricans, Cubans, and Brazilians to realize "Caucasian/white" simply does not encompass the enormous diversity of their physical appearance.

Defining Latinos as Caucasians was socially significant because U.S. census results are often used to help formulate national policies, including federal funding for various programs. Latinos are overrepresented in U.S. society in areas such as unemployment and lack of health care, and hiding the true numbers and circumstances of Latinos affected the scope and funding of

numerous federal programs aimed at institutionally discriminated-against groups.

Combining Latinos with Anglos not only masks patterns of
discrimination but also hides other significant consequences for
them as a group. For example, when viewing Latinas as a group,
Flores and his colleagues pointed out that cervical cancer rates for
Latinas are significantly higher than for Anglo women (Flores et
al., 1990). While the causes are so far unknown, Flores's research
enables other investigators to focus on factors that are specific to
rural Latinas.

It took politicians years to learn what many social scientists
have known for some time; that race is too difficult to define and,
as an objective concept for grouping people, is essentially useless.
Most social scientists now use the concept of *ethnicity* to represent a more inclusive notion of diversity.

THE "SOCIAL CONSTRUCTION" OF RACE

Constructing Race and Racism

The concepts of *race* and *ethnicity*, in and of themselves,
have no intrinsic, universal meaning. Societies differ in what
constitutes a racial and ethnic group, differ in the meanings of
race and ethnicity, and differ in the social consequences of race
and ethnicity. In this sense, social scientists say that the
definitions and meanings of race and ethnicity are "socially constructed"; that is, each society decides for itself what arbitrary
meanings race and ethnicity will have for that society.

Barely one hundred years ago western Europeans still believed that the human species could be adequately grouped into
different races that roughly corresponded to the major landmasses of the world. The classification that was most widely accepted
separated humans into three major categories: Negroid, with dark
skin and woolly textured hair, located primarily in Africa south
of the Sahara; Caucasoid, with light skin and straight or wavy

hair, located primarily in Europe; and Mongoloid, with yellowish skin and a unique skin fold around the eyes, located mostly in Asia and North and South America.

However, Sheilagh Brooks pointed out there are many peoples who simply do not fit neatly into these simplistic categories of white, black, and yellow peoples.

According to anthropologist Ralph Linton (1936):

> It seems slightly ludicrous that the main exponents of the theory of . . . pure strains should be inhabitants of Europe, one of the most hybridized regions in the world . . . . The Huns, a yellow tribe from far eastern Asia, raided almost to the Atlantic and, after their defeat, dissolved into the European population. Other Asiatic tribes . . . settled large areas of eastern Europe. . . . The Romans brought in Negro slaves while . . . the Mohammedan conquerors of Spain and Sicily had more than a tinge of black blood. (p. 351)

According to most social and biological scientists, then, race as a concept has little or no scientific meaning. Yet the intense interest in race in U.S. society, from Tocqueville in the early 1800s to William Julius Wilson in the 1990s, emerges from its significance as a *social* rather than biological fact. While the term *ethnicity* or *ethnic* group might be more useful scientifically, race has been the most profound way of classifying people throughout U.S. history. Racial prejudices have justified genocide against Native Americans, enslavement of Africans, and ongoing institutionalized discrimination against virtually all non-Anglos.

Influences on U.S. Racism

As we have already discussed, groups of people are valued differently in all societies, and often this stratification and inequality have stemmed from perceived racial and/or ethnic differences. But it was not until western European expansion and colonization four hundred years ago that the social consequences of race, or more accurately skin color, became a linchpin in an ideological system that allowed and even encouraged not only colonialization and exploitation, but slavery and genocide on a world scale.

This period of western European expansion brought together peoples of different cultures and origins on a scale and with an intensity that was unprecedented in human history. But it was a very unequal cultural exchange. At the height of this expansion, western Europeans "colonized," or "owned," virtually all of Africa, Oceania, part of Asia, and the entire Western Hemisphere. The saying "The sun never sets on the British Empire" was a fact.

The conquest, enslavement, and destruction of native peoples and cultures was massive in scope. Rival European societies vied for the legal ownership and subjugation of entire continents, and of all the peoples and resources indigenous to those lands, usually with the open encouragement and blessing of Christian church leaders. For example, the native population of North America at the time of European expansion is estimated at several million (figures range from 5 to 40 million). By the mid-1800s the number of Native Americans was approximately 250,000. The native population of Tasmania, an island off Australia, survived only seventy-three years of British colonial rule before the Tasmanian race was completely exterminated, described as but "one chapter in the triumph of 'civilization' over 'savagery' " (George Murdock, in Preston and Smith, 1989, p. 305).

What was needed was a moral and scientific justification for exploitation and destruction on a continentwide scale. The Europeans' ability to defeat and subjugate native nonwhite peoples was justified as a sign of a racial superiority that was "natural" and "morally right." Their concept of the "white man's burden," driven by Christian missionary zeal, unbounded greed, and a notion of native people as less than fully human, focused on racial differences to provide much of their rationale.

Europeans found the necessary justification in the ideology of *racism,* with its fundamental premise that some *races* are culturally, intellectually, or morally superior to others. As we mentioned earlier, ideas of dividing people according to inherited biological traits have existed for centuries but were not part of an organized worldview until sixteenth-century Europeans needed to justify their wholesale destruction of nonwhite people and cultures.

Early-sixteenth-century Spanish attitudes toward native tribes exemplify the general European sense of moral and racial superiority and the outrages it excused:

> Before entering a new area, Spanish generals customarily read a *requiremiento* (requirement) to the inhabitants. This long-winded document recited the history of mankind from the Creation to the division of the non-Christian world by Pope Alexander VI and then called upon the Indians to recognize the sovereignty of the reigning Spanish monarch. "If you do so . . . we shall receive you in all love and charity." If this demand was rejected, "we shall powerfully enter into your country, and . . . shall take you, your wives, and your children, and shall make slaves of them. . . . The death and losses which shall accrue from this are your fault." This arrogant harangue was read in Spanish and often out of earshot of the Indians. When they responded by fighting, the Spaniards decimated them, drove them from their lands, and held the broken survivors in contempt. (Garraty, John, in Broom et al., 1990, pp. 250–251)

Domination by the Europeans served as a sign from God, demonstrating their racial and cultural superiority. Even annihilation of native peoples by European-carried diseases provided proof of the necessity that white Europeans bring Christian "salvation" to non-European people. The ideology of superiority is demonstrated by a historian writing in the early 1900s: "There befell a great mortality among [the Indians]. . . . By this means, Christ, whose great and glorious works throughout the earth are all for the benefit of his churches and chosen, not only made room for his people to plant, but also tamed the hearts of these barbarous Indians" (W. C. MacLeod, in Preston and Smith, 1989, p. 287).

European anthropologists scientifically legitimized some of

the abusive attitudes and actions toward colonized peoples. The "discovery" and tidy categorization of people into three different and distinct races, roughly corresponding to the major landmasses, proved too attractive to ignore for those wishing even more ways to rationalize and excuse inhumane treatment of colonized people.

The first explicit European racism focused on the question of whether Native Americans were actually human, or some intermediate species between humans and beasts. Largely through the efforts of Bartolomé de Las Casas, known as the Apostle of the Indians, Pope Paul III proclaimed American Indians as "truly men" who should not be enslaved (Gossett, 1963, pp. 13–14).

Africans never found such powerful defenders and suffered grievously as a result. The first Africans imported into English colonies came into a society largely comprising white bond-servants. As England reduced the term of service for white servants, to encourage emigration to and colonization of America, the demand for cheap labor for picking tobacco rose dramatically. The enslavement of Africans became an economic "necessity." By 1670, Virginia law specified that "All negroes ... shall serve *Durante Vita*," that is, were to be slaves for life (Jackson and Tolbert, 1989, p. 30).

The early enslavement of Africans was largely defended along religious lines. In the early 1700s, Cotton Mather admitted that slavery was a "spectacle that shocks humanity." However, he speculated that it was part of God's plan to Christianize these heathens (Jackson and Tolbert, 1989, p. 31). As slavery came under more attack, by the late 1700s the religious justification for oppression of Africans was replaced by a "scientific racism" that "proved" blacks to be an inferior race. This justification is explored more fully in Chapter 3.

Consequences of U.S. Racism

The U.S. Declaration of Independence states that "all men are created equal"—a claim that is more hopeful than factual. Vestiges of a racist European ideology that justified control, conquest, and destruction of nonwhite peoples and cultures are seen throughout U.S. history. Apart from brutalizing Native Americans and slaves, U.S. culture evolved its own variations and themes of racial and ethnic superiority that are present throughout U.S. history.

In addition to the devastating impact racism has on non-Anglos, the U.S. legacy of prejudice and discrimination also has dangerous consequences for Anglos. For example, in 1990, the University of Chicago's National Opinion Research Center found that over 50 percent of non-African-American and non-Latino respondents said African Americans and Latinos were less intelligent than whites. These prejudicial stereotypes have been consistently reported among whites. In 1991, longtime pollster Lou Harris reported a troubling, though very consistent, finding: "There is a hardcore 25 percent of whites in the country" who don't feel African Americans can learn (p. 3A).

In yet another study in 1990, Latinos and African Americans were judged more harshly than whites according to such categories as "lazy," "violence-prone," "intelligence," and "living off welfare" (Smith, 1990, pp. 9–10). The acceptance of such prejudiced attitudes permeates all aspects of contemporary American culture. In a 1991 *USA Today* poll rating athletic skills, white respondents rated white athletes highest for "leadership," followed by "thinking," and finally "instincts." The highest skills of African-American athletes were "instincts," followed by "thinking" and "leadership" (Meyers, 1991).

While it is true there are more middle-class and affluent African Americans than in the past, African Americans are still worse off than whites on virtually all measures, including poverty, education, health care, and life expectancy.

Figure 1.5 offers graphic evidence focusing on the different rates of infant mortality, maternal deaths, and life expectancy for whites and African Americans.

While we have focused on African Americans in discussing race and racism, we could have concentrated on any non-Anglo

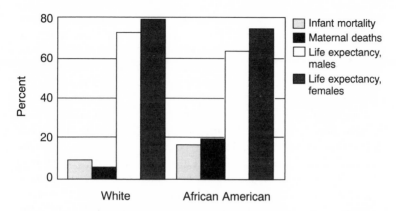

Figure 1.5. Indicators of relative health, according to race, 1990. The rate is the number per 1,000. Infant mortality is the number of deaths per year of infants under one year old per 1,000 live births. Source: *Statistical Abstract of the United States*, 1991.

group in American society; the results would be the same. The consequences of continuing racial prejudice and discrimination are intolerable for *all* non-Anglo groups.

Chapter 2

Prejudice and Hatred
A Common Experience

ETHNOCENTRISM AND PREJUDICE

Many social scientists use the concept of *ethnocentrism* to explain the existence and persistence of prejudice, discrimination, and hatred, whether it is aimed at racial or ethnic groups or at any other groups accorded "minority" status in American society. *Ethnocentrism* is a term coined by U.S. sociologist William Sumner (1906), who described it as the "view of things in which one's own group is the center of everything and all others are scaled and rated with reference to it" (p. 13).

Most if not all groups are ethnocentric to some degree. People are born into and raised in an already-existing culture in which the values and norms of their society are embedded so thoroughly and internalized so early in life as to be taken for granted as natural and morally right. That these norms and values come to be seen as almost inevitable was elegantly described by anthropologist Ralph Linton (1936): "It has been said that the last thing which a dweller in the deep sea would discover would be water. He would become conscious of its existence only if some accident brought him to the surface and introduced him to air. . . . The ability to see the culture of one's own society . . . calls for a degree

43

of objectivity which is rarely if ever achieved" (Robertson, 1987, p. 66).

Ethnocentrism has been benignly described as a potentially positive, even necessary, social force. Some claim it is needed to create belief in one's own group and to repel outside incursions, thus establishing social unity, identity, and cohesion. But because its definition implies that the values, norms, and behaviors of one's own group are *superior* to those of another, the negative consequences far outweigh any positive functions ethnocentrism produces in U.S. society. This attitude of the superiority of "the ways of one's group" has dire consequences for any society; it helps produce and perpetuate attitudes of prejudice and hatred and acts of discrimination and violence.

ETHNOCENTRISM AND PREJUDICE CROSS-CULTURALLY

Whereas Sumner expressly described ethnocentrism as using the values and norms of one's own *group* to judge another group, social scientists have usually taken this to mean using the values and norms of one's *society* to judge those of another, described as *cross-cultural prejudice*. Even when applying the concept to U.S. culture, there is a tendency to approach from a cross-cultural perspective. For example, a favorite method of introducing the concept of ethnocentrism to beginning U.S. college students is Horace Miner's anthropological article, "The Body Ritual among the Nacirema" (1956):

> The supplicant entering the temple is stripped of all his or her clothes. In every-day life the Nacirema avoids exposure of his body and its natural functions. Bathing and excretory acts are performed only in the secrecy of the household shrine, where they are ritualized as part of the body-rites. Psychological shock results from the fact that body secrecy is suddenly lost upon entry into the *latipso*. A man, whose own wife has never seen him in an excretory

act, suddenly finds himself naked and assisted by a vestal maiden, while he performs his natural functions into a sacred vessel. This sort of ceremonial treatment is necessitated by the fact that the excreta are used by a diviner to ascertain the course and nature of the client's sickness. Female clients, on the other hand, find their naked bodies are subjected to the scrutiny, manipulation, and prodding of the medicine men. (pp. 505–506)

Some readers have realized Miner was describing *American* culture (*Nacirema* spelled backward). The point is that traditional uses and examples of ethnocentrism tend to compare different cultures or use entire societies as frames of reference. Textbooks use the pre–World War II Japanese occupation of Korea and attempts to eradicate Korean culture as an example of extreme ethnocentrism, referred to as *cultural genocide.* Nazi Germany's attempt to exterminate Jews as the "final solution" is the most widely used example of ethnocentrism carried to the extreme. The Nazis "justified" their atrocities as necessary to ethnically cleanse Germany of anyone not fully "Aryan."

Cross-cultural examples of ethnocentrism are not always violent and are often more attitudinal than behavioral. The intense economic competition between the United States and Japan has rekindled anti-Japanese and anti-American attitudes across both countries. Weekly Japanese television comedy shows regularly include jokes about "lazy" and "unskilled" U.S. workers. One widely reported American joke has Japanese tourists in San Francisco asking an American on the street for directions to the Golden Gate Bridge. The American retorts, "You didn't have any trouble finding Pearl Harbor. Find it yourself."

U.S. history is replete with societywide and cross-cultural examples of the prejudices and violence that often emanate from ethnocentric attitudes. The most obvious domestic example is the Civil War, still the most violent conflict in U.S. history. Cross-cultural examples that readily come to mind are the 1848 war with Mexico, which cost Mexico one-third of its land, and the Spanish-American War of 1898.

The Spanish-American War is a particularly good example of the power and influence of ethnocentrism. This war was the first tangible national policy test of Herbert Spencer's notion of "social Darwinism," that American victory not only represented the survival of the fittest but also helped "prove" that superior cultures were produced by superior races. Spain was cynically portrayed in the William Randolph Hearst–influenced media as a backward culture ruled by rigid social classes, a corrupt monarchy, and superstitious Roman Catholicism. The appeals to American prejudices toward a non-Anglo, non-Protestant culture were so blatant, virulent, and *successful* that "yellow journalism" became part of our cultural heritage. Defeating Spain (and acquiring its worldwide empire, including Cuba, Puerto Rico, and the Philippines) was seen as part of our God-given "manifest destiny."

As important as these extreme cross-cultural examples are, they mask some of the most powerful consequences of ethnocentrism. Much of the prejudice, discrimination, hatred, and violence that occur *within* the United States can be directly traced to ethnocentric attitudes and behaviors. The continuum of prejudice perpetuated by such attitudes and behaviors is found at all levels of society, from cultural to personal.

ETHNOCENTRISM AND PREJUDICE
WITHIN THE UNITED STATES

The question often arises: Why, thirty years after the civil rights movement and twenty years after the women's movement, is U.S. society still plagued by racism and sexism? Much of the answer lies in the unexamined influences of ethnocentric attitudes and beliefs that have become embedded within the very fabric of U.S. society, attitudes and beliefs that emerge as discrimination and even violence on a cultural, institutional, and personal level.

CULTURAL PREJUDICE

What allows the spectrum of prejudices based on race, ethnicity, gender, class, and sexual orientation to continue to thrive in U.S. society are the social values and meanings we have assigned to various groups of people within U.S. society. This is what ethnocentrism within a society looks like. We as a culture essentially rank-order the relative value of specific cultural groups, including their norms and values. Over two hundred years ago, U.S. culture was dominated by Europeans of English ancestry. White, Anglo-Saxon (middle-class male) Protestants (WASPs) became the group whose physical appearance, values, and norms became the standard by which all other groups were to be judged. We as a culture have socially decided that African Americans, Latinos, Native Americans, women, working-class people and poor, and gays, lesbians, and bisexuals are "less" favored groups, and that it is therefore acceptable to treat them unequally.

There is a direct connection between the ethnocentric attitudes of early European settlers that condoned genocidal policies toward native peoples and contemporary attitudes of indifference and hostility toward Native American peoples and cultures; a direct connection between ethnocentric beliefs that legitimized the enslavement of millions of Africans as a reasonable course of action for a "Christian" people and the often abysmal social, economic, and political conditions of millions of African Americans today; and a direct connection between centuries-old European sexist beliefs that women not should *be* but *were* subservient to men because it was "natural" and "God's law" and the startling FBI statistic that 40 percent of *all* U.S. women murdered are killed by their intimate partners.

The systematic destruction of American Indian cultures and the enslavement of Africans are profound examples of the consequences of cultural prejudice, hatred, discrimination, and violence that are rooted in and justified by ethnocentric values. Less obvious, but equally pervasive, historical examples are found in the typical immigrant group's experiences in confronting pressures exerted by the dominant Anglo culture.

Though tension and conflict with immigrant groups had long existed, it was not until the 1880s that immigration was widely perceived as a threat to the dominant Anglo culture. The earlier bulk of immigrants had come from northern Europe: England, Scotland, Ireland, Germany, and Scandinavia. They had increased the foreign-born population of the United States but its culture remained overwhelmingly Anglo-Saxon and Protestant.

From 1880 to 1920, the U.S. population increased from 50 to 100 million, and 30 million of the increase came from southern and eastern European immigrant groups. They were clearly different from the dominant culture: non-Anglo, non-Protestant, non-English-speaking, and non-middle-class. Judged from an essentially Anglo cultural perspective, these outsiders were seen fearfully as "masses of clannish and suspicious aliens." The romanticism of the United States as a "melting pot" gave way to the reality of a culture *enforced* on non-Anglos. Anglo Conformity, a classic example of ethnocentrism, permeated all major U.S. institutions. For example, the public schools "demanded complete renunciation of the immigrant's [children's] ancestral culture in favor of the behavior and values of the Anglo-Saxon core group" (Gordon, 1964, p. 88). Business also added its voice to the clamor for conformity. The first thing non-English-speaking employees of Ford Motor Company's night school learned was how to say in English, "I am a good American." In Ford's factory school, workers were taught that they "walk to the American blackboard, take a piece of American chalk . . . walk to [their] American home, [sit] down with [their] American family to their good American dinner" (Carlson, 1987, p. 88).

The ugliest aspects of ethnocentrism fanned fears and suspicions about non-Anglo immigrants. One authority wrote in 1916, "We have found that our forces for assimilating this foreign element have not been working. . . . We have suddenly been made to realize that . . . many of these . . . are not strangers to the hand that stabs in the dark" (Higham, 1988, p. 242). Fears that immigrants were "mongrelizing" American society and the white race were prevalent themes in popular culture. For example, the YMCA (originally, the Young Men's Christian Association) warned that "Unless we Americanize them they will foreignize us" (Carlson, 1987, p. 86). The racial prejudices fostered by these ethnocentric attitudes became so great that immigration from southern Europe and Asia was halted in 1917.

Contemporary examples of prejudice, fed by unseen ethnocentric prejudices of group superiority and subordination, are easy to find. When groups are ranked by categories such as race, ethnicity, gender, class, and sexual orientation, the effects of prejudice, discrimination, and hatred are seen across the spectrum of social indicators. There is an alarming consistency of prejudice-inspired discrimination, hatred, and violence directed against undervalued groups in the United States.

We have documented violence against racial and ethnic minorities, women, gays, and lesbians. Violence against working-class and poor Americans is more subtle, but equally deadly. In the early part of this century, federal troops were regularly used to break labor strikes. Often these confrontations turned violent, such as the "massacre" of Peabody Coal Co. workers and their families in Telluride, Colorado, in the early 1900s. Currently many poor communities are used as toxic dumping grounds, having much higher concentrations of local dumps, low-level toxic waste sites, power plants, and other polluting industries. The resulting higher rates of exotic cancers are often ignored. For example, Nogales, Arizona, a largely poor Latino community, has had a cancer rate over twice the national average since 1980. Yet it was only in 1994 that the state took notice and then congratulated itself for appropriating $100,000 for medical intervention at the same time the state was trying to convince its citizens to pay $150 *million* to finance a major-league baseball stadium.

The repulsive radiation experiments of the late 1940s–1970s illustrate some of the consequences of membership in low social classes. Many of the "subjects" of the hideous government and university research projects were victims of "injustice" and "bias" and constituted "society's have-nots" (Healy, 1994).

INSTITUTIONAL PREJUDICE AND DISCRIMINATION

By *institutionalized discrimination*, we mean how prejudiced beliefs about groups of people become embedded in the institutions that dominate our society. Again using race as our illustration, we see that racism became institutionalized in U.S. society in more ways than slavery (and beyond) because many major institutions—such as legal, educational, congressional, and economic institutions—incorporated and thus perpetuated racial prejudice.

Legal Institutions

The myth of racial superiority became a more conscious element of the prejudice and discrimination expressed through Anglo-conformity attitudes, and for hundreds of years, federal and state courts provided a legal rationale for the hateful practices of racism. In North Carolina in 1831, for example, it was against the law to teach a slave to read, punishable by "39 lashes on his or her back" (Rothenberg, 1988, p. 265). In the *Dred Scott* decision of 1857, the Supreme Court concluded that African Americans were not people but property and therefore could not be citizens of the United States. In *Plessy v. Ferguson* (1898), the U.S. Supreme Court declared the segregation of African Americans the law of the land. It ruled that any institution could exclude African Americans if separate accommodations were provided. Segregated public schools were not only legal but were required in seventeen states and the District of Columbia as recently as 1950. It wasn't until the 1954 *Brown v. Board of Education* decision that the legality of school segregation was challenged.

Educational Institutions

Many U.S. history textbooks perpetuate the myth that Columbus "discovered" a continent empty of civilization. When texts discuss the "settlement" of the western United States, it is invariably and exclusively from the perspective of the Anglo settlers and military, never from the point of view of those already there.

Traditional U.S. prejudice against the existence, let alone the validity, of Native American cultures is seen in the comments of Harvard University president James Bryant Conant. In a 1948 speech, he stated, "This nation, unlike most others, has not evolved from a state founded on a military conquest.... On the contrary, we have developed our greatness in a period in which a fluid society overran a rich and empty continent" (Novak, 1971, p. 5).

By 1920, "scientifically designed" educational curricula differentiated by racial and ethnic origins had been instituted, often using a special, *nonacademic* curriculum for southern and eastern European and African-American students. According to one public-school English teacher, "Think of asking the Jew from Russia to read *The Courtship of Miles Standish* with the same zest and appreciation as is felt by the little girl in Virginia in whose veins runs the blood of Miles Standish" (Carlson, 1987, p. 90).

Congressional Institutions

The "three-fifths compromise" in Article 1, Section 2 of the U.S. Constitution allowed three-fifths of the slaves to be counted for taxing and representation purposes, but both slaves and free African Americans were denied citizenship.

Since the founding of the republic, Congress has played a major role in promoting racial prejudice. The 1790 Naturalization Act granted the right to become a U.S. citizen through naturalization to whites only. Although the Fourteenth Amendment to the U.S. Constitution (passed to give African Americans citizenship) granted citizenship to all people born on U.S. soil, a congressional citizenship prohibition applied to Asians until the 1950s.

The immigration laws of the late 1800s to the early 1900s legally restricted the migration into the United States of Asians and southern and eastern Europeans, but *not* western and northern (read Anglo-Saxon Protestant) Europeans. Women were denied the right to vote until the suffrage movement forced Congress to "grant" women the "right" to vote. Congress has failed to pass the Equal Rights Amendment giving women rights equal to those of men.

Economic Institutions

There are countless current examples of institutional prejudice and discrimination based on race and ethnicity. African Americans and Latinos are much more likely than whites to be rejected for mortgage loans, regardless of the applicants' income, as shown in Figure 2.1. In 1990 high-income African Americans were rejected over 21 percent of the time and Latinos nearly 15 percent of the time, while whites with the same income were turned down only 8 percent of the time.

Single parents, overwhelmingly women, are the single most predictably impoverished group in American society. This trend has been described as the *feminization of poverty*. Many employment and leave policies contribute, as they are so restrictive that it is difficult for single parents to find and keep jobs that meet their specific needs.

PERSONAL PREJUDICE AND DISCRIMINATION

Americans tend to view prejudice as an individual phenomenon, as some*one* who is racist, or sexist, or heterosexist. Our typical solution to sexist and racist situations is to focus on the individual perpetrator and/or victim. This focus addresses only symptoms and overlooks more fundamental root causes.

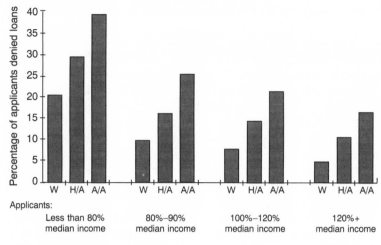

Figure 2.1. Percentage of applicants denied mortagages, 1990. Source: Henslin (1993), p. 321.

Personal prejudice and discrimination, still based on under-lying ethnocentric ideas, occur when individual people use ra-cial, ethnic, or gender stereotypes to explain their or someone else's actions. In 1993, Marge Schott, owner of the Cincinnati Reds professional baseball team, was reported to have described some of her players as "my million-dollar niggers" and warned employees to look out for "money-grubbing Jews." When asked about the Nazi swastika armband at her home, Schott replied, "I don't think it's a symbol of evil." She also said Hitler had the right idea "but went too far" ("Schott: Racism," 1993, p. D2).

Schott also claimed racism was a creation of the media and "really isn't there." When asked if she was racist, Schott appeared offended: "No, I'm not racist. Absolutely not" ("Schott: Racism," 1993, p. D2). Yet, when asked by Diane Sawyer on ABC television's *PrimeTime Live* if she had indeed used the word *nigger*, Schott said, "Everyone uses it. Haven't you used it, Diane?" Replied Sawyer, "No, Marge, I have never used that word" (*PrimeTime Live*, 1993).

Barely a year later, Schott was at it again. Talking about the appearance of today's baseball players, she said she didn't want her ballplayers to wear earrings because "only fruits wear earrings" ("Schott's Take on Ballplayers," 1994, p. C4).

In 1988, a Florida jury, half of whom were women, acquitted a man of kidnapping and raping a woman at knifepoint because, in the words of the jury foreman, "We all feel she asked for it for the way she was dressed." Her clothing was "too enticing," he said. The woman was stunned by the jury's verdict: "I can't understand how anybody could think I deserved to be cut up with a knife, raped multiple times, knocked out and almost killed in a car crash" ("Jury Says Victim Asked," 1988, p. A3).

We do not mean to imply that the three levels of prejudice are cleanly divided; in fact, it is difficult to tell where one stops and another begins. A graphic example of the intertwining of cultural, institutional, and personal prejudice occurred recently in Texas. A state judge, Jack Hampton, gave a lighter sentence to a murderer partly because the two victims were gay. "These two guys that got killed wouldn't have been killed if they hadn't been cruising the streets picking up teenage boys," Hampton told the *Dallas Times Herald*. "I don't care for queers cruising the streets picking up teenage boys. I've got a teenage boy." Hampton said the homosexuality of the two murder victims played a part in his decision to give the eighteen-year-old murderer a thirty-year prison sentence rather than the maximum life sentence ("Judge Lightens Sentence," 1988, p. A2).

Though there was immediate pressure and protest from Dallas's gay community, Judge Hampton remained on the bench. The lack of city- or statewide outrage and Hampton's continued term as judge indicate conformity between his actions and broader cultural prejudices toward gay men. The lighter sentence due to the victims' sexual orientation is an obvious example of institutional discrimination. And Hampton's own words are eloquent testimony to his personal prejudices and hatreds.

Another blending of the three levels of prejudice occurred in a rural Alabama county. When the local high school principal threatened to cancel a school dance if interracial couples attended, Revonda Bowen, a sixteen-year-old student, asked who she should bring to the dance, since her mother was African American and her father white. Principal Hulond Humphrey replied, "That's just it. Your mom and dad made a mistake, having you as a mixed-race child. I don't want any more mistakes" ("NAACP Wants Principal," 1994, p. A7).

Humphrey's personal prejudice is all too evident. As principal, he was also able to translate his personal prejudice into institutional discrimination. He had the power and influence to set school policy, such as canceling a dance, and in effect to legitimize such biased attitudes. Though initially suspended, Humphrey was quickly reinstated by the county school board. Though more difficult to see, his reinstatement illustrates the power of underlying cultural beliefs about racial differences and particularly about "mixing" races.

Because we've focused extensively on race and racism to help illustrate these three levels of prejudice, we want to emphasize that these prejudices are at work against other unequally valued and treated groups. The founding of a gay, lesbian, and bisexual college club serves as an excellent case study to broaden the understanding of prejudice as it relates to the three levels.

THE GAY, LESBIAN, AND BISEXUAL CLUB: A CASE STUDY IN THE INTERPLAY OF CULTURAL, INSTITUTIONAL, AND PERSONAL PREJUDICE

Heather

We have orders to contact you by letter that because of your life stile [sic] you have 30 days to make one of three choices

[*sic*] #1 change your life stile [*sic*] #2 leave the tri states #3
or die

A of I [Army of Israel]

In February 1993, a group of students at Southern Utah University (SUU) established that school's first homosexual campus organization, the Gay, Lesbian, and Bisexual (GLB) Club. The letter to "Heather" was received by one of the club's founders in early March 1993, ostensibly from the Army of Israel, a racist Aryan skinhead group located in southern Utah and also part of the Christian Identity movement. The Army of Israel's reaction to the existence of an openly gay campus group was not an isolated objection, only the most overtly threatening. For the next several months, public controversy raged on campus and in the surrounding community over whether this club should be allowed on campus.

With 5000 students, SUU is located in Cedar City, a southern Utah community of eighteen thousand. The surrounding population (as well as the school population) is mostly rural and conservative, having cast more 1992 votes for Ross Perot than for either Bush or Clinton.

The community and university response to the GLB Club offers a good example of the interplay of prejudice on cultural, institutional, and personal levels.

Cultural Prejudice

Much of what happened to the GLB Club was a result of deeply rooted cultural values and prejudices. Club members were acutely aware of the general social hostility toward homosexuals; consequently, most of the first two meetings was spent in finding an appropriate name for the club. The members wanted other campus gays and lesbians to recognize the club by its name but did not want the name to attract the wrath of those violently opposed to gays and lesbians. The club members were concerned about being attacked, and they took measures to protect themselves against letter bombs. Consequently, the first several names were purposefully vague; Out, Coming Out, Alternative Lifestyles, and Alternatives were but a few. They settled on GLB. The reticence of club members about being too public is understandable. Prejudice against gays, lesbians, and bisexuals is so deeply rooted in U.S. culture that it is often difficult to see. The cultural norm of heterosexuality is so taken for granted that is has become *enforced* heterosexuality, referred to as *heterosexism*, and is the last of the great "isms" (along with racism, sexism, ageism, and classism) to be culturally and legally acknowledged. Racism, sexism, ageism, and even classism have all been socially acknowledged, and racism, sexism, and ageism have been legally acknowledged, though to varying degrees. For example, the military has been racially and sexually integrated (in April 1993 the U.S. Navy proposed opening combat positions previously closed to women), and affirmative action programs are aimed at hiring and promoting of non-Anglos and women.

However, though often victimized, gays, lesbians, and bisexuals have yet to be seen as an identifiable and discriminated-against group, let alone offered specific legal protections. When "Heather" received her death threat, the local police were apathetic. But she and other club members took it much more seriously. They had learned to be more vigilant: Only a few years before, a local gay college student had been brutally raped with a tire iron and murdered. The victimization of gays and lesbians is extensive and often violent. The first national study examining violence against homosexuals found that 94 percent of over two thousand sampled had experienced some form of victimization (including verbal abuse, physical assault, and property vandalization) and that 19 percent reported having been beaten, punched, or kicked at least once because of their sexual orientation (Herek and Berrill, 1992, pp. 19–20).

One example of the antihomosexual values and norms in U.S. culture was the attempt to establish an inclusive multicultural curriculum in the New York City public schools in 1992–

1993. There was no debate over the so-called Rainbow Curriculum including traditionally excluded groups such as women and non-Anglos. However, adopting textbooks depicting lesbians and gay men as a "normal" segment of U.S. society created enormous debate, anger, and threats. Ironically the fight to continue to exclude gays, lesbians, and bisexuals as normal elements of society was led by African Americans, who were offended that homosexuals could be placed in the same category with themselves, thus maintaining prevailing cultural values and norms of antihomosexuality. So we see that cultural prejudice against gays and lesbians, or the ideology of enforced heterosexism, is the overriding value system that animates and justifies institutional and individual prejudices.

Institutional Prejudice

Cultural norms are usually reflected in major social institutions; prejudice against homosexuals as a group is found in many institutions of U.S. society. For example, in 1993, federal courts upheld a ban on homosexuals marching as a group in the New York City St. Patrick's Day Parade; in most cities and states, longtime relationships of gays and lesbians are not legally recognized, a circumstance depriving surviving partners of these couples of health insurance and other benefits accorded to legally married heterosexual (including common-law) couples.

The institutional responses to the emergence of the GLB Club at SUU also reflected the underlying antihomosexual values of U.S. society. Several SUU students circulated a petition to deny the GLB Club official club status. The petition was aimed at the university's financial donors, students and citizens alike, and warned the university to remove the "undersigned's names and those of other civic, business, campus, and community members" from fund-raising lists because "it would be inappropriate to monetarily support" campus organizations as a whole if the university continued to support the GLB Club ("GLB Club Fire Blazes," 1993, p. 3).

SUU administrators were less than enthusiastic in their support of the club, even in the face of the death threat to "Heather." The vice president of student affairs put those trying to eliminate the club on equal footing with the club members: "It is [the protestors'] right to not support them, just as it is their [GLB] right to organize the club. . . . We would hope that students and the community at large would understand the position the university is placed in." And in a letter to Friends of Southern Utah University, the chief fund-raising group, the university president was even more reluctant in his support: "Recognition of a club or organization does not constitute approval or sanctioning of the purpose of the club or organization" (*Daily Spectrum*, 1993, p. A1). This memo to a main fund-raising group came *after* the death threat, of which the president made no public acknowledgment or condemnation.

The local daily newspaper, while not necessarily mirroring cultural prejudice, did its best to inflame the issue of the club's being on campus. Its first mention of the group was in the Sunday (and largest) edition, a blazing headline directly under a multicolored masthead: "Homosexual Club on Campus." Other article headings, which *all* ran on page 1, included "Gay Club Fire Blazes on at SUU," "Students at SUU Mount Protest to Campus Club for Homosexuals," and "Gay Club Leaders Flee Cedar," which was a blatant lie.

Individual Prejudice

Individual prejudice is prejudice that exists on an interpersonal or individual level and is also a reflection of underlying cultural prejudices and values. The death threat to one of the GLB Club members is a powerful example. But it is critical to realize this death threat was *not* an isolated event but is intimately linked to prevailing social prejudice toward and hatred of gays and lesbians. In a subsequent survey of people's attitudes, nearly 10 percent of those who filled out an anonymous questionnaire felt *death* for homosexuals was appropriate. Comments included

"They should all be lined up against a wall and shot," "The death penalty should be applied [to homosexuals]," and "Anyone who is a fag should be killed."

Letters to the editor in the local and campus newspapers were less hate-filled but equally prejudiced. Common phrases found in these letters include "aberration," "counterfeit minority," "illness," "deviants," responsible for loosening "the fabric of which an orderly society is composed," and "not something that can or should be defended."

The anti–GLB Club protests stopped, the university did not lose any financial support, the local newspaper stopped fanning the flames of hate, and the GLB Club continues to flourish—all because a small group of people refused to be intimidated by prejudice and threats.

Chapter 3

The Intellectual Basis of Racism and Prejudice

Hoping to spark a race war in Los Angeles in 1993, eight members of the white Aryan Resistance, the Church of the Creator, and the Fourth Reich Skinheads plotted to bomb Los Angeles' largest black church, the First African Methodist Episcopal Church, machine-gun its congregation, and kill Rodney King. Fortunately, the eight white racists were arrested by the FBI on July 14, 1993. FBI agents had infiltrated the group and also learned they planned to murder other leading black and Jewish leaders, including officials of the NAACP and rap music stars ("Agents Break Up Skinhead Plot to Spark Race War," 1993, p. A1).

How do white racial supremacists justify and prepare themselves to kill other people they deem inferior? Regrettably the basis for many types of racial, social-class, and cultural prejudice is often manufactured in the ivory towers of U.S. academia.

RACISM, BIAS, AND SOCIAL SCIENCE

Reporting on the results of a 1990 National Opinion Research Center (NORC) poll and a 1990 Gallup Poll, *U.S. News & World*

Report ("Whites' Myths about Blacks," 1992, pp. 41, 43–44) summarized the NORC's and the Gallup Poll's findings on whites' perceptions of African Americans. A majority of whites (62 percent) rated African Americans as lazier than whites and most whites (78 percent) "thought [African Americans] more likely to prefer welfare to being self-supporting." Regarding the relation of African Americans to crime, 50 percent of whites saw "African-Americans as more violence-prone than whites." Most whites (75 percent) believed that "African-Americans have as good a chance as white people in my community to get any job for which they are qualified," and 50 percent of the white people polled thought African Americans actually got "too much consideration in job hiring." When asked "Do African-Americans blame everyone but themselves for their problems?" a majority (57 percent) of whites agreed.

In his review of Carleton Coon's book, *The Origin of Races* (1962), anthropologist Theodosius Dobzhansky (1963) stated:

> Scientists living in ivory towers are quaint relics of a bygone age. . . . The work and writing of scientists is . . . vulnerable to misuse. Race prejudice is a psychological and social disease and is not based on reason, yet those who suffer from it have repeatedly sought the support of bogus "science." (p. 171)

This chapter is about how theories and concepts from social and behavioral science may be the origin and rationalization for various forms of popular prejudice and hatred. Various examples of theories and concepts from sociology, psychology, anthropology, and political science are reviewed to show how they generate or reinforce bias, prejudice, and racist thinking.

How do we explain the persistence of bias, prejudice, racism, and discrimination? What are the appropriate evaluations of their victims and consequences? There is, of course, no lack of explanations. One could easily become lost in the myriad theories surrounding prejudice. Two issues generate controversy regarding racist and prejudicial theories: their scientific validity and their ideological role.

Survival of the Fittest

In 1859 Charles Darwin published *Origin of Species,* in which he presented his version of evolution, which he called the "theory of natural selection." Basically, natural selection favors the members of a species that can best adapt to and survive in particular environmental conditions, and that can continue to reproduce and pass on their characteristics to their offspring. As an illustration, imagine a population of giraffes living 100 million years ago on the savanna plains of Africa. Within this population of early giraffes (as in almost any population of organisms), there is a lot of individual variation in coloring, leg size, weight, height, and neck length. The giraffes obtain one of their main sources of food by grazing on the leaves of various trees. Once the animals eat all of the leaves on the lower branches of the trees, those with slightly longer necks and legs will be able to reach up a bit higher and consume the leaves on the upper branches. When leaves are scarce—during times of drought or because of changing environmental conditions—those individual giraffes that are able to survive because they can obtain leaves that their shorter siblings cannot stand a greater chance of passing their longer necks and legs on to their offspring. This process is repeated many times over millions of years. Also, genetic mutations add to the changes. A giraffe may be born with an exceptionally long neck and exceptionally long legs; therefore, if environmental conditions demand, this exceptional giraffe may survive over its siblings and pass on its genes.

Social Darwinism applies these concepts of natural selection to human social conditions. This theory claims that those classes and races that are most successful economically, socially, and politically succeed because they are biologically superior both as individuals and as groups. Thus social stratification reflects the "survival of the fittest." Social institutions and the distribution of income, wealth, and power are viewed as manifestations of biological laws. Since the laws of nature, and consequently their reflection in society, cannot and should not be altered, inequality is an inevitable feature of human societies.

William Graham Sumner (1840–1910) taught the first U.S. sociology class at a university in 1875. Sumner was an ordained Episcopal priest and a Yale professor. He was a stimulating lecturer and read voraciously in thirteen languages. Sumner was also America's leading social Darwinist and racist as the twentieth century began. He described his theories as the "science of society."

Sumner, one of the founding fathers of American sociology, was guilty of the worst kind of intellectual reductionism, which is the reducing of complex phenomena to overly simplistic explanations. In this case, Sumner reduced the complexity of the U.S. social and economic system down to the mechanisms of Darwin's theory of natural selection. Social stratification was merely a reflection of a natural process ordained by God to ensure that the "fittest" human individuals and groups would dominate society. Those at the bottom of the stratification (especially those who were nonwhite) were exactly where they should be, because they were unfit biologically, socially, and morally to compete successfully in a capitalist free-market system. As Sumner put it, describing the attitude of social critics concerned about inequality, they

> seem to be terrified that distress and misery still remain on earth and promise to remain as long as vices of human nature remain. Many of them are frightened at liberty, especially under the form of competition, which they elevate into a bugbear. They think it bears harshly on the weak. They do not perceive that here "the strong" and "the weak" are terms which admit of no definition unless they are made equivalent to the industrious and the idle, the frugal and the extravagant. (Hofstadter, 1965, p. 57)

Sumner didn't hesitate to compare the struggle for survival among animals with human competition in a capitalist economy. Richard Hofstadter (1965) believes Sumner's version of social Darwinism supplied the growing U.S. capitalist economy of the late 1890s with an ideological rationale for its abuses, saying,

"The competitive order was now supplied with a cosmic rationale" (p. 57).

Just as racists today disdain democracy and majority rule, Sumner argued that equality, democracy, and natural rights were ridiculous and unnatural. Sumner and other early social Darwinists laid the foundation for contemporary racist and elitist theorizing. Many of the founders of U.S. social science built racist thinking into the fabric of U.S. social thought. It is not surprising, then, that racism and elitism pervade the American view of society.

Most racist and prejudicial theories share common threads in social Darwinism. Social Darwinism has been dismissed by the majority of contemporary social scientists as a type of reductionism. As mentioned earlier, reductionism attempts to use simplistic ideas to explain complex phenomena. For instance, radical vegetarians who believe that most human behavior is primarily the result of what people eat often contend that major social problems such as crime, aggression, and wars could be eliminated if humans would stop eating meat. Certainly the food we ingest affects our chemistry and metabolism and influences our moods and behavior. To maintain, however, that all the complexities of social life and society are simply the products of biology and chemistry creates an incomplete and inadequate explanation of human affairs: It is an example of reductionism. In their book *Not in Our Genes: Biology, Ideology, and Human Nature* (1984), Lewontin, Rose, and Kamin critique biological determinism and social Darwinism, stating:

> Broadly, reductionists try to explain the properties of complex whole molecules, say, or societies in terms of the units of which those molecules or societies are composed. They would argue, for example, that the properties of a protein molecule could be uniquely determined and predicted in terms of the properties of the electrons, protons, etc., of which its atoms are composed. And they would also argue that the properties of a human society are similarly no more than the sums of the individual behaviors and tendencies of

the individual humans of which that society is composed.
(p. 5)

Social Darwinism is reductionist because it attempts to explain the complexities of social stratification and racism not in their own terms, but in terms of biological factors and characteristics of individuals or families.

From Social Darwinism to Functionalism

One of the major contemporary schools of American sociology is known as *functionalism*. Functionalists study social phenomena (e.g., institutions, organizations, and groups) by asking: What is the function of this or that social condition or institution for society? When functionalists attempt to explain social differences, they ask: What is the function of social stratification?

What is now considered the classic position of functionalism on stratification was written fifty years ago by Princeton University sociologists Kingsley Davis and Wilbert E. Moore in their article "Some Principles of Stratification" (1945). The similarity of the propositions of Davis and Moore and current American ideology regarding racial inequality is striking. Davis and Moore maintained that social stratification is a "universal necessity" and that stratification has always been present in human societies, is present in all contemporary societies, and will always be present in future societies.

They argued that some social positions are more "functional" for society than others. By this, they meant that certain occupations are more vital or important to society than others. For example, a medical doctor's contribution to society is more significant than that of a ditch digger. The doctor's work involves saving lives and preventing illness and requires many years of education and training as well as the application of expertise in difficult situations. In addition, not just anyone has the intelligence and discipline to become a doctor; only a few select individuals have that potential. In short, a doctor's position is more functional for "societal survival." The work of digging ditches requires no education or expertise and can be performed by just about anyone.

Therefore the function or purpose of social stratification, or economic and social inequality, is to ensure the proper allocation and distribution of social rewards (high income, wealth, prestige, and power) and social punishments (low pay and low prestige). Consequently the stratification system serves as a mechanism for placing and motivating the best individuals to fill the most functional positions. As Davis and Moore (1945) put it, "Social inequality is thus an unconsciously evolved device by which societies insure that the most important positions are conscientiously filled by the most qualified person" (p. 244).

Doctors receive high pay, prestige, and power because they have earned it the old-fashioned way, through hard work, dedication, sacrifice, and the market value of their services (i.e., the more functional nature of their occupation for society). Thus everyone in society more or less reaches the social position for which she or he is fit and receives appropriate social rewards or punishments. Inequality is, then, not only functional for society but also morally just and fair.

Although the functionalist theory of inequality is allegedly a sociological viewpoint, Davis and Moore (1945) succumbed a little to biological determinism by implying that inherent capacity is a major contributor to why different individuals end up in high or low social positions (p. 243).

The ideological relevancy of the functionalist theory of inequality is obvious. It is the basis for the popular conservative, commonplace view that the rich are rich because they deserve it and the poor and homeless deserve to be where they are because they are lazy, unproductive, and pathological. Because inequality is inevitable and universal, the implication is that the poor will be always with us, and that's OK because it's functional for "societal survival."

THE RACISM OF ANTHROPOLOGY

Cultural Inferiority

Although 69 percent of America's poor are white, the popular misconception is that most of the poor and the majority of welfare recipients are nonwhite. Anthropologist Oscar Lewis first suggested the concept of a "culture of poverty" in his 1959 book, *Five Families: The Children of Sanchez*. By the mid-1960s, with the publication of *La Vida: A Puerto Rican Family in the Culture of Poverty* (1965), Lewis had systematically clarified the "culture of poverty" and had addressed issues regarding the proper use of this concept.

According to Lewis (1965), the culture of poverty manifests itself at three levels: the individual, the family, and the community. His characteristics of individuals living in a culture of poverty include a "strong feeling of marginality, of helplessness, of dependence and of inferiority. . . . Other traits include a high incidence of maternal deprivation, of orality, of weak ego structure, confusion of sexual identification, a lack of impulse control, a strong present-time orientation with relatively little ability to defer gratification and to plan for the future, a sense of resignation and fatalism, a widespread belief in male superiority, and a high tolerance for psychological pathology of all sorts" (pp. xlvii–xlviii).

Families in the culture of poverty are characterized by a high incidence of abandonment by the fathers or other adult males. Consequently there exists a trend toward female- or mother-centered families, and the children in these families do not experience a "specially prolonged and protected stage in the life cycle." At the community level, we find poor housing conditions, crowding, and "gregariousness," but most important, a minimum of organization beyond the level of the family.

This litany of characteristics, if true, is certainly enough to convince anyone that the nonwhite poor are indeed a pathetic and pathological horde. But, Lewis contends, the culture of poverty actually has positive adaptive functions for the poor. It provides adaptive mechanisms by helping to reduce frustrations, thus making the deprivation of poverty tolerable.

Unfortunately politicians, a variety of social scientists (Moynihan, Banfield, Herrnstein, and others; see discussion below), and journalists who adopted Lewis's "culture of poverty" concept failed to heed the exceptions and qualifications regarding it. The culture of poverty idea became a pivotal concept around which many other theories and U.S. government documents on social problems attempted to explain why Latinos and African Americans in particular are disproportionately among the disadvantaged. Nevertheless, Lewis (1965) admitted from the very beginning that, although economic and material poverty were pervasive, the culture of poverty was not widespread: "There is relatively little of what I would call the culture of poverty. My rough guess would be that only about 20% of the population below the poverty line in the U.S. have characteristics which would justify classifying their way of life as that of a culture of poverty" (p. li).

For the minorities who did live in a culture of poverty, Lewis found evidence that "When the poor become class-conscious or active members of trade-union organizations, or when they adapt an internationalist outlook on the world, they are no longer part of the culture of poverty, although they may still be desperately poor" (p. xlviii). Before the development of cultural inferiority theories, anthropologists developed various evolutionary and physical-biological explanations for nonwhite inferiority. Among these theories was the idea that nonwhites' evolution was slower to full human status and that their brain size and consequently their intelligence were inferior to those of whites.

Racial Inferiority Based on Evolution, Brains, and Genes

One of the most distinguished American anthropologists of the 1950s and early 1960s was Carleton Coon. Coon was elected president of the American Association of Physical Anthropologists in 1961. The following year, Coon's *The Origin of Races* was published, and it unleashed a storm of controversy. Coon argued that different human races had had separate evolutionary developments that crossed the line to *Homo sapiens* at different rates. The race that crossed the line to the human species first, the white race, was obviously more advanced culturally and intellectually. Coon (1962) wrote:

> Each major race had followed a pathway of its own through the labyrinth of time. Each had been molded in a different fashion to meet the needs of different environments, and each had reached its own level on the evolutionary scale. (p. xvii)

Coon further stated that

> the subspecies which crossed the evolutionary threshold into the category of Homo sapiens the earliest have evolved the most, and that the obvious correlation between the length of time a subspecies has been in the sapiens state and the levels of civilization attained by some of its populations may be related phenomena. (p. x)

In other words, Coon proposed different rates of becoming fully human and subsequent cultural achievements. Coon also made provocative comments regarding the evolutionary role assigned to women:

> As far as reproduction is concerned, all the sexual activity that takes place among human beings, except at ovulation, is a waste of time, energy, and attention. . . . The sexual behavior of the human female is oriented more toward the maintenance of the social structure than toward reproduction. It tends to create a family, an economic unit built around the feeding, care, and education of children, and to secure the continued interest of husbands. (p. 84)

Racial and Sexual Inferiority Based on the Size of Brains

Craniology, the science of the comparative measurement of skulls, brains, and the volume of the empty brain cavity of a human skull, was a popular nineteenth-century "scientific" anthropometric method of demonstrating that nonwhites and women were naturally inferior to white men. One method of measuring brain capacity was to stuff mustard seeds into a skull through the opening at its base (the foramen magnum). Measurements could then be taken by comparing the weight of the removed mustard seeds from one skull with those from another skull. Leading scientists (Paul Broca, Le Bon, and Spitzka) of the latter part of the nineteenth century came to conclusions based on these methods that nonwhites and women had smaller cranial capacities than white males, and that their smaller brain size was proof of inferior intelligence. It is the studies of the nineteenth-century craniologists that became the foundation for the contemporary "IQ" theories of nonwhite inferiority that will be examined below.

Stephen Gould's *The Mismeasure of Man* (1981) presented a fascinating description and critique of some of the leading nineteenth-century craniologists. What follows is a brief review of Gould's account of the work of two of the nineteenth century's best-known craniologists, Samuel George Morton and Paul Broca.

Crania Americana

When Samuel George Morton died in 1851, the *New York Tribune* stated, "Probably no scientific man in America enjoyed a higher reputation among scholars throughout the world, than Dr. Morton" (Gould, 1981, p. 51).

By the time of his death, Morton had amassed one of the world's largest collections of human skulls, numbering more than one thousand. Human skulls were the data Morton used to test his theory that the ranking of races and sexes could be based on an empirical and objective measurement of brain size as indicated by cranial capacity. However, Morton's objectivity remains in question. Prior to the publication of his major works, *Crania Americana* of 1839 and *Crania Aegyptraca* of 1844, he had published several articles defending the theory that the human races were created as separate species (Gould, 1981, p. 52). Not only were his biases already formed, but despite his claim of adherence to the rigors of the scientific method and logic, his method of measuring skulls to infer social inferiority or superiority would prove to be riddled with illogic and less than objective measurement.

Morton believed he could objectively measure intelligence by measuring brain size via cranial capacity. His methodology was to fill the cranial cavity with white mustard seed and then infer the skull's volume from the amount of seed it could hold. Later he switched to one-eighth-inch diameter "BB" shot, because it packed better.

His results (see Table 3.1) demonstrated to his satisfaction that whites had bigger brains and more intelligence and consequently were superior to other races. His findings were reprinted many times during the nineteenth century to prove with "hard data" the natural superiority of whites.

Paul Broca

Another leading craniologist, Paul Broca, a medical doctor who in 1859 founded the Anthropological Society of Paris, carried on in the tradition of Morton. Broca claimed to demonstrate

Table 3.1. Cranial Capacity by Race (Morton's Data)

Race	Number n	Mean	Internal capacity (in^3)	
			Largest	Smallest
Caucasian	52	87	109	75
Mongolian	10	83	93	69
Native American	147	82	100	60
African	29	78	94	65

Source: Based on Stephen Gould (1981), *The Mismeasure of Man*. New York: W. W. Norton, p. 54.

not only that whites are superior to other races, but also that men, across races, are superior to women:

> In general, the brain is larger in mature adults than in the elderly, in men than in women, in eminent men than in men of mediocre talents, in superior races than in inferior races. . . . Other things equal, there is a remarkable relationship between the development of intelligence and the volume of the brain. (Quoted in Gould, 1981, p. 83)

Broca's studies on the differences between male brains and female brains were based on autopsies performed in Parisian hospitals. Broca found male brains weighed on average 181 grams more than female brains. This finding supported Broca's prejudice that women were less intelligent than men (see Table 3.2).

In 1977 Stephen Gould (1981) reanalyzed Morton's data and found that "Morton's summaries are a patchwork of fudging and finagling in the clear interest of controlling *a priori* convictions" (p. 54). For example, Morton's sample of Native American skulls was strongly biased by an overrepresentation of small-brained Incan Peruvians: "Morton included a large subsample of small-brained people (Inca Peruvians) to pull down the Indian average, but excluded just as many small Caucasian skulls to raise the mean of his own group" (p. 60).

However, possibly the most serious flaw in Morton's method was his logic. He simply did not control for brain size relative to

Table 3.2. Broca's Data Comparing the Weights of Male Brains with Female Brains

Sex	Number n	Mean weight of brains
Males	292	1,325 grams
Females	140	1,144 grams

Source: Based on description of data in Gould (1981), p. 10.

body size. If absolute brain size was the source of intelligence, then whales and elephants would have more "intelligence" than humans.

Because today they are considered less than scientific, the theories, methods, and logic of craniology have been largely dismissed by the scientific community. For example, in one incident it was discovered that, when the mustard seeds were put in the skull of a white man, the seeds were packed in tightly, while the skull of a nonwhite man was filled loosely. Of course, the careful measurements of the mustard seeds from the two skulls revealed that the white skull had a superior cranial capacity. In addition, modern scientists know that brain size, without consideration of its relative size to overall body size, bears no relation to intelligence.

One nineteenth-century craniometrician, French psychologist Alfred Binet, published nine journal articles on the value of craniometry before his studies of the measurements of the heads of schoolchildren led him to lose faith in brain size as an index of intelligence. He found the differences in the "cerebral volume" of children who had been labeled dumb or smart were negligible (Gould, 1981, p. 146). The French government asked Binet to devise a method to determine which children were likely to fail in school so that steps could be taken to prevent their failure. Since he had abandoned brain size as a determining factor in measuring intelligence, Binet turned to the study of photographs of children's faces in an attempt to discover correlations between types of faces and school failure. When the face method also proved unsuccessful, he turned to palmistry—the reading of lines in the hands—to predict intelligence (Blum, 1978, p. 56).

Inferring Character and Behavior from Lips and Skin Color

With the decline in the popularity of craniology, other attempts were made to link physical characteristics to race, behavior, and social standing. In 1921 Rand McNally & Company published a set of booklets on the "science" of characterology by

L. Hamilton McCormick. McCormick (1921) described characterology as:

> An exact science for the reason that by observing the rules
> and tenets herein formulated all possible combinations of
> features, cranial as well as facial, can be analyzed and the
> traits to which they refer named, and if errors are not made
> in the application of such rules, mistakes in diagnosis can-
> not occur. . . . By means of this science [one] can obtain a
> more nearly complete knowledge of the personality of an
> individual in a few moments. . . . Judged by its utility, Char-
> acterology ranks with mathematics, economics, chemistry,
> medicine and law. (pp. 12–13)

This now discarded "science" alleged that traits such as hon-
esty, dishonesty, criminality, insanity, musical ability, and art
aptitude could be linked to the physical features of individuals.
Everything from ear, eye, and nose shape to the configuration of
the head, the skin complexion, the thinness or thickness of the
lips, and hair color and texture, for example, was claimed to be
scientifically linked to various social behaviors, including occupational status and material success.

An example of characterology's claim to infer behavioral and
cultural attributes from physical features is the following description of the relation of lip thickness to cultural traits:

> Many traits of character are evidenced by the lips. . . .
> Excessively thick, protruding lips, unless there are counter-
> balancing signs, refer to grossness, slothfulness, love of
> food, sensuality, lack of breeding, and an unenterprising,
> indolent disposition.
>
> Negroes whose lips are large and thick are fond of bril-
> liant colors which harmonize with their bronze complex-
> ions, and furthermore, they have the sense of taste highly
> developed; they consequently excel in cooking, knowing
> instinctively the kind and amount of flavoring required. Ne-
> groes and natives of tropical countries, as the fullness of
> their lips indicate, are affectionate, musical and religious.
> (McCormick, 1921, pp. 7–8)

On skin complexion, McCormick wrote, "The black (or dark brown, as pure black skin does not exist) complexion of the African and certain Oriental races implies affection, lethargy, music, love of brilliant colors, and lack of initiative" (p. 25). McCormick observed this about Asians: "A large percentage of Orientals, who, owing to centuries of training, have remarkable memorizing power but are not noted for originality, possess brains which are high and narrow, deficiency with them being evident in the antero-lateral or principal reasoning district" (p. 31).

Even hair was for the characterologist an indicator of superiority. In the following quote McCormick contrasted Caucasians with Asians and Native Americans:

> Straight hair, when fine, as is typical with the Caucasian race, is associated with the Memo-Mental temperaments; it is a mark of refinement, of a serious disposition, and if extra fine, of a delicate constitution. Coarse, straight hair, such as is possessed by the Orientals and American Indians, betokens lassitude. (p. 29)

This crude biological reductionism of characterology is essentially dismissed by psychologists today. However, many psychologists still attempt to link measurable traits of individuals to make inferences about whole groups, classes, and races of people. Nevertheless, the concepts and assumptions of craniology and characterology, while mostly rejected by modern science, captured the imagination of the public and obviously form the basis of many racial stereotypes.

THE RACISM OF PSYCHOLOGY

IQ Tests: Craniology and Characterology in a New Form

Blatantly neosocial Darwinism theories are those in the discipline of psychology focusing on the alleged lower intelligence of nonwhites, particularly poor African Americans, as an explanation for their low social standing as a group. Of course, African Americans were alleged to be less intelligent than whites long before contemporary "mental measurement professionals" claimed they could scientifically explain the disproportionate number of African Americans among America's poor on the basis of "inherently inferior" African-American intelligence. For example, a popular nineteenth-century U.S. school geography textbook informed students:

> The home of the black or "Negro" race is central and southern Africa and some of the Australian islands. The peoples of this race have coarse woolly or kinky hair, protruding lips, and dark brown or black skin. The black race includes some of the most ignorant people in the world. (Redway and Hinman, 1898, p. 29)

The former craniologist Alfred Binet is better remembered today as the creator of the first "IQ" test in 1908. Its contemporary version is known as the Stanford–Binet Intelligence Scale because of updates done at Stanford University. Binet's IQ test was composed of questions that he believed reflected various tasks normal children should be able to perform in school. To Binet's credit, he never contended that a student's IQ score was anything other than an indication of what a student had learned in class and how well the knowledge had been applied. Nevertheless, the idea that "intelligence" tests measured innate fixed intelligence became widespread. By 1917 U.S. psychologist Robert Yerkes had administered IQ tests to two million army recruits.

In the 1920s Stanford University professor Lewis M. Terman revised and updated the Binet test, the result being the current popularity and widespread use in the United States of the Stanford–Binet IQ test. Terman summed up his views on intelligence differences between the races in *The Measurement of Intelligence* (1916), which was dedicated "To the Memory of Alfred Binet":

> Their dullness seems to be racial, or at least inherent in the family stocks from which they come. The fact that one meets

this type with such extraordinary frequency among Indians, Mexicans, and negroes suggest quite forcibly that the whole question of racial differences in mental traits will have to be taken up anew and by experimental methods. The writer predicts that when this is done there will be discovered enormously significant racial differences in general intelligence, differences which cannot be wiped out by any scheme of mental culture. (pp. 91–92)

Terman also believed that intelligence differences between social classes resulted primarily from biological differences: "That children of the superior social classes make a better showing in the tests is probably due, for the most part, to a superiority in original endowment" (p. 72). Furthermore, he wrote:

The common opinion that the child from a cultured home does better in tests solely by reason of his superior home advantages is an entirely gratuitous assumption. Practically all of the investigations which have been made of the influence of nature and nurture on mental performance agree in attributing far more to original endowment than to environment. Common observation would itself suggest that the social class to which the family belongs depends less on chance than on the parents' native qualities of intellect and character. (p. 115)

These ideas were popularized by many other books, including S. J. Holmes's *Human Genetics and Its Social Import* (1936). In Chapter 14, titled "The Social-Problem People," Holmes summarized the view of geneticists regarding the relation of low intelligence and social problems:

Low mentality tends to go along with poor education and an inferior economic and social status. Pauperism, vagabondage, illegitimacy, and intemperance tend sooner or later to become a part of the traditional mores of the group. People of this class are prone to mate with their own kind, and as a result whole communities grow up characterized by a large amount of consanguinity which brings out undesirable recessive traits. (p. 186)

The passage by Congress of the Immigration Restriction Act of 1924 was supported by the "IQ research" of Terman and his followers: The immigration of southern and eastern Europeans should be limited because they supposedly scored low on the Stanford–Binet IQ test (Gould, 1981, p. 232).

Current theories attempting to explain contemporary American racial stratification as stemming from inborn differences in intelligence rely heavily on results from the Stanford–Binet test. A brief review of how IQ scores are calculated is appropriate. IQ, an abbreviation of *intelligence quotient,* is derived from the formula: IQ equals mental age (which is derived from the "IQ" test scores) divided by chronological age and multiplied by 100 or

$$IQ = \frac{MA}{CA} \times 100$$

For example, if a ten-year-old child scores a "mental age" of thirteen years, as measured by a standard IQ test such as the Stanford–Binet, we then calculate the child's IQ as follows:

$$\frac{13}{10} \times 100 = 130$$

This child would have an above-average IQ, since a "normal" ten-year-old should have at least a ten-year-old mental age. The normal ten-year-old's IQ would be figured this way:

$$\frac{10}{10} \times 100 = 100$$

Consequently, an IQ score of 100 is normal. However, the IQ score of a ten-year-old who scored a mental age of eight years would be 80, which is below normal:

$$\frac{8}{10} \times 100 = 80$$

Arthur R. Jensen, a psychologist and a self-described "mental measurement professional" at Harvard University, has undoubtedly been one of the most infamous advocates of the ideology that social stratification results from innate IQ differences. One of the basic tenets of Jensen's (1981) position is that "there is no rational basis for the a priori assumption of racial equality in any trait, physical or behavioral" (p. 197). He attributed the observed differences in average group IQ scores between African Americans and whites to "genetically conditioned behavioral differences between human races that show many other signs of evolutionary divergence" (p. 199).

Throughout his research, Jensen contended that the average African-American–white IQ difference was about 15 points. Based on his review of the identical twin studies by British psychologist Sir Cyril Burt, Jensen concluded that 80 percent of IQ was inherited and the remaining 20 percent was influenced by the environment. However, after his death in 1971, Burt was "accused of fraud, of having faked much of his research, of reporting tests that were never done, and of signing fictitious names as coauthors" (Eitzen, 1982, p. 294).

Furthermore, Jensen believed, U.S. society had bent over backward to remove all social, cultural, and legal barriers that inhibited African-American achievement. The federal government had funded numerous remedial programs, like Head Start, to help African-American children. Despite society's efforts, African Americans had continued to represent a disproportionate number of poor people, welfare recipients, criminals, and so on, and their IQ test scores remained lower than those of whites. If the fault did not lie in the structure of U.S. society, then the only explanation left was that the fault lay in the genetic structure of African Americans:

> The plain truth is that compensatory programs have not resulted in any appreciable, durable gains in IQ or scholastic

achievement for those youngsters who have taken part in them. This is an important discovery, and the fact that we do not like this outcome or that it is not what we expected neither diminishes its importance nor justifies downplaying it.

The error lay in believing that the disadvantage with which many poor or culturally different children entered school—and the disadvantage that compensatory education was intended to remedy—was mainly a deficiency in knowledge.

I suspect that a substantial part of the individual variance in IQ and scholastic achievement—probably somewhere between 50 percent and 70 percent according to the best evidence on the heritability of IQ—is not subject to manipulation by any strictly psychological or educational treatment. The reason for this, I assume, is that the main locus of control of the unyielding source of variance is more biological than psychological or behavioral. (Jensen, 1981, p. 20)

Other writers have expanded Jensen's claims to explain more than just racial differences in the United States. For example, Stanley Burnham wrote in *Black Intelligence in White Society* (1985):

This high correlation between IQ and SES [socioeconomic status] seems entirely relevant, then, in finding a cause for the pervasiveness of black poverty throughout the world. A lower standard of living among blacks is not just an American problem, but may be found across the globe from Tanzania to California. For in no country, nor in any recorded epoch of history, has the overwhelming majority of the black population ever known anything except hand-to-mouth survival at a subsistence level. (p. 48)

Richard Herrnstein, another Harvard psychologist, helped popularize Jensen's views. Herrnstein (1971) summarized his argument by means of a syllogism:

1. If differences in mental abilities are inherited, and
2. If success requires those abilities, and
3. If earnings and prestige depend on success, then
4. Social standing (which reflects earnings and prestige) will be based, to some extent, on inherited differences among people. (p. 58)

Herrnstein contended that, because an ideology of egalitarianism dominates our society, we are under constant pressure to eliminate social barriers to status mobility. Thus, as social barriers to mobility decrease, the only remaining obstacles to social mobility must be inborn. In addition, the gap between the rich and poor will increase because, if there are any intelligent people in the lower classes, they will, naturally, drift up into the higher classes. Herrnstein pointed to Edward Banfield's *The Unheavenly City* (1970) as an example of one alert social scientist's description of the consequences of the innate inferiority of the lower class. Herrnstein (1971) concluded:

> Greater wealth, health, freedom, fairness, and educational opportunity are not going to give us the egalitarian society of our philosophical heritage. It will instead give us a society sharply graduated, with ever greater innate separation between the top and the bottom, and ever more uniformity within families as far as inherited abilities are concerned. (p. 64)

Herrnstein suggested we greet the ascent of an IQ meritocracy with enthusiasm because it results in a society where natural abilities match social functions. When asked in an interview what he thought of Herrnstein's prediction regarding the rise of a meritocracy in the United States, Arthur Jensen (1976) responded, "I think his prediction . . . is quite right" (p. 66).

William B. Shockley, Nobel-prize-winning scientist, expanded the "lower intelligence as the cause of social stratification" argument one step further. In the 1970s, Shockley and four other prominent scientists joined millionaire physicist Robert K. Graham in establishing a "sperm bank" as a depository for "superior sperm." The bank's purpose was to create a "master race" that would solve America's leading social problems. The sperm bank, officially called the Repository of Germinal Choice, is located in Escondido, California. The *New York Post* described the events as follows:

> Three super intelligent women were impregnated last year with the frozen sperm of the scientists in an experiment which is likely to become the most controversial in the nation's history. . . . Each woman was able to choose the sperm of her "mate scientist" on the basis of his IQ, age, weight, height, skin, hair, color of eyes and history of bearing healthy children. (Seifman, 1980a, p. A13)

Shockley explained to the *New York Post* that his efforts were directed at "saving the human race from the genetically disadvantaged." Shockley also stated his belief that "genetic defects in African-Americans are responsible for their criminal tragedies," and that he was "endorsing the concept of increasing the people at the top of the population" (Seifman, 1980, p. A13).

IQ AS DESTINY

Harvard psychologist Richard Herrnstein would go on to write *Crime and Human Nature* (1985) with another Harvard conservative, James Q. Wilson. The conclusions of *Crime and Human Nature* were foreshadowed by Herrnstein's 1971 *Atlantic Monthly* article on the IQ meritocracy. The epidemic of street crime in the United States is disproportionately the result of the pathology of lower-class African Americans who are afflicted with innate inferior levels of intelligence that made them constitutionally unable to defer gratification and obey the law. Back in 1986, Leon J. Kamin, among others, clearly exposed the flawed research and methodology of the Wilson/Herrnstein thesis on crime. Kamin further went on to place *Crime and Human Nature* in its sociopolitical context, stating:

The Wilson and Herrnstein work ought not to be judged in
isolation; their selective use of poor data to support a mud-
dled ideology of biological determinism is not unrepresenta-
tive of American social science in the sixth year of the Reagan Presidency. The political climate of the times makes it
easy to understand why social scientists now rush to locate
the causes of social tensions in genes and in deep-rooted
biological substrate. (Kamin, 1986, p. 27)

Herrnstein's mentor at Harvard was the famous behaviorist
B. F. Skinner. Among Skinner's last works was *Beyond Freedom
and Dignity* (1971), in which he reduced the values of democracy
and individual freedom to personal and political illusions. Skinner's argument was that an orderly society could be produced by
replacing democracy and individual freedom with appropriate
reinforcement schedules to produce conformist behaviors.

In 1994, shortly before his death, Herrnstein coauthored with
conservative political scientist Charles Murray, a senior fellow at
the right-wing think tank American Enterprise Institute, an 845-
page tome entitled *The Bell Curve* (1994). *The Bell Curve* is essentially a rehash of the earlier Jensen, Shockley, and Herrnstein
theories of the 1960s and 1970s, updated to suit mid-1990s conservative ideology and politics.

The contentions of the Murray and Herrnstein book are simple. Major social pathologies—crime, poverty, dependence on
welfare, unwed teenage mothers, and the growing polarization of
the U.S. socioeconomic stratification system—are primarily the
result of a 15-point (one standard deviation) difference between
white IQ scores and African-American scores. The IQ differences
and their subsequent social and economic consequences are fun-
damentally genetically determined differences between whites
and African Americans.

Affirmative action, government intervention, and welfare
programs make no difference in modifying inherent biological
differences and their outcomes. African Americans should not be
offended, but instead focus on their "clan" membership and its
unique strengths—for instance, sports and music. The reality of

society, no matter how upsetting, is that a "cognitive elite" rules and the lower classes simply do not and will not have the cognitive skills to guarantee social and economic success.

Murray and Herrnstein view the complexity of the social stratification system in simple biological terms. They state: "The trouble is that socioeconomic status is also a result of intelligence, as people of high or low cognitive ability move to high and low places in the class structure" (Murray and Herrnstein, 1994b, p. 31). They also suggest that private discussions among the upper classes are often characterized by negative attitudes toward minorities, especially African Americans. As they put it:

> The private dialogue about race in America is far different from the public one, and we are not referring just to discussions among white rednecks. Our impression is the private attitudes of white elites toward blacks is strained far beyond any public acknowledgment, that hostility is not uncommon and that a key part of the strain is a growing suspicion that fundamental racial differences are implicated in the social and economic gap that continues to separate blacks and whites, especially alleged genetic differences in intelligence. (Murray and Herrnstein, 1994, p. 27)

The Bell Curve has been described by various reviewers as a "historical oddity, wrong-headed, politically incorrect, indecent, philosophically shabby and dangerous pseudoscience racism." Leon Kamin describes *The Bell Curve* as a political statement: "to treat it as science is a delusion" (Sege, 1994, p. 91).

Time magazine writer Richard Lacayo adds:

> Specialists in the intelligence field complain that Herrnstein and Murray all but ignore what is known about brain development before and after birth. "When it comes to science, the book could have been written a hundred years ago," complains Harvard education professor Howard Gardner. A pregnant mother's nutrition or drug abuse can have a crucial impact on her child's eventual intellectual capability, which could go far to explain the lower IQs of inner-city children. (Lacayo, 1994, p. 67)

Ironically, Murray, in a *New York Times Magazine* interview, surprisingly called his theories on IQ "social science pornography" (DeParle, 1994, p. 50). Murray went on to explain that his book may have an appeal to "closet racists" because his research "demonstrates scientifically" the cognitive and social inferiority of African Americans. The *New York Times Magazine* concluded that Murray may not be a politically powerful conservative, "but he may well be the most dangerous" (October 9, 1994, p. 50).

In contrast to Murray and Herrnstein, social scientists have long known that social status is not simply a result of IQ. For example, Bowles and Gintis have concluded from their empirical research on the relation of IQ to social standing that

> the fact that economic success tends to run in the family arises almost completely independently from any inheritance of IQ, whether it be genetic or environmental. Thus, while one's economic status tends to resemble that of one's parents, only a minor portion of this association can be attributed to social class differences in genetic endowment. (1976, p. 120)

Bowles and Gintis empirically examined the relationships of IQ scores, education attainments, family status, and social standing of several thousand individuals. What they found was when you controlled (held constant) IQ scores, the social standing of individuals was best predicted by their social class of origin, not their IQ scores or cognitive skills. In other words, people at the lower end of the stratification system, no matter how high or low their IQ, have a greater probability of staying in the same class they were born into. On the other hand, upper-class individuals, despite their low, average, or high IQs, usually end up in the same strata they were born into. As Bowles and Gintis conclude:

> Our empirical results will reinforce our contention that the emphasis on IQ as the basis for economic success serves to legitimate an authoritarian, hierarchical, stratified, and unequal economic system, and to reconcile individuals to their objective position within this system. (1976, p. 116)

MORE SOCIAL SCIENCE RACISM

In *How the Other Half Lives: Studies among the Tenements of New York* (1890), Jacob Riis wrote about African Americans living in New York City:

> Poverty, abuse, and injustice alike the negro accepts with imperturbable cheerfulness. His philosophy is of the kind that has no room for repining. Whether he live in an Eighth Ward barrack or in a tenement brown-stone front and pretensions to the title of "flat," he looks at the sunny side of life and enjoys it. (p. 151)

In a 1924 sociology textbook, *Sociology and Modern Social Problems*, Charles Ellwood argued that it was the "racial heredity" of blacks that resulted in their character and led to "social problems":

> Since heredity affects the conduct of each individual, so must racial heredity affect the conduct of a race.... The tropical environment of the negro failed to develop in him an energetic nature, but favored the survival of those naturally shiftless and lazy. (p. 249)

In more recent years other social scientists have elaborated on the alleged inferiority of minorities, especially African Americans. Edward Banfield, appointed by President Richard M. Nixon to head a task force on model cities during the early 1970s, expounded on the inferiority of races. Once again, poverty—especially African-American poverty—and, in Banfield's opinion, nearly all other urban social problems could be explained by the unique characteristics of the people who were poor. Banfield's controversial *The Unheavenly City* (1970) is an ideological tract that blames the victim and lacks any pretense of humanitarian heart-bleeding. According to Banfield, poverty is caused by a combination of inferior biology and a "culture of poverty" (i.e., a belief system of negative personal and moral values). Banfield's analysis of poverty viciously proposed the idea that a possible solution to the perpetuation of poverty would be to reduce the children of the poor to marketplace commodities:

> As a matter of logic, the simplest way to deal with the problem—and one which would not involve any infringement of parents' rights—would be to permit the sale of infants and children to qualified bidders both private and public. (p. 231)

Banfield arrived at such a conclusion through a curious theory of social class. Rather than define social class by some set of objective social criteria, as most social scientists do, Banfield defined social class as "one primary factor, namely, psychological orientation toward providing for the future." Banfield (1970) further explained that "The more distant the future the individual can imagine and can discipline himself to make sacrifices for, the "higher" is his class" (p. 47). Based on this one factor, Banfield came up with a description of the stratification of American society and its heavy concentration of African Americans in the lower and working classes (see Table 3.3).

Banfield (1970) believed poor people enjoyed their condition:

> The lower-class individual lives in the slum and sees little or no reason to complain. He does not care how dirty and dilapidated his housing is either inside or out, nor does he mind the inadequacy of such public facilities as schools, parks, and libraries: indeed, where such things exist he destroys them by acts of vandalism if he can. Features that make the slum repellent to others actually please him. (p. 62)

According to Banfield's logic, the source of our serious urban social problems was lower-class African Americans. Crime, youth gangs, the drug problem, racial tensions, welfare fraud, urban decay, and just about all our urban problems could be attributed to the culture of poor African Americans in our central cities:

Table 3.3. Class and Race

	African Americans (%)	Whites (%)
Upper	1	12
Middle	4	21
Working	37	50
Lower	58	17

Source: Based on Banfield (1970), p. 266.

So long as the city contains a sizeable lower class, nothing basic can be done about its most serious problems. Good jobs may be offered to all, but some will remain chronically unemployed. Slums may be demolished, but if the housing that replaces them is occupied by the lower class it will shortly be turned into new slums. Welfare payments may be doubled or tripled and a negative income tax substituted, but some persons will continue to live in squalor and misery. New schools may be built, new curricula devised, and the teacher-pupil ratio cut in half, but if the children who attend these schools come from lower-class homes, they will be turned into blackboard jungles, and those who graduate or drop out from them will, in most cases, be functionally illiterate. The streets may be filled with armies of policemen, but violent crime and civil disorder will decrease very little. (pp. 234–235)

Therefore wasn't it the right and the responsibility of society to protect the interests of the majority? Hadn't the United States previously been required to infringe on the rights of a minority to protect the majority?

If abridging the freedom of persons who have not committed crimes is incompatible with the principles of free society, so, also, is the presence in such society of persons who, if their freedom is not abridged, would use it to inflict serious injuries on others. There is, therefore, a painful dilemma. If some people's freedom is not abridged by law-enforcement agencies, that of others will be abridged by law breakers. The question, therefore, is not whether abridging the freedom of those who may commit serious crimes is an evil—it is—but whether it is a lesser or a greater one than the alternative. (p. 184)

Unfortunately, the urban crisis then confronting us required a similar response. Realizing that selling infants probably wouldn't be acceptable, Banfield proposed a five-point program:

1. Encourage the Black person to realize that he—and not society or racism—are responsible for their ills.
2. Get him out of school at age 14, and place the ones who are unable to get jobs into the army or a "youth corps."
3. Give cash subsidies to the "competent" poor, but only goods to the "incompetents," and encourage or force the "incompetents" to reside in an institution or a semi-institution, such as a "supervised public housing project."
4. Provide "intensive" birth control "guidance."
5. Increase police powers in black areas and toward Black people, including more "stop and frisk" procedures and similar tactics, including jailing those persons "likely" to commit violent crimes. (p. 246)

Banfield's use of the "culture of poverty" as a partial explanation for the condition and behavior of lower-class African Americans was derived from the theory developed by anthropologist Oscar Lewis.

The Pathology of the "Negro" Family

Shortly after Lewis introduced the culture of poverty idea into discussions of poverty and social problems, the government published *The Negro Family* (1967), now known as the "Moynihan Report." It explains African-American society in terms of a culture of poverty.

During the decade of struggle for civil rights and African-American urban rebellions in many cities, Daniel Patrick Moynihan, then Assistant Secretary of Labor, prepared *The Negro Family*.

What became a problem was how the government and the nation understood why poor African Americans seemed stuck in perpetual poverty. The Moynihan Report provided an explanation. Moynihan (1967), while saying the conditions of poor Negroes were historically related to slavery, nevertheless emphasized that "At the heart of the deterioration of the fabric of Negro society is the deterioration of the Negro family" (p. 5). Moynihan's insights came from the importance of the family in psychoanalytic theory. Consequently his report emphasized personal and family pathology as the cause of the condition of poor African Americans. The statistical basis of his argument was that one-fourth of urban African-American marriages had dissolved, one-fourth of African-American births were illegitimate, and one-fourth of African-American families were headed by females.

Although Moynihan did mention, in passing, the historical oppression of African Americans, the fear many whites exhibited toward African Americans, the lack of capital afforded African Americans, and white organized crime as factors producing the "Negro condition," he maintained that African Americans themselves were basically responsible for their status:

> Nonetheless, at the center of the tangle of pathology is the weakness of the family structure. Once or twice removed, it will be found to be the principal source of most of the aberrant, inadequate, or antisocial behavior that did not establish, but now serves to perpetuate the cycle of poverty and deprivation. (p. 30)

Based on this explanation, Moynihan's case for national action to correct the condition of poor African Americans concluded: "In a word, a national effort towards problems of Negro

Americans must be directed towards the question of family structure. The object should be to strengthen the Negro family so as to
enable it to raise and support its members as do other families" (p.
47).

In other words, the African-American family could be
strengthened through psychotherapy! Once that was accomplished, African Americans would be like other people, and many
of America's social problems would be solved. Many civil rights
leaders of the time objected strongly to Moynihan's analysis.
James Farmer's response represents a good summary of the African-American community's reaction to the report:

> This well-enough intentioned analysis provides the fuel for
> a new racism. . . . It succeeds in taking the real tragedy of
> black poverty and serving it up as an essentially salacious
> "discovery" suggesting that Negro mental health should be
> the first order of business in a civil rights revolution.
>
> Nowhere does Moynihan suggest that there may be
> something wrong in an "orderly and normal" white family
> structure that is weaned on race hatred and passes the word
> "nigger" from generation to generation. (Rainwater and
> Yancy, 1967, p. 410)

Reducing Racial Oppression to Mental Illness

One of the great political and social science evasions of the
1990s is the failure to publicize the fact that the vast majority of
America's homeless are African Americans and other minorities.
That this is the case disguises the role of racism in creating the
American disgrace of homelessness.

"On July 7, 1986, a homeless Cuban refugee aboard a Staten
Island ferry unwrapped a sword and began hacking and stabbing
other passengers. Before he was subdued, Juan Gonzalez had
killed two people and wounded nine others. After his arrest, he
informed police God had told him to kill" (Chapman, 1989, p. 7B).
This account of the mental illness of a homeless person typifies
some of the highly distorted and biased mass-media images of the

homeless crisis. It is an image derived from the pronouncements of a select group of psychiatrists who have attempted to convince the public that the complex causes of homelessness, and the fact that a majority of America's homeless population is nonwhite, can be simplistically reduced to a mental illness issue and thus to a genetic issue.

The newspaper commentary went on to present its analysis of the causes of homelessness: "One of the most durable myths about the homeless is that there is nothing wrong with them that cheap apartments wouldn't fix. . . . Many of the homeless are people who would have trouble keeping a roof over their heads if you gave them a mansion on Rodeo Drive" (Chapman, 1989, p. 7B). Where did this newspaper commentator get his information from? He found it in *Nowhere to Go: The Tragic Odyssey of the Homeless Mentally Ill* (1988), by psychiatrist E. Fuller Torrey. Torrey claimed that there are "vast hordes of mentally ill homeless persons" populating our cities. He described the bulk of the homeless population as "lazy individuals who will do anything to avoid work . . . alcoholics and drug addicts . . . newly arriving immigrants [and] recently released denizens of jails" (pp. 6–7).

Throughout the Reagan–Bush era, and to a lesser extent today, various "experts" have attempted to shift the focus on the causes of minority homelessness away from larger economic and social processes and onto alleged characteristics and attributes of homeless individuals. Most of the initial literature on the new homeless of the 1980s was well grounded in reductionism and racism. Psychiatrists have played a prominent role in "medicalizing," "psychologizing," and "biologizing" the origins of homelessness. Perhaps unwittingly, these psychiatrists have succumbed to the ideological requirements of very conservative political administrations.

Ellen Bassuk, a Harvard psychiatrist, is the chair of the Better Homes and Gardens Magazine Foundation for homeless families. In a *Better Homes and Gardens* article (Daly, 1988, pp. 21–24), she claimed that "Homelessness is ultimately a local issue, dealt with by local organizations." In 1984 she authored an article that appeared in the prestigious *Scientific American*. She posited that deinstitutionalization from mental hospitals and chronic mental illness were the primary causes of homelessness. The evidence given by Bassuk for these claims was weak, and the conclusions lacked solid scientific reliability or validity. According to Bassuk (1984), "Homelessness is often the final stage in a lifelong series of crises and missed opportunities, the culmination of a gradual disengagement from supportive relationships and institutions" (p. 43). Frankly it is difficult to understand why such a notable scientific journal would publish this piece; it was clearly more speculative and ideological than scientific. Much of Bassuk's subsequent research focused on homeless families and children. Although she admitted more recently that the lack of decent low-income housing plays a role, she has basically concluded that homeless mothers and children suffer from "personality disorders" or "difficulties in relationships," which contribute significantly to their homelessness (Bassuk, Rubin, and Lauriat, 1986).

In 1988, the National Academy of Sciences published *Homelessness, Health, and Human Needs,* prepared by the academy's Institute of Medicine. This study contained a comprehensive review of research about who the homeless were but had a disappointing explanation of the causes of homelessness. The Institute of Medicine apparently either forgot about or became confused regarding the meanings, distinctions, and relationships between *necessary* and *sufficient* causes in its discussion of the origin of poverty and homelessness. It claimed, under a section of its document titled "Health Problems That Cause Homelessness," that, in many cases, health problems *are* the cause of homelessness. The document states, "Some health problems precede and causally contribute to homelessness . . . the most common of [which] are the major mental illnesses. In addition to accidents, various common illnesses such as the degenerative diseases that accompany old age can also lead to homelessness" (p. 39). Certainly, mental illnesses and various other health problems occur among the homeless, but to maintain that they are either necessary or sufficient causes of homelessness constitutes poor logic, reductionism, and pseudoscience.

Of course, there is no question that a physical or mental illness may contribute to increasing an individual's vulnerability to becoming homeless. But illness is neither a necessary nor a sufficient cause of homelessness. In science, a necessary cause is one that *must* be present for the effect under study (in this case, homelessness) to occur. For example, in order for a human to become pregnant, she must be female, even though not all females will become pregnant. A sufficient cause is one that, when present, inevitably leads to the effect under study.

Although many of the homeless suffer from health problems, and some of them have serious psychological problems, illness of any kind does not inevitably lead to homelessness. To argue otherwise is not science but ideology. In addition, such arguments unwittingly perpetuate blaming-the-victim views of homelessness. These approaches obscure the real causes of homelessness and play into the hands of political reactionaries.

In December 1986 psychiatrist E. Fuller Torrey participated in a national conference on the homeless held at George Washington University in Washington, D.C. The panel attempted to address the causes of homelessness. Torrey's position was clearcut: Homeless people were mentally ill and had either been released from mental hospitals or should be placed in them. In a later article, Torrey, in a fashion reminiscent of craniology and characterology, asserted that three factors cause homelessness: bad brains, bad genes, and bad luck. Torrey never acknowledged the epidemiological fact that the majority of the homeless were nonwhite and what that might imply for his theory.

Torrey also maintained that one-third of the homeless had "bad brains," which meant, in Torrey's reductionist view, they had mental diseases such as schizophrenia. Absolutely no scientific or psychiatric research exists adequately documenting such a sweeping claim. A review of research literature on mental illness among the homeless shows that no more than 15 percent of the homeless have a diagnosis of schizophrenia or bipolar disorder combined, and even then the validity of the diagnoses is in question (Ropers, 1988).

Torrey (1988) further theorized that another one-third of the homeless were afflicted with alcoholism, drug abuse, criminal behavior, marginal IQs, and personality disorders. He argued that all of these conditions were evidence of "bad genes." The remaining one-third, Torrey conceded, were victims of "bad luck," for example, individuals displaced from jobs because of changes in technology.

There is, however, no consensus among the scientific research community that one-third of the homeless are schizophrenic or manic-depressive. In fact, most of the research in the latter part of the 1980s and the early 1990s, including the psychiatric research, indicates that the vast majority of the homeless do not suffer from any form of chronic mental illness, nor are they former mental patients or individuals who should be institutionalized.

As for the "bad luck" explanation, it suggests that haphazard events select individuals and cause some homelessness. The homeless, however, are not victims of chance occurrences; they are victims of clearly identifiable and patterned national economic, social, and political trends, such as underemployment, cutbacks in social welfare, and the lack of low-income housing.

The public pronouncements of psychiatrists like Bassuk and Torrey are based on highly flawed research and, in some cases, on no research at all. Undoubtedly the prestige of the medical profession played some role in the early acceptance of these views. More likely, however, the ideological role of these psychiatric positions provided them with wide acceptance. Blaming homelessness on bad personalities, brains, and genes fit well into the extremely individualistic and entrepreneurial ideologies of the Reagan and Bush administrations. Contending that homelessness is primarily caused by mental illness opens the door to the idea it is biologically determined. David Tomb, professor of psychiatry at the University of Utah Medical School and medical director of the Western Institute of Neuropsychiatry, maintains that, because genetics causes schizophrenia, and most of the homeless are schizophrenic, homelessness is therefore caused by a biological pathology (Palmer, 1986). Because professionals such as Tomb and Torrey do not understand the severe manifestations of U.S. social and racial inequality, they contend that homelessness is mainly a mental health issue. They as well as other many psychiatrists take a blame-the-victim approach and advocate psychotherapy as a solution, but they ignore or dismiss the structural racial injustice of the U.S. stratification system.

One factor that contributes to the confusion regarding the relation of race, homelessness, and mental illness is the documented misdiagnosis of African-American people. William B. Lawson (1986), a doctor, found that "Recent research suggests that Blacks and other minorities are at a greater risk than whites of being misdiagnosed" (p. B2). Psychiatrist B. Jones, director of psychiatry at the Lincoln Medical and Mental Health Center in the Bronx, New York, stressed that cultural differences in the expression of emotion and behavior may result in the misdiagnosis of blacks because psychiatric diagnosis rests "almost entirely" on observations of behavior (Jones and Gray, 1986).

The stereotype that most of the homeless are nonwhite undeserving bums and derelicts or that some personal form of pathology (e.g., alcoholism, drug abuse, mental illness or retardation, and divorce or separation) was the primary cause of homelessness was used by the Reagan–Bush administrations to divert attention from racism and the serious structural problems of the economy. Through the political activity of the homeless and their advocates and scientific research, a more accurate picture of who the homeless are helped overthrow the ideologically inspired stereotypes.

What we do know is that the homeless are mostly nonwhite displaced and unwanted members of the lower and working classes who are victims of national social and economic trends beyond their control. Compared to previous generations of "skid row" homeless, today's homeless are younger and better educated; the majority are nonwhite; and if there is one institution most homeless men have been in, it isn't a mental hospital, it is the U.S. military! One-third to one-half of homeless men, depending on location, are veterans. A fifth of the homeless are working full or part-time, while another three-fifths actively look for work. The majority received no public assistance before becoming homeless, and at least through most of the 1980s, most received no assistance while they were homeless. Although about a third of the homeless may have various problems with alcohol, that isn't very different from the extent of alcohol problems among the general population.

All of the "social science" theories reviewed above have several themes in common. They all are reductionist because they account for the complex social conditions of the status of nonwhites, inequality, and stratification in terms of genetic, biological, attitudinal, or personality defects and pathology. They are overly simplistic and limited in their scientific validity, and they support conservative and even reactionary right-wing racist politics. They are part of the great evasion of primary social and racial injustice in the United States.

Chapter 4

Social Conditions in the United States

After hundreds of years of struggle and endless political pronouncements about equality, democracy, freedom, civil rights, material abundance, well-being, and unlimited opportunities, U.S. society remains permeated with economic, social, and racial injustice and the gross inequality of its citizens.

Despite the widespread belief among Americans that they live in the richest nation in the world, the World Bank reports that the United States ranks only seventh relative to per-person gross national product. As Table 4.1 indicates, Switzerland ranks number one.

Although part of the American-dream mythology promotes visions of unlimited upward social mobility, rags-to-riches is the exception, not the rule. A *New York Times* report concluded:

> But modern Horatio Algers not withstanding, a wave of recent studies show that rags-to-riches remains the economic exception, not the rule. Though many doors and many rewards are open to talent, being rich or poor is more likely than not to carry over from generation to generation, and certainly from year to year.
>
> If anything, economists say, the climb out of poverty has become harder in the last decade or two. The United

Table 4.1. Per-Person 1990 GNP by Country
(Using Market Exchange Rates)

1. Switzerland	$32,688
2. Finland	$28,640
3. Japan	$25,430
4. Sweden	$23,680
5. Norway	$23,120
6. Germany	$22,320
7. United States	$21,790

Source: *New York Times*, March 8, 1992.

States' economy has become less and less hospitable to the young, the unskilled and less educated. It is highly unlikely that this year's rich man will be next year's pauper—or vice versa. (Nasar, 1992b)

White middle- and working-class citizens often seem to psychologically and politically block out and rationalize the constant emotional and social tension—generated by conflict between racial, ethnic, class, and alternative lifestyle groups—that has its roots deeply planted in economic competition. As hard economic times increase the competition for limited economic resources (such as jobs, housing, medical care, education, and welfare), the stage is set for more racial, ethnic, and lifestyle tensions.

The U.S. reality is that over a third of the population lives near or below government poverty guidelines. In 1990, ninety-four million Americans lived in households where the annual income was less than $15,000.

The United States is grossly stratified and polarized in its distribution of wealth and income. For example, the top fifth (20 percent) of the population receives 46.1 percent of the before-tax income, while the bottom fifth receives only 3.8 percent. This is the lowest percentage of income of any bottom fifth of a population in any industrialized nation.

When the pretax income received is broken down in population fifths by the share received by each major racial group, African Americans and Latinos make up larger percentages of the lower income fifths than whites (see Table 4.2).

As U.S. troops were sent to Somalia to feed the hungry, Patti Carr, an unemployed office manager on her way to the United Christian Food Pantry for food handouts, stated, "I think it's wonderful that we put our effort into helping the people in Somalia, but I also wish they'd put half as much effort into helping people at home." John Hammock, an Oxfam famine-relief organization spokesperson, said, "You don't have to go overseas to find the Third World. The Third World exists in the United States, and in urban as well as rural areas" ("Hungry Say Relief Needed at Home, Too," 1992, p. A1). The U.S. Conference of Mayors reported that requests for emergency food assistance had increased 26 percent in major U.S. cities ("Relief Agency to Attack Hunger in U.S.," 1992, p. 12).

The Tufts University Center on Hunger, Poverty and Nutrition claimed hunger had increased by 50 percent in America since the mid-1980s. The number of hungry Americans in 1985

Table 4.2. Percentages of Racial Groups among Income and Population Fifths

Population fifths	White	African American	Latino
Top fifth	21.3	8.7	11.0
2nd fifth	20.5	13.5	15.6
3rd fifth	20.5	17.5	20.4
4th fifth	19.5	22.8	24.7
Lowest fifth	8.1	37.6	28.3

Source: *Measuring the Effect of Benefits and Taxes on Income and Poverty* (1988). U.S. Department of Commerce, Bureau of the Census, Washington, DC.

was twenty million; today it is thirty million. The Harvard School of Public Health and the Physician Task Force on Hunger in America defined hunger as "chronically short of the nutrients necessary for growth and good health" (Brown, 1987, p. 37).

THE PLIGHT OF U.S. CHILDREN

The condition of a society's most vulnerable group, its children, is a good index of the state of that society's social conditions and relations. "The Economics of Life and Death" (1993), a report published in the *Scientific American* by Amartya Sen, says:

> The more conventional criteria of measuring economic success can be enhanced by including assessments of a nation's ability to extend and to improve the quality of life. (p. 40)

> Analyzing mortality data can help in the economic evaluation of social arrangements and of public policy. This perspective can be particularly useful in elucidating crucial aspects of social inequality and poverty and in identifying policies that can counter them. One of the more immediate problems that must be faced in the U.S. is the need for a fuller understanding of the nature of economic deprivation. Income is obviously a major issue in characterizing poverty, but the discussion of American poverty in general and of African-American poverty in particular has frequently missed important dimensions because of an overconcentration on income. (p. 45)

> Black male children in Harlem are less likely to reach the age of 65 than male babies in Bangladesh. Even though poor Black Americans live materially better than the poor in third world countries, like Bangladesh and China, the higher mortality of Black American males "reflects deaths caused by violence. Violence is a significant part of social deprivation in the U.S.A." (p. 46)

African-American life expectancy has actually declined. In 1990 it was reported that African Americans could expect to live, on average, only 69.2 years, down from 69.7 years in 1984. However, white life expectancy had risen from 75.3 years to 75.6 years.

INFANT MORTALITY AND LIFE EXPECTANCY

The death rate of infants is unfortunately a valid measure of the health and social condition of a population. There are significant infant mortality differences between racial groups in the United States. In 1992 the *New York Times* reported that a study by Robert A. Hahn, a doctor at the federal Centers for Disease Control, indicated that death rates of minority infants were underestimated. The *Times* story stated:

> The study, for 1983 to 1985, found that infant mortality was slightly overreported for whites, but underreported for all other races and ethnic groups. . . . The researchers found that true infant mortality was overreported for whites by 2.1 percent, and underreported for all other races: 3.2 percent for blacks, 46.9 percent for American Indians, 33.3 percent for Chinese-Americans, 48.8 percent for Japanese-Americans, 78.7 percent for Filipino-Americans and 8.9 percent for Hispanic-Americans. ("Death Rates for Minority Infants Underestimated, Study Says," 1992, p. A14)

Children in Poverty

In 1990 one in five American children lived in poverty. If current trends continue, by the year 2000 one in three children will live in poverty (see Table 4.3). Nearly sixteen million are just 25 percent above the poverty line and live in conditions similar to those of the "official" poor, but they are not technically con-

Table 4.3. Children at Risk, 1977–1991

Children in poverty	1977–1981 (%)	1989–1991 (%)	Percentage change (average), 1977–1991
United States	16.9	19.8	17
Whites	10.4	11.4	9
Blacks	42.0	44.1	5
Latinos	30.3	37.9	25

Source: Barazia (1993), p. B1.

sidered living in official poverty. A 1990 study, conducted by the National Center for Children in Poverty at Columbia University, examined families with children that were living in near-poverty conditions. The study found that "many of these families have as much difficulty as officially poor families. When we look closely at children living in near-poverty, we find they are often indistinguishable from children living in poverty" ("Twenty-five Percent of Children under Age 6 Live below Poverty Line," 1990, p. 2).

For minority children the situation is drastic. An astonishing 43 percent of African-American and 37 percent of Latino children live below the poverty line. Nearly 30 percent of the 18.5 million children who live in the central cities live in poverty. Most of these poor children (71 percent) live in families with two parents present, and with one or both parents working.

A three-hundred-page report by the House Select Committee on Children, Youth, and Families (*Report: Children Locked in Poverty*, 1989) found that children make up the largest segment of the U.S. poverty population. Among children, the poverty rate rose from 15 percent in 1970 to 20.5 percent in 1989.

CRIME

The FBI's 1992 *Uniform Crime Report* revealed that during 1991 the number of violent crimes reported to the police exceeded 1.9 million offenses, the highest number ever recorded. Violent crimes include murder (1 percent), rape (6 percent), robbery (36 percent), and aggravated assault (57 percent).

The murder rate reached an all-time high in 1991, at 24,703, one of the world's highest murder rates! New York City averaged about two thousand homicides per year, and Los Angeles averaged about one thousand homicides per year. Over half (53 percent) of the murder victims were acquainted with their murderers. Among females killed, 28 percent were murdered by husbands or boyfriends. A third of the murders were preceded by arguments.

In 1992 the *New York Times* reported that gun homicides were highest among African-American men from the ages of fifteen to nineteen (see Table 4.4). In Washington, D.C., the rate was 227 deaths for every 100,000 people; Los Angeles County was next with 226. The lowest rate in the study was found in Dade County, Florida, which includes most of the Miami metropolitan area.

The U.S. Department of Justice reported in 1993 that the state and federal prison populations had reached a record high of 883,592 inmates ("Drug Crimes Push Prison Populations to New Levels," 1993, p. A5). This represented a 7.2 percent increase over the previous year. The federal prison population had grown by a rate of 12.1 percent to 80,259 inmates, and the state prison population had risen by 6.8 percent, to 803,334.

There is also the plague of youth gangs. For instance, in the city of Los Angeles there are approximately seventy thousand gang members. In a 1994 Associated Press national poll on crime, 60 percent of the respondents indicated that "being a victim of crime" was something they were personally worried about. When asked, "Is there an area within a mile of your home where you

Table 4.4. Firearm Homicides among Young
African-American Males

City	Rate per 100,000
Washington, DC	227.2
Los Angeles, CA	226.0
Wayne, MI (Detroit)	220.8
Duval, FL (Jacksonville)	97.8
Orleans, LA (New Orleans)	178.3
Henrico, VA (Richmond)	169.4
Brooklyn, NY	164.9
Jackson, MO (Kansas City)	152.0
St. Louis, MO	148.2
Broward, FL (Fort Lauderdale)	43.1
Baltimore, MD	132.3
New York, NY	32.2
Suffolk, MA (Boston)	30.4
Dade, FL (Miami)	129.3
Caddo, LA (Shreveport)	26.6
Alameda, CA (Oakland)	21.0
Genesee, MI (Flint)	119.1
Maricopa, AZ (Phoenix)	114.9
Queens, NY	110.4
Philadelphia, PA	103.4

Source: *New York Times* (June 11, 1992).

would be afraid to walk around at night?" again 60 percent of the
respondents answered yes.

LOS ANGELES: A CASE STUDY OF AN
AMERICAN MELTING-POT FAILURE

The city of Los Angeles serves as an excellent case study of
the declining social and economic conditions of the 1990s in U.S.

society. The worst urban riot in modern history was ignited by the Rodney King criminal trial in which four white LA cops were found not guilty of abusing their powers when they beat him. The riot's aftermath left fifty-three people dead and $500 million in property damage.

As we were writing this chapter, the nation anxiously awaited the jury's verdict in the Rodney King civil trial held in federal court. The eyes of the nation were on America's second largest city, Los Angeles, where, at the time of the jury's delibera-tion, the sale of assault rifles was at an all-time high, small busi-nesses were boarding up their windows, the LA police were going through intensive riot-control training, and the California Na-tional Guard was bivouacked in warehouses preparing to put down a possible urban revolt. On April 19, 1994, Rodney King was awarded $3.8 million in compensatory damages by a Los Angeles jury ("King Gets $3.8 Million, Goes after Officers," 1994, p. A6).

In the subsequent civil suit brought by King against fifteen police officers, Officer Tim Wind, who admitted clubbing King ten times and kicking him six times, contended he had been ordered to do so by Sergeant Stacey Koon. Wind testified that Koon ordered, "Hit him! Hit him!" ("Officer Says He Was Ordered to Hit King," 1994, p. A5).

This situation contrasts starkly with a city that was once thought to be a model of the U.S. racial and ethnic melting pot. *Time* described Los Angeles as "a map of bunkered [ethnic] en-claves" (Lacayo, 1993, p. 28).

In response to *Time*'s April 19, 1993 cover story, "Los An-geles: Is the City of Angels Going to Hell?" reader Jennifer Ehren-berg wrote the following letter to the editor:

> I've lived in Los Angeles County for only 18 months. During this time I have had a number of uniquely L.A. experiences, including lying on the floor during a gang shoot-out after which eight bodies were carried from a neighboring house; "losing" the tires and wheels from my car; witnessing a gang-related stabbing at the beach; fleeing from bottle-

throwing youths at the start of last year's riots; and waking
up to two earthquakes and several floods. Why was anyone
surprised by the '92 riots? L.A. went to hell long before then.
("Los Angeles: Is the City of Angels Going to Hell?" 1993,
p. 9)

Los Angeles's plight is really not unique; rather, it is in-
dicative and representative of the state of the nation. At the root
of Los Angeles's racial and ethnic conflict, soaring crime rate, and
huge homeless population is the increasing polarization of wealth
and poverty. The poverty rate for residents in LA's South Central
District is higher in the 1990s than it was during the Watts riots
in 1965. Disinvestment in manufacturing and defense industries
has changed the face of the occupational structure of the United
States and has hit Los Angeles particularly hard. About 160,000
of LA's defense-industry jobs were lost during the early 1990s,
and at least 70,000 manufacturing-related jobs in LA's largely
African-American-populated South Central (Lacayo, 1993).

Carlton Jenkins, manager of Founders National Bank, the
only African-American-owned bank in Los Angeles, stated, "The
Rodney King incident was the match that lit the fire that exposed
the increasing disparity between the haves and the have-nots. It's
been a situation festering for some time in the economically disenfranchised communities who live every day with the knowledge that they've gotten everything they're ever going to get"
(Stevenson, 1992, p. 23).

The *New York Times* described South Central Los Angeles as
an economic wasteland, where the per capita annual income in
1990 was $7,600 (52.6 percent lower than for Los Angeles County
as a whole). The unemployment rate for South Central was 7.1
percent, compared to 5.8 percent for Los Angeles County (see
Table 4.5).

A research group at the UCLA School of Architecture and
Urban Planning conducted a comprehensive study of the causes
and conditions of poverty in Los Angeles (Ong, 1989), which,
with a population of about nine million, is one of the largest
urban areas in the United States. The study found that with

Table 4.5. South Central Los Angeles Compared to Los Angeles County, 1990

	South Central	Los Angeles County
Population	523,156	8,863,164
Manufacturing (total employment)	23,756	657,955
People for each manufacturing job	18.8	13.7
Unemployment	7.1	5.8
Median household income	$20,357	$37,904
Percentage of households with income below $7,500	17.0	7.6

Source: Based on *New York Times* (May 6, 1992), p. 23.

nearly 30 percent of its labor force engaged in manufacturing, the Los Angeles percentage of manufacturing-related jobs ranks higher than the national average. While other major cities, such as New York and Chicago, saw their manufacturing labor force shrink, that in Los Angeles has increased (see Table 4.6). The Los Angeles service-sector work force has also grown and now represents 56 percent of all jobs.

The growing disparity of poverty and wealth in Los Angeles epitomizes the economic and social transformation occurring throughout the nation (see Table 4.7). Despite economic growth

Table 4.6. Manufacturing Jobs (Thousands)

	1969	1987
New York	921	461
Chicago	983	551
Los Angeles	881	907

Source: Based on Ong (1989), p. 130.

Table 4.7. Poverty Rates in Los Angeles and the Nation
(Percentages)

	1969	1987	1993
Los Angeles	11.0	15.6	17.0
National	12.1	13.5	15.1

and increasing jobs, Los Angeles has not avoided a gross disparity between income and wealth that has a direct bearing on racial and ethnic relations in that city. In the late 1960s the Los Angeles poverty population of 11 percent was lower than the national average of 12.1 percent, but by the late 1980s it had increased to 15.6 percent and exceeded the national average of 13.5 percent.

The increasing poverty in Los Angeles and its resulting racial and ethnic tensions result partially from "deindustrialization in the high-wage sector and reindustrialization in the low-wage sector" (Ong, 1989, p. 16). Low-wage jobs make up the majority of new jobs in the manufacturing and service sectors in Los Angeles. For example, deindustrialization in African-American areas of Los Angeles has created high rates of unemployment, a primary cause of poverty among minorities.

In the late 1970s and the early 1980s, Los Angeles lost over fifty thousand industrial jobs to plant closures in the auto, tire, steel, and nondefense aircraft industries. These industries traditionally offered high-paying blue-collar employment to large numbers of minorities. Many of these plants were located either within ghettos or nearby. South Central, which forms the core of the African-American community in Los Angeles, experienced a loss of 321 firms from 1971 to 1988 (Ong, 1989, p. 203).

High statistical correlations exist between unemployment, poverty, and minority status. A perfect correlation is 1.00, and the correlation between unemployed African-American males and poverty is .65; it is .81 for African-American females (Ong, 1989, p. 202).

Ironically, poverty in the Hispanic barrios in Los Angeles is associated not with deindustrialization, but with low-wage *reindustrialization*. In recent years, good-paying blue-collar industrial jobs, formerly located within the vicinity of the barrios, have been replaced by low-paying labor-intensive jobs in the apparel and furniture industries.

Low income disproportionately affects African Americans, Latinos, women, and the young. African-American and Latino men in Los Angeles earn, on the average, 30 percent and 20 percent less, respectively, than white men with comparable education and skills. Women, particularly minority women, earn about 33 percent less than white men (Ong, 1989, p. 19). The unfair treatment of African-American and Latino men and women in the labor market reflects, according to the UCLA study, "both overt and deinstitutionalized discrimination":

> [Poverty in Los Angeles] represents the extreme outcome of income inequality: the lack of an income needed to achieve a minimum standard of living. Poverty is the result of the cumulative failures of our society to prepare people for meaningful work, of . . . wage discrimination, of an inadequate safety net, and of changing household structures. Despite this multitude of causes and mediating factors, there is, nonetheless, a direct and significant link between the economy and impoverishment. Given the rise in inequality in the labor market, it is not surprising that the poverty level has also risen. Poverty is a problem of both low wages and joblessness. (Ong, 1989, p. 19)

The position of African Americans and Latinos in the labor market contributes to the explanation of the creation of many of the social problems confronting the Los Angeles African-American ghettos and Latino barrios that trouble middle-class white Americans. Good-paying, steady employment is unavailable in the ghettos and barrios, and racism and discrimination prevent many nonwhite citizens from getting and keeping good jobs outside the poverty neighborhoods. Minority youth, as well as white working-class youth, often feel alienated by the prospect of working at menial jobs. One consequence of this alienation is the growth of youth gangs and youth crime. Youth gangs offer a system of respect and status to their members and often provide illegitimate opportunities for them to make large sums of money, such as in drug dealing. Another consequence of the concentration of the large African-American and Hispanic poverty population in Los Angeles has been the creation of one of the largest nonwhite homeless populations in the nation.

Time writer Richard Lacayo (1993) summarized the relationship of a troubled Los Angeles economy to its racial tensions:

> What has aggravated the city's racial divisiveness is the lack of a strong economy to rebuild on. Los Angeles remains mired in a three-year recession, with a countywide 10.4 percent unemployment rate, three and a half points higher than the U.S. average. In poor black neighborhoods, the rate is as high as 50 percent. The peace dividend of the post-cold war era has landed like a bomb in the Los Angeles area, wiping out 110,000 defense-industry jobs so far and possibly another 50,000 more by the end of next year. Many manufacturing jobs, which supported the city's working class, have evaporated because of corporate cutbacks. L.A.'s South Central District lost more than 70,000 jobs in the 1970's and '80s; the poverty rate for area families now is higher than it was at the time of the Watts riots in 1965. (p. 28)

THE PLIGHT OF U.S. MINORITIES

Minority Poverty

African-American families are 3.5 times more likely to live in poverty than white families. Almost 30 percent of the African-American population lives in poverty; only 6 percent of the white population does. Almost half of poor African-American families are headed by women. Over a quarter of Latinos live in poverty; nearly half of the families are female-headed.

Homeless Minorities

The scourge of homelessness is perhaps the most unfortunate and unsightly symptom of the ills of the U.S. social, racial, and economic landscape. A 1993 Columbia University study found that 13.5 million Americans "have been on the streets or stayed in homeless shelters at some point in their life" (Safety Network, 1993, p. 1). Another study, by Dennis Culhane of the University of Pennsylvania, found that in 1992 African-American children were at "highest risk of homelessness" in New York City and Philadelphia (Safety Network, 1993, p. 1).

Public perceptions of the homeless have been dominated by negative stereotypes and conservative political mythology regarding the causes of homelessness and the composition of the homeless population. Since the mid-1980s a prominent stereotype has been that the majority of the homeless are suffering from chronic mental illness and have been deinstitutionalized from mental hospitals or should be institutionalized in mental hospitals. Other stereotypes and explanations of the homeless population center on drug abuse and alcoholism. All these generalizations about the causes of homelessness and the makeup of the homeless population have been scientifically disproved by numerous research studies (Ropers, 1991). Public opinion is beginning to catch up to the research findings. For example, a national survey by *Parade Magazine* (1994, pp. 4–6) found that "56 percent of those surveyed think that most of the homeless are not responsible for the situation they're in." In addition, 82 percent of the survey participants believed "the homeless should not be prohibited from public places, such as libraries, parks and mass transit," and 63 percent agreed with the statement that "the main reason for homelessness is the breakdown of the American family." Much has been written on the new urban homeless, but little attention has been given to the large numbers of minority group members among the contemporary homeless population.

It is well documented that homeless Americans from the 1950s through the 1970s were predominantly white males (Bogue, 1963). In the past, African Americans and Latinos, while overrepresented among the poor, were underrepresented among the "skid row" homeless. The new urban homeless population of the 1980s and 1990s, however, is composed of larger percentages of nonwhites than ever before. As the U.S. Department of Housing and Urban Development's report on homelessness in America (1984) concluded:

> The minority population (Black, Hispanic, Native American, etc.) is overrepresented among the homeless, a significant change from 20 years ago. Forty four percent of the shelter population is minority according to the national shelter survey, compared to a figure of 20 percent in the national population. (p. 29)

As long as economic and social inequality between races exists, so will racism. Racial conflict and social conflict in U.S. society is deeply rooted in the reality of gross social and economic inequality.

Chapter 5

Learning Prejudice, Learning Hate

I came to live with my father when I was eight. I had lived
in New Haven all my life. . . . When I landed at Salt Lake
City airport, I was terrified: There were no black faces, only
white—even the sky caps were white! My half-sister had
lived in Orem, Utah, all her life, so she didn't know. I wasn't
surprised, but she didn't know how white folk could be. She
was six before she first heard it. She didn't know what it
meant. She was hurt because her best friend told her she
couldn't be her friend anymore because my sister was a
"nigger." She was crying. She didn't know what the word
meant, but she knew she'd lost her best friend. Yeah. *I*
wasn't surprised. *I* was from New Haven. (Angela, 1993)

A woman told us this story about her family's experience as
African Americans living in an almost exclusively white community. Angela's sister's friend had finally learned the beliefs and
norms of her insulated community: that your skin color makes a
difference. Introduced to the social rules about race in the United
States, Angela abruptly entered the world of prejudice, hate, and
discrimination learned through the lifelong process called *socialization,* which teaches the prevailing social rules and practices of
every culture and sets many of the boundaries on who we are as
individuals.

SOCIALIZATION OF U.S. VALUES AND NORMS

Socialization is necessary for any group or society to survive and grow, for it reflects and transmits—through near-universal social institutions such as the family, education, and religion—the essential social values and rules that maintain the cultural continuity of every society and group in different ways. Too frequently, these institutions teach rules and values that reflect underlying cultural values of prejudice, fear, and hate.

But socialization is more than learning the ways of one's group or society (as if even this is "easy"). It is so encompassing and fundamental that it shapes how we think and reason, as well as our perceptions about our talents, abilities, and the world around us; it even shapes our emotions.

While it might seem strange, each culture has "norms of emotion" (Clark, 1991) that define the proper expression of emotion for a certain culture. This can be easily observed if you stand in an international airport and watch, say, close friends who are reuniting after a considerable separation. If you are watching Americans only, you will immediately notice an enormous difference in the emotional responses between two women and those between two men. The women will embrace warmly, and often for a considerable time. Men, on the other hand, will either shake hands vigorously, or perhaps indulge in a brief embrace with usually one or maybe two pats or slaps on the back. If your observations include men of different cultures, you will notice Japanese men bowing formally to each other, while French men, Russian men, and Arab men embrace and kiss each other.

Equally interesting is to observe the differences in how often couples of different cultures touch each other. Social researcher Sidney Jourard did just this and discovered substantial differences based on nationality and geographical region. For example, Americans and northern Europeans touched each other much less frequently than members of Mediterranean cultures. When he went to different cities and kept track of touches between couples, he counted 180 touches in an hour in San Juan, Puerto Rico; 110 in Paris; 2 in Gainesville, Florida; and 0 in London (Thayer, 1988).

These descriptions of socialization sound harmless, but contrast them with this chilling example of how prejudice and hatred are also socialized: as a young couple is being interviewed, a small child is heard in the background. The mother leafs through a book, then places it on the table: it is about Adolf Hitler. She readily acknowledges they read to their child from it. As everyone walks into the child's room, the camera zooms in on a large flag above the crib: a Nazi flag. German neo-Nazis? No, they are a young Pennsylvania couple, raising their child to be a racist (Cochran, 1994).

Socialization reflects and reinforces cultural *myths* and *inequalities* as well as values. Social scientists and other observers of our social condition have long recognized the enormous gulf between what we say and what we do. Although American culture professes freedom and equality as fundamental cultural values, there is little in our nation's past or present to indicate these values are universally applied. Unfortunately, much of American history reads like a litany of *in*equality and prejudice. Not only were the first white settlers unable to leave Native Americans in peace (or alive), but they were also unable to leave other *white* settlers in peace. We hold onto our romantic ideas that Europeans came to North America and established the religious freedom they had been denied in their homeland, but the truth is that many of the colonies were intolerant of and bigoted against other views and values. For example, the Puritans of Massachusetts in the 1600s not only conducted the infamous Salem witch trials, executing twenty innocent people and terrorizing countless others, but also literally chased Roger Williams from Boston to Rhode Island because he wanted to allow, among others, *Catholics* to settle in the colony. There was religious freedom only for those willing to subscribe to a narrow doctrine determined by a few—hardly religious "freedom"—and ironically, they practiced many of the same persecutions from which they had so diligently escaped.

From our earliest roots, then, Americans have been socialized to be prejudiced—to be suspicious of people who look, act, and have beliefs outside prevailing cultural norms and values. It is not surprising, then, that deep-rooted prejudice exists in every U.S. institution, from the family to education, from the law to the job market.

In earlier chapters we discussed the dismal situations of various racial, ethnic, and cultural groups in U.S. society, So, how do we as Americans "learn" or become socialized that prejudice and discrimination are not only acceptable but are as "American as apple pie" (Riga, 1993)?

THE SOCIALIZATION OF PREJUDICE

Socialization is a lifelong process, though it is most crucial and powerful in an individual's early years. Aristotle is reputed to have claimed, after teaching the boy who was to become Alexander the Great, "Give me a child for his first five years and he will be mine for life."

Several crucial social institutions are involved in this learning and teaching process, each offering somewhat different messages about how individuals and groups are supposed to act and feel in given situations, and about how social rewards (such as wealth and power) should be distributed. The family and education are two of the most important in passing on social knowledge from one generation to the next. We could examine any of the major socializing institutions—religion, the mass media, the law, or peer groups, to name a few—and uncover how we raise, train, and teach our children to accept prejudice and discrimination as at least "normal," and at times "natural" and "morally correct." A brief look at just the family and education provides us many examples of the power and pervasiveness of American prejudice.

SOCIALIZATION WITHIN THE FAMILY

The family is, without doubt, the most important socializing institution in virtually all societies, no matter how different the specific rules and norms of behavior, thought, and emotions are. Because human infants cannot survive alone, food and shelter are provided, language is learned, intimate emotional ties are established, and society's values and norms become part of a child's self-identity.

Because children are unable to compare or evaluate what they learn with what other children learn or what other adults teach, they are often left overly vulnerable to whatever messages are taught by their parents. Children are also born into existing social positions and roles *within the family*. They learn society's meanings of their and others' positions, roles, and norms, including how society groups people based on social class, race, gender, and sexual orientation. They learn that those groups are treated unequally both within and outside the family and often internalize those meanings into their own concept of themselves.

Learning and Reflecting Social-Class Prejudice

> In several experiments, scientists injected toxic plutonium into gravely injured hospital patients. In another, they exposed indigent cancer patients to whole-body radiation 10 times more powerful than that recommended as treatment for leukemia. They dangled prison inmates' testicles in irradiated water, and served poor pregnant women cocktails containing radioactive iron filings. (Healy, 1994, p. A1)

Was this tax-financed testing done by Nazi Germany? No, these "tests" were conducted in the United States of America—and some of our most prestigious research institutions demonstrated a "little of the Buchenwald touch" (Healy, 1994, p. A1). These so-called scientific experiments were all the more outrageous because of *who* the guinea pigs were. They were not the scientists themselves, nor their families, nor were they patients at private hospitals such as the Mayo Clinic. No, they were those already victimized once in society: they were mostly poor.

What is it in our nation that allows radiation experiments on our poorest citizens? It is a cultural prejudice against those without money, power, or prestige—what social scientists call prejudice based on social class.

The traditional American prejudice against the working class and the poor is rooted in the ideology of society as a "meritocracy." The basic belief in this ideology is that all Americans enjoy essentially equal opportunity to succeed. In the American belief system, equality of opportunity means one's social class, whether upper or working class, rich or poor, is a "natural" reflection of one's ability, intelligence, talents, and morals.

Applying Herbert Spencer's phrase "the survival of the fittest" to one's social class has long legitimized America's prejudice toward those at the bottom of the economic ladder. To test whether Americans still held these beliefs, a 1986 nationwide survey asked people to rank a list of reasons for poverty in the United States. The most frequently cited reasons for poverty were that poor people were lazy and stupid. For example, laziness and immorality were cited as reasons for poverty nearly twice as frequently as prejudice (Kluegel and Smith, 1986). As seen in Figure 5.1, when asked if rich and poor had equal opportunity to succeed in America, nearly as many of the poorest Americans agreed with this statement as did the richest (Robertson, 1987).

These results demonstrate how effective socialization can be, as children of all classes adopt the dominant cultural values and beliefs, beliefs that justify the continued exploitation and oppression of America's poorest and most powerless citizens. Beginning in early childhood, working- and lower-class children are taught values that "explain" why their own class is among society's least "fit."

While different social classes have different social values, they also produce different discipline styles. According to Kammeyer, Ritzer, and Yetman (1994), working-class children are punished directly after they misbehave, no questions asked. In

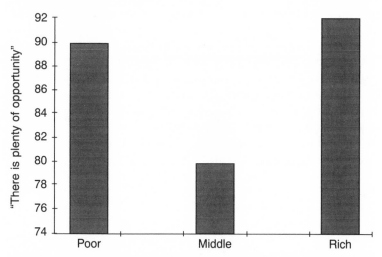

Figure 5.1. Americans' beliefs about opportunity to succeed, controlling for income. Source: Robertson (1987), p. 248.

contrast, middle-class children are more likely to be punished according to how parents evaluate the child's *intention*. Working-class children are punished if they violated a *rule*. The long-term parental goal is obedience—to rules and to authority. Middle-class children are punished (or not) if they violate the long-term parental goal of self-direction.

Since the late 1960s, social scientist Melvin Kohn (1969; Kohn, Naoi, Schoenbach, Schooler, and Slomczynski, 1990) has explored the influence of social class on child-rearing and socializing practices. He has found that many working-class parents emphasize their children's outward conformity—that is, being obedient, following the rules, and staying out of trouble—while many middle-class parents stress curiosity, exploration, and self-expression in their children.

Kohn also found that parents' work experiences play a major part in these child-rearing practices. Many working-class jobs emphasize conformity and obedience to authority, and these parents, generally expecting their children will work at blue-collar jobs similar to their own, teach them to function well in work settings where they do what they are told, when they are told to do it. In contrast, many middle- and upper-middle-class jobs, especially professional and management positions, emphasize initiative, self-expression, and autonomy. Expecting their children to work in similar white-collar and professional settings, these parents teach them to function well in work settings that expect initiative and responsibility.

By pushing working-class children toward working-class jobs, child-rearing practices help perpetuate the U.S. class system. It is a testament to the power of socialization that many working-class families not only believe in the rightness of a system that is prejudiced against them but raise their children to maintain this discriminatory system.

Kohn's research shows how parental socialization helps perpetuate the discrimination inherent in the U.S. class structure. Working-class parents not only teach their children to be obedient to rules and external authorities, but also push their children toward jobs that pay less and have less power and less social status. They teach their children to know, expect, and accept their "place" as unequals within the U.S. social class system.

Family socialization can also lead to other types of prejudice and discrimination. For example, members of the middle and upper middle class tend to have more liberal attitudes about civil liberties than working-class families, especially around issues such as affirmative action programs for non-Anglos and women. As long as affirmative action programs were aimed at trade unions and other working-class occupations, they received tremendous support from those whom sociologist Robert Merton called fair-weather liberals. But when elite graduate and professional schools began using affirmative action guidelines for admissions, many middle- and upper-middle-class members criticized these programs as "reverse discrimination." In other words, as long as middle-class Anglos didn't have to be confronted by the presence or influence of working-class or poor in their daily or working lives, personal prejudices, fears, and hatred remained "underground."

Learning Racial Prejudice

> "Mommy, I want to be white." Imagine my wife's anguish and alarm when our beautiful brown-skinned three-year-old daughter made that declaration. We thought we were doing everything right to develop her self-esteem and positive racial identity. We overloaded her toy box with black dolls. We carefully monitored the racial content of TV shows and videos. . . . Yet now our daughter was saying she wanted to be white. . . . How had she got that potentially soul-destroying idea and, even more important, what should we do about it? (White, 1993, p. 48)

This is an excellent example of how quickly and completely a culture's values and norms are integrated into a person's identity. That a three-year-old is ready to absolutely reject a fundamental aspect of who she is—a person of color—is a profound statement of the power of the negative messages of hate, fear, and prejudice aimed toward her.

One of the primary effects of early childhood socialization is the *internalization* of dominant cultural messages into one's self-concept. Anglo-American parents may not give this much thought, but nonwhite American parents have an added burden: They must socialize their children into a culture that defines them as unequal and inferior to whites. The dilemma is how to transmit broad social values and meaning without teaching their children to internalize, and thus believe and participate in, their own inequality.

Latino, Native American, African-American, and Asian-American parents have to struggle with their own level of allegiance to a social system that does not fully embrace them and their children and, at worst, brutalizes and despises them. The ambivalence and tensions produced by this dilemma are experienced not only by parents, but also by their children.

One consequence of this dilemma is that some children of color adopt the negative label that Anglo culture has put on their race, a condition described as *self-hate*. In the famous 1947 "doll" experiment, psychologists Mamie and Kenneth Clark asked 253 black children between ages of three and seven to choose between a black and a white doll; two-thirds of the African-American children preferred to play with the white doll. No matter their age, many of the youngsters commented that the white dolls were "nice" and that the black dolls "look bad" (McLemore, 1991, p. 148).

In 1985 psychologist Darlene Powell-Hopson repeated the doll test using black and white Cabbage Patch dolls; again, 65 percent of the African-American children preferred the white dolls. Many of their comments were very similar to those of an earlier generation of African-American children; one child explained, "Black is dirty" (White, 1993, p. 48). Often the lessons children learn are transmitted unknowingly. According to Powell-Hopson, "This does not indicate that they want to be white, but reflects their knowledge that society prefers a skin color other than their own" (White, 1993, p. 99). Philosophy professor Laurence Thomas (1990) described this preference of skin color as a "scar of distrust [that] becomes the fountainhead of low self-esteem and self-hate" (p. 84).

Researchers put some of the blame on how parents socialize their children. The doll study was again repeated, and after reading *positive* stories about black dolls, a majority of African-American *and* white children chose a black doll. American society's prejudice against nonwhites is both pervasive and subtle, and there is a danger that parents' socialization of their children will reflect society's disdain for people of color. According to Powell-Hopson, "Many of us [African-American parents] perpetuate negative influence of family on messages, showing preference for lighter complexions, saying nappy hair is bad and straight hair is good, calling other black people 'niggers,' that sort of thing"

(White, 1993, p. 49). In some way, this is a chilling example of how difficult it is for anyone to behave differently from how they were socialized themselves—even if it means perpetuating "self-hate" in their children.

Zena Oglesby, founder and executive director of the Institute of Black Parenting, an African-American adoption agency, helps prospective African-American parents deal with fears about adopting darker-skinned children. He estimates that over 40 percent of the couples who come into his agency prefer a light-skinned child, regardless of their own complexions ("Why Skin Color," 1992). This is another painful reminder of how U.S. society is prejudiced toward dark skin.

But much of the pressure and preference for lighter skin reflects how U.S. society devalues people with nonwhite skin, and how minorities have internalized this racist devaluation of their own color. African-American film director and cultural leader Spike Lee, in his films *School Daze* and *Jungle Fever*, openly acknowledged this painful phenomenon, for which he received some rancor from African-American community members. Lee showed tremendous courage by exposing how African Americans also mirror society's prejudiced preference for lighter skin. In an ironic twist, in April 1994, Lee's father publicly acknowledged his estrangement from his son because of the *father's* interracial marriage.

Other research using pre-school-aged children supports the idea that African-American, Latino, Native American, and Asian-American children accept the social evaluation of themselves as members of an inferior group. It was exactly this idea that helped the U.S. Supreme Court challenge school segregation in the 1954 *Brown v. Board of Education of Topeka* case. In that ruling, the Court declared that segregating children because of race "generates a feeling of inferiority as to their status in the community that may affect their hearts and minds in a way unlikely ever to be undone. . . . Separate . . . facilities are inherently unequal."

Latino, African-American, Native American, and Asian-American families struggle to help their children contend with the daily experiences of prejudice, what psychiatry professor Alvin Poussaint called "mini-assaults" (Peterson, 1992, p. 7D). He stressed the importance of these families' dealing with the tension and conflicts without turning the social prejudice back onto non-white children. What families must teach is that "There is not something wrong with the child. There is something wrong with the bigots."

Learning Gender Prejudice

> Frogs and snails and puppy-dogs' tails,
> And that are little boys made of.
> Sugar and spice and all that's nice,
> And that are little girls made of.
> Sighs and leers, and crocodile tears,
> And that are young men made of.
> Ribbons and laces, and sweet pretty faces,
> And that are young women made of.

As a result of countless generations of socialization, traditional roles and expectations of women and men have come to be seen as "natural" and "morally right." Institutionalized as a dominant ideology, it is not surprising that these roles and expectations are transmitted, often unknowingly, from parents to their children. The consistent transmission of these *different* roles and expectations is later reflected in social institutions that discriminate against women.

Contrary to popular belief, traditional gender roles are still very much a part of most U.S. families. Women continue to be largely defined as mothers, wives, and managers of the household, while men continue to be viewed as wage earners outside the home. Even when both partners work eight-hour days outside the home, the man does one hour of housework daily and the woman five. Economist Rajani Kanth, in the introduction to his book *Devaluing Women: The Uncharted Domain of Domestic Drudgery* (1995), describes how his stepmother would pray every evening after finishing her housework. When he asked her what she prayed for, she replied, "To be born a man in my next life" (Wright, 1993, p. 1A).

Often, morality is used to legitimize pressures on and expectations of women to adhere to traditional, and often discriminatory, roles. In one widely distributed religious pamphlet, the spiritual leader of the Mormons sternly reminded his female followers, "Women are to be an assistant to the husband. . . . It was never intended by the Lord that married women should compete with men in employment. . . . Wives, come home from the typewriter, come home from the factory. No career approaches in importance that of wife—cooking meals, washing dishes, making beds for one's precious husband" (Benson, 1987, p. 6).

Traditional roles are still strongly reinforced within the family. Studies continue to demonstrate that parents still reward passivity and dependence in female children and activity and independence in males: Preschool boys are allowed to roam farther from home than their sisters; boys are encouraged to play more roughly, to get dirtier, and to be more defiant; and girls are encouraged to be emotionally expressive while boys are often punished for similar behavior. The legacy of prejudice and discrimination is not found in the traditional roles themselves, but in how our culture *values* the different roles traditionally given to women and men. Underlying the seemingly "natural" difference between women and men is the fundamental message that males and masculine activities are more highly valued than females and feminine activities.

This unequal valuing is part of a vicious circle: Low value for women translates into low-paying, low-prestige jobs. Conversely, males have a powerful interest in keeping the inequality system alive; it gives men greater wealth, power, and prestige.

Children's attitudes are often a good barometer of widely held cultural attitudes because they haven't learned to censor what they say or feel. In a study on how children would feel if they were to wake up the other sex, Alice Baumgartner of the Institute for Equality in Education found children in Grades 3 to 12 held a fundamental contempt for females—attitudes held by both boys *and* girls. The boys' comments about being better than girls are to be expected. However, the responses of the girls showed how pervasive our cultural prejudice extends, and how early boys and girls internalize this social reality. One fourth-grader said, "If I were boy, I would be better treated." A third-grader commented, "I could do stuff better than I do now." From another third-grader, "If I were a boy, my whole life would be easier." Perhaps most tellingly, one sixth-grader said, "If I were a boy, my daddy might have loved me" (Tavris and Baumgartner, 1983).

In learning to "be a man," many boys are taught to avoid any behavior deemed feminine, from crying to intimacy. Though research is only just beginning, we assume that there are connections between this early socialization into masculinity and adolescent behaviors, some of which are devastating, such as juvenile male crime rates and suicide rates. As researcher Ruth Hartley (1959) showed, the intense pressure on boys to avoid anything associated with girls and women often translates into hostility *against* girls and women. One boy remarked, "I don't trust women doing anything." Another commented, "They're getting too smart now." One boy was very definite in his feelings about girls and women: "I don't care for females. I don't like females." Explaining the epidemic levels of violence against women in U.S. society can be partly traced to this early socialization into masculinity. We are not able to see masculine and feminine merely as "different" or "separate"; recall Supreme Court Chief Justice Earl Warren's declaration that separate is inherently unequal. By valuing females less than males, we put half of our population in various levels of danger.

Parents' attitudes and behaviors have a strong influence on reinforcing traditional gender differences, norms, and expectations. A recent University of Colorado study showed how parents' stereotypic gender expectations "predestine" their children's future accomplishments in math, reading, and sports. For example, researchers found that parents who believed that boys were "naturally" better at math than girls *perceived* their daughters' objective math scores to be *lower* than they actually were and subsequently guided them away from potentially lucrative math-related careers ("Parents' Beliefs," 1991, p. A1). Our attitudes are so embedded that even reality cannot permeate them or alter our behavior.

Learning Heterosexual Prejudice

Children usually first learn within the family that homosexuality is one of U.S. culture's most stringent taboos.

> Jason was a junior in high school when he sat beside her one night and asked, "Mom, would you love me no matter what?" She got a scared look on her face. "Mom, I'm gay."
> She didn't say a word, just got up, went into her bathroom, and threw up. She walked out of the bathroom, stiff-legged, down to the kitchen. Like bombs exploding, she threw every glass in the cupboard at the wall. She started slapping me and raking her fingers across my face. Then she threw herself down and wailed. It was such an eerie sound. She looked up with this, this crazy look on her face.
> "You cannot—you will not," she gasped, and started scratching her own face, making it bleed. (Bartocci, 1992, p. 78)

Socially labeling and treating gay and lesbian children as *not* healthy and normal has powerful consequences. It can lead to extreme reactions from parents who not only know their children deeply but who have also been encouraged by society to love and accept their children unconditionally.

Hartley (1959) touched on this when she talked about the pressures on boys to conform to a negatively presented role. What was punished so severely was any behavior outside what we have defined as traditionally masculine. The cultural definition of masculinity deems "homosexual" as *not* masculine, and violating that definition can have harsh consequences. Research has shown that by age five, boys are punished, often severely, for engaging in behavior determined to be "not masculine" (Hartley, 1959). The same research also shows that, by age six, boys *and* girls react more harshly toward boys acting "feminine" than toward girls acting "masculine."

This information is useful but not persuasive when one is trying to understand the type of prejudice and fear that Jason's story highlights. The AIDS epidemic has brought a renewed prejudice and fear toward homosexuals, and parents are not immune from these reactions. But even deeper than this is that gay, lesbian, and bisexual children fall outside society's definition of an acceptable or "normal" girl and boy:

> Having been branded a sissy by neighborhood children . . .
> I was often taunted with 'hey sissy' or 'hey faggot' or 'you
> hoo honey' (in a mocking voice when I left the house). To
> avoid harassment, I spent many summers alone in my room.
> I went out on rainy days when the street was empty. . . . I
> didn't need anyone, I told myself over and over again. I was
> an island. Contact with others meant pain. Alone, I was
> protected. (Avicolli, 1988, p. 202)

For many parents, gay and lesbian children almost cease to exist because they have no place in our social groupings. As one father described it, "When your child comes out [reveals his or her gayness], it's like death—the death of the child you thought you knew" (Bartocci, 1992, p. 77).

As we saw with racial and gender prejudice, once a *group* of people are socially defined as "less than," they often become literal targets of others' prejudice and hatred.

In an extreme example of society's antagonism toward gays, an American sailor who admitted beating to death a gay shipmate told U.S. Navy investigators he was "disgusted by homosexuals" and that his victim "deserved it." Allen Schindler was beaten so savagely his mother said "[The body] was so badly destroyed that there was no way of knowing it was my son." The Navy physician who performed the autopsy described the condition of Schindler's body as similar to the consequences of "a high-speed automobile accident or a low-speed aircraft accident" (Howlett, 1993a, p. 3A).

This type of violence is not an isolated, individual act. Antigay and antilesbian harassment and hate crimes are on the rise in the United States. According to an annual crime survey of five metropolitan areas, hate crimes against lesbians and gays had increased 172 percent between 1987 and 1992 ("Survey: Anti-Gay Crimes Up," 1993, p. 3A). These hate crimes range from physical menacing to homicide and are found in every institution of U.S. society, including the family.

Some of the lessons children learn about prejudice, discrimination, and hate are neither unintentional nor without severe consequences. In surveys measuring antilesbian and antigay violence by relatives, between 16 and 41 percent of gay respondents had experienced verbal insults or intimidation by relatives and 4 to 8 percent had encountered physical violence as well (Herek and Berrill, 1992). In April 1993 a twenty-seven-year-old Fort Worth man beat his two-year-old son to death because he was worried his son was becoming a homosexual. The father killed his son for playing with dolls and holding his hands in an "effeminate" manner ("Child Killing," 1993, p. 3A). While tempting to dismiss this example as a crazy father rather than a hate crime, what it signals is how extreme the reaction is to someone who violates what we as a society think "manly" is all about. This father mirrored our cultural prejudice and hatred against "effeminacy" with violence and murder.

SOCIALIZATION WITHIN EDUCATION

As a result of the Industrial Revolution, by the late 1800s many social philosophers were concerned about the massive changes taking place. Societies were moving from largely agrarian, rural communities marked by a strong sense of shared values, norms, and institutions to urban industrial cities marked by anonymity and a lack of traditional cohesion.

French sociologist Émile Durkheim felt that, among all possible social institutions, including the family, public schools could best stem this potential "moral disintegration" by teaching values that would be shared by most of society. Nearly one hundred years ago, Durkheim recognized the power of compulsory, mass public education. He claimed, "The man who education should realize in us is not the man such nature has made him, but as society wishes him to be" (quoted in Meighan, 1986, p. 234).

For many children, school marks the beginning of long-term social interaction outside the influence of the immediate family. It is often the beginning of a child's socialization into the broader values of an entire culture, not just the particular values of a child's family. Too often, the prejudices, discrimination, and even violence many children learn in family settings are not *unlearned* in school.

As a social institution, education is merely a microcosm of society, reflecting the values, meanings, and norms of the larger culture. The racial and sexual prejudices and violence, the unequal distribution of economic property and power, and the discrimination and violence against gays and lesbians are also present in the social institution of education.

Many social scientists have researched the day-to-day school routines that encourage, and sometimes force, students to learn acceptable, and often prejudicial, social norms. Education researchers recognize the power and influence schools have in teaching children the "moral knowledge" of their culture. Some educators even see this as education's primary role. As one educator claimed, education should teach children "what the norms are, to accept those norms, and to act according to them" (Dreeban, 1968, p. 46). Described as the *hidden curriculum*, these pressures on students include virtually all aspects of social life, from the unofficial three R's of "rules, routines, and regulations," to specific norms and prejudices based on social class, race and ethnicity, gender, and sexual orientation. One of the most important functions of the hidden curriculum is to turn social inequalities into educational inequalities, teaching the idea that such inequalities are "natural" and "morally right."

Learning Racial Prejudice

On Martin Luther King's birthday, barely five years ago, a particularly scurrilous incident at the University of Colorado pointed to the unceasing examples and effects of racism and sexism on college and university campuses. A fraternity rush poster appeared surreptitiously on campus in the early morning hours. An obese, naked African American woman dared readers, "Hey Big Boy! Bad Mama Jamma Says Come Rush Sigma Chi." Those fraternity members responsible apologized, saying they did not realize anyone would be offended by such a "harmless" prank. (Pence, 1993)

Education reflects the racism that pervades U.S. society. It helps teach the acceptability of prevailing ideas and norms about racial and ethnic prejudice. Institutional discrimination is indicated by several factors: who attends school, who attends what schools, what is taught, and how students are treated.

Who Attends School

Institutional racism can be seen in attendance and graduation rates among various racial groups. According to the Southern Regional Educational Board, the numbers of African-American students in college in the 1990s will decline from the numbers in the 1970s. From 1967 to 1976 African-American college-student enrollment increased 246 percent. But by 1986 the rate of increase had reached a "virtual standstill" (Jaschik, 1986, p. 1). Equally disturbing, African-American, Latino, and Native American students leave college without diplomas at much higher rates than whites. Only 32 percent of African Americans graduate within six years, compared to 56 percent of white students (Kelly, 1994).

The reasons for this decline are complex. Among them are

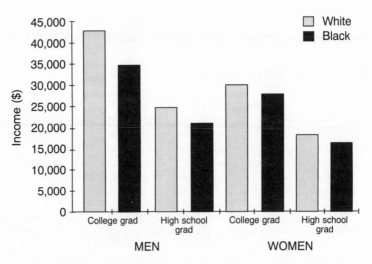

Figure 5.2. Black–white income gap, 1992.

the sharp reduction in federal college grants to poor students during the Reagan–Bush era and the continuing wage discrimination against minorities. Figure 5.2 uses U.S. Census Bureau data to show that college-educated African-American men earn barely two-thirds what college-educated white men with similar backgrounds earn. Political scientist Ronald Walters said the Census Bureau study dealt "a devastating blow" to the notion of a decline in racism. According to Walters, "Race as a factor is growing, and racism accounts for . . . some of this" (quoted in Usdansky, 1993, p. 3A). African-American students clearly see the U.S. meritocracy for the hoax it is, as fewer African-American students are willing or able to graduate from colleges. Further evidence of their disbelief in equal opportunity emerged when whites and blacks were asked how many agreed with the statement, "There is equal opportunity in America." Ninety percent of poor whites agreed, nearly the same percentage as that of rich whites who agreed. In contrast, the percentage of poor and middle-class African Americans who agreed never approached 50 percent (Robertson, 1987).

Who Attends What Schools

In another example of institutional discrimination, students' race and ethnicity determines to a large extent who attends private preschools and nursery schools. Parents whose children attend private preschools are overwhelmingly white. This preschool attendance gives the children an enormous advantage when they enter the first grade.

Often having no prior school experience, many children of color who enter kindergarten not only are behind in learning the hidden curriculum but are also confronted with a system basically structured along the lines of middle-class white values and norms. For instance, the hidden curriculum has already taught white children the importance of self-control, deferred gratification, "proper" work habits, and "correct" ways of interacting with other children and teachers, yet the everyday values and behavior of nonwhite children are often used against them, both inside and outside the classroom. Social scientist William Madsen noted that, because of their deep religious faith, some Mexican-Americans temper the cultural value of progress with an understanding and acceptance of things as they are. Madsen claimed many do not subscribe to the white value of mastering the physical environment nor value as heavily the white reliance on technology. There is also some evidence that emphasis on family involvement keeps some Mexican-American students from the levels of extracurricular school activities that remain dominated by white students (Bryjak and Soroka, 1994).

What Is Taught

What is taught in schools is also a powerful tool for students' learning to accept racial discrimination. For example, *Discovering Utah*, a fourth-grade text used in Utah schools, not only states in its title that Utah was "undiscovered" before whites settled there but it implies that the thousands of years before whites came are unimportant—certainly not important enough to be studied in school. This statewide text includes only one chapter on Native Americans who inhabited the state before it was "discovered" by whites. The taking of tribal lands and the exile of the Native Americans to small reservations are summarized in a *few paragraphs*, trivializing and minimizing a significant turning point in the history of Utah (Fenton and Wilson, 1992).

Both minority and white students often learn an inflated importance and place of whites in history, even when focusing on U.S. history. For example, the cover of the brochure for the 1993 Utah Archeological Conference, a statewide, week-long conference sponsored by the professional state archaeological association, showed a Native American wearing a white-style hat, underneath the conference heading (and topic): "Utah Prehistory." *Prehistory* means *before white people*, as if native peoples either had no history prior to whites or are not considered part of history themselves!

The consequences of this enduring racism and ignorance are felt by both students and faculty. The sociology department chair at the University of Colorado publicly criticized two of the three Latino faculty members for stressing Chicano/Chicana issues in their courses and research. He commented that focusing on Latinos and Latino culture was not an adequate sociological perspective, apparently ignoring and oblivious of the state's four hundred years of Latino history and traditions and of the 20 percent of the state's Latino population (but less than 5 percent of the university enrollment), and even ignorant of the origins of the state's name, which comes from the Spanish word for "red." It is not surprising that, nearly two years after their professional work had been publicly denounced, the three Latino department members accused the department of "institutional racism." Denouncing the climate of racism, they demanded to be reassigned to another university department (Baca, 1994, p. B3).

Omitting much of the depth and essence of the experiences

of nonwhites leaves many white students to form images of contemporary life among nonwhites from the mass media, not based on knowledge and information. For example, in response to the question, "What are some *personal* consequences of attending a school with a student population that is only one percent African American?" one naive University of Colorado student sincerely responded, "We don't have a very good basketball team." This comment reflects the overwhelming majority of images of African Americans—as athletes, entertainers, and gang members—in the mass media. When African-American perspectives and experiences are omitted from textbooks, white students with little contact with African Americans often embrace such laughable but dangerous stereotypes, dangerous because they easily feed into prejudice and help perpetuate discrimination in all aspects of U.S. society. Educator James Banks (1984) warned about this isolation and ignorance among white students: "Individuals who only know, participate in, and see the world from their unique cultural and ethnic perspectives are denied important parts of the human experience and are culturally and ethnically encapsulated" (p. 105).

Minority students learn the same important lesson as working-class and poor students about U.S. society: only middle- and upper-class whites count when the American story is told.

How Students Are Treated

Racial and ethnic prejudice is also reflected in how students of color are treated by the educational system as a whole, including their fellow students and administrators. Since the mid-1980s, there has been an alarming increase of racist incidents, some of them violent, on U.S. college campuses. This trend has emerged at small, private eastern liberal-arts colleges, such as Dartmouth and Amherst. It has also surfaced at large state universities in Pennsylvania, Michigan, Colorado, and Arizona. For example, in 1993 at the State University of New York at Oneonta, "Being a black male . . . didn't just mean you were part of a minority group. It meant you were a suspect in a local assault" (Willock, 1993, p. 6). After blood-stained towels were found on campus following a local assault reportedly by an African-American male, the vice president for administration released a list of all African-American male students to local and state police to aid in their investigation. Following community outcries, the college president suspended the administrator for a month for violating the federal Buckley Amendment, designed to protect students' privacy.

The power of school administrators can also reflect racial prejudice. In 1994 a Wedowee, Alabama, high school principal told a school assembly he would cancel the senior prom if interracial couples planned to attend. Even more astonishingly, the principal, suspended for a short time, was quickly reinstated by the county school board (Marshall, 1993, p. 13).

Other than the family, schools are the most important socializing agent in U.S. culture. Because of what is taught and how students are treated, education not only mirrors but also promotes racial prejudice and discrimination.

Learning Gender Prejudice

> It's been 20 years since Barbie has spoken her little plastic mind. Now Teen Talk Barbie, introduced in July 1992 by Mattel Inc., is chattering away in playrooms across the country, and this is what she has waited so long to say: "Math class is tough."
>
> Maybe, Barbie, but math teachers are not amused.
>
> "It's a subtle form of brainwashing," said Nancy Metz, a math teacher at Watkins Mill High School in Gaithersburg, Md. "It's a very young person hearing that, and that's not what we want young women to hear." ("Barbie Speaks," 1992, p. A2)

As a near-universal institution, education exerts enormous influence on U.S. culture. Part of that influence unfortunately helps legitimize prejudice and discrimination based on gender.

Institutional sexism is seen in who teaches, what is taught, and how students are treated.

Who Teaches

Institutional sexism is easily seen in the distribution of teachers by gender and the grade taught. Among preschool teachers, with the lowest pay and the lowest status among all educators, the vast majority are female; among elementary-school teachers, also with the lowest pay and least status among public-school teachers, again the vast majority are women, particularly in kindergarten through fourth grade. Most men involved in elementary education are either teachers in Grades 7 or 8 or are school administrators, both positions providing more prestige and money than female-dominated elementary-education positions. This promotes prejudice because the institutional discrimination based on gender shown in these statistics is clear: Higher-status positions in education mean more men and higher pay than in positions dominated by women.

What Is Taught

Gender bias is also reflected in what school curricula teach. Research since the mid-1970s focusing on school textbooks has shown little change in the sex-stereotypical images: Females are ignored and marginalized in textbook portrayals. In a 1972 study of books rated "excellent" by the American Library Association, Weitzman, Eifler, Hokado, and Ross (1993) found male characters outnumbered females by 11 to 1, and in the case of animals, the ratio of males to females was 95 to 1. The roles were equally stereotypical: Girls helped Mom in the kitchen or worried about getting their clothes dirty, while boys played, had fun, or were adventurous and daring.

Ten years later, Samuel (1981) illustrated that science textbooks also taught the legitimacy of the stereotypical gender divisions and inequalities found in society. The overwhelming majority of pictures and illustrations in high school science texts showed boys and men in active roles and girls and women in passive roles. Hoffman's (1975) analysis of sex education text-books found similar biases and prejudices.

According to a more recent study analyzing the Caldecott Medal winners for most distinguished picture book of the year for the 1980s, "The most telling finding is the near unanimity in conformity to traditional gender roles. Not only does Jane express no career goals, but there is no adult female model to provide any ambition. One woman in the entire 1980s collection of 24 books has an occupation outside the home, and she works as a waitress at the Blue Tile Diner (Finsterbusch and Schwartz, 1993, p. 64).

How Students Are Treated

A powerful element of institutional prejudice is how female and male students are treated. Studies reporting subtle and overt gender biases in schools are voluminous, the range vast: Boys interrupt girls more, boys' ideas are given more credence, boys are called on more and are given other types of attention more than are girls, and girls are given less constructive feedback on their performance, according to reports cited by the Congressional Caucus for Women's Issues ("Girls Harassed," 1993, p. A6).

In addition, elementary-school students are still often seg-regated by sex, with girls primarily taking home economics clas-ses and boys taking shop and mechanics classes. Female high school students continue to be tracked away from potentially high-paying and high-status careers in traditionally "masculine" technical fields, such as the sciences and computer technology, and into traditional "feminine" (and low-paying, low-status) ca-reers as elementary-school teachers and secretaries.

The lingering rationale is that more boys than girls will be-come breadwinners, so *his* education is considered more impor-tant than *hers,* and high schools should be more concerned with *his* academic success and *his* going on to college. The reality, however, is depressingly different. Over 55 percent of women will be *full-time* employees while they have pre-school-aged children; more mothers with small children work full time in the labor force than stay at home full time. Because over 50 percent of marriages end in divorce, and because 97 percent of all children who live with single parents live with their mothers, this continuing bias makes even less sense (Einbinder, 1992).

Yet another way students are treated is with unequal access to educational resources. Institutional sexism is the rule rather than the exception, even with tax-dollar spending and students' fees at the college level. According to a National Collegiate Athletic Association (NCAA) Gender Equity Task Force, women's college athletics still receive only 60 percent of the institutional financial support of men's programs, over twenty years after Title IX prohibited such inequality. Yet female students make up *over* 50 percent of all college students, whose fees help subsidize college athletic programs, most of which operate in the red.

A final example of sexism in schools is how students feel about and treat each other. In 1959, Hartley began tracing a connection between disdain for women on a broad scale and adolescent boys' hostility toward women. These examples of prejudice and discrimination reflect America's broad cultural disdain for women.

In 1983, nearly twenty-five years after Hartley's groundbreaking research on boys' attitudes toward girls and women, Alice Baumgartner and her colleagues measured the progress in erasing gender prejudice in U.S. education (Tavris and Baumgartner, 1983). After all, there had been over a decade of attempts to eliminate sex prejudice in the textbooks children read, the lessons teachers present, and the counseling provided to students. To gauge the results, nearly two thousand schoolchildren were asked a single question: "If you woke up tomorrow and discovered that you were [changed to] a (boy) (girl), how would your life be different?"

The results were sad and shocking, for again there appeared to be a fundamental contempt for females—held by both boys *and* girls. The elementary-school boys often titled their answers with phrases such as "The Disaster" or "Doomsday." Their descriptions were even more telling. One boy said, "If I were a girl, everybody would be better than me, because boys are better than girls." And this terse comment, "If I were a girl, I'd kill myself." From a fourth-grader, this might not seem very out of place. But imagine this statement if it came from a twenty-nine-year-old man who had been beating his wife for nearly ten years.

But perhaps the most surprising responses were from the girls, because they also felt boys were better, or at least better off, than girls. For example, an eleventh-grader commented, "People would take my decisions and beliefs more seriously." Girls and boys are aware of another enormous disadvantage of being female: the prevalence of violence against women. Even the youngest girls frequently mentioned that if they were boys, they would not have to worry about being raped or beaten, and the boys feared for their safety if they became girls.

In the process of learning to "be a man," many boys are taught to avoid any behavior deemed feminine, from crying to intimacy. As Hartley and Baumgartner showed, the intense pressure on boys to avoid anything associated with girls and women often translates into hostility *against* girls and women. Part of the explanation for the epidemic levels of violence against women in U.S. society can be traced to this early socialization into masculinity. The connection between males as more highly valued and a sense of male hostility against females is illustrated in the results of a late-1980s poll of seventeen hundred Rhode Island sixth- to ninth-graders who attended assault awareness programs across the state. One-third of the boys and *one-sixth of the girls* said it was acceptable for a man to force a woman to have sex if he had spent money on her. And these were students who had just attended a rape awareness workshop ("Survey Finds," 1988, p. 1B). At such a young age, boys (and girls) are socialized to view women as a purchasable commodity. Women "owe" men sex, and if they don't "pay up," men have the license to force them. This frightening social rule helps us understand why the United States has the highest rape rate in the industrialized world.

Galvanized by such high-profile cases as the Clarence Thomas–Anita Hill Senate hearings and the charges against Senator Robert Packwood (Oregon), much of the nation's attention is focused on sexual harassment in the workplace. But there is also a growing trend toward examining harassment where it first surfaces: in American schools. In March 1993 a *Seventeen* magazine poll of forty-two hundred readers ("Survey: 80% of Teens," 1993, p. 1A) found sexual harassment "rampant in elementary and secondary schools." In June of the same year, the American Association of University Women released a report that echoed *Seventeen's* findings. Based on a survey of over sixteen hundred grade school and high school students, Anne Bryant, executive director of the association's education foundation, described the level of sexual harassment in schools to be of "epidemic proportion" (Quoted in Kelly, 1993, p. 2A).

Schools, then, are places where boys learn and practice sexual harassment, and places where girls learn that sexual harassment is a part of everyday life—to be tolerated and accepted.

Learning Heterosexual Prejudice

A homeroom in a high school in South Philadelphia. The boy sits quietly in the first aisle, reading a book. He does not look up, not even for a moment. He is hoping no one will remember he is sitting there. He wishes he were invisible. Suddenly, a voice from beside him. "Hey, you're a faggot, ain't you?"

The boy doesn't answer. "Faggot, I'm talking to you!"

To look up is to meet the eyes of the tormentor. Suddenly, a sharpened pencil point is thrust into the boy's arm. He jolts, aware there is blood seeping from the wound. "Why did you do that for?" he asks timidly. "Cause I hate faggots," the other boy says, laughing.

Some other boys begin to laugh, too. A symphony of laughter. The boy feels as if he's going to cry. But he must not. Must not cry. (Avicolli, 1988, p. 203)

On an individual level, schools encourage homophobia, a fear, dislike, and loathing of, or, in short, prejudice against, homosexuals. On an institutional level, they produce heterosexism, institutional discrimination against homosexuals. These two terms can be confusing; just remember them as one (homophobia) being a feeling and thus a prejudice and one (heterosexism) being a behavior and thus discrimination. Institutional discrimination against gay, lesbian, and bisexual students is seen in how students are treated and what is taught.

How Students Are Treated

In 1959 Hartley identified some profound socialization pressures on boys. She hinted at a deeper, fundamental fear driving boys: hostility against girls and women not as an end in itself, but as a mask of boys' own fears and insecurities that they did not measure up *as males.*

In schools, homophobia is usually directed against boys rather than girls. There is controversy over why, but one reason is that males are perceived as the preferred sex and masculine as the "dominant" gender, so more attention and pressure is on boys' conforming or not conforming to society's roles. The pressure that homophobia puts on boys to be "manly" is seen in evidence that many 11-year-old boys who score highest on masculinity scales also score high on anxiety scales (Pence, 1992).

The easiest example of different pressures on schoolchildren in terms of homophobia is that girls who play "boy" games or with boys can be "tomboys," while boys have no similar counterpart ("susiegirls"?). *Tomboy* can be used as a putdown to a girl, but it is at best a half-hearted attempt at enforcing gender roles. In fact, many times this tag is a compliment, an "honor" boys bestow on girls for not being a "girl," and it is often seen as such by the girl and even by her parents.

Conversely, it is impossible, within the confines of U.S. culture, to imagine a boy being called a conceptual name similar to *tomboy.* Over the past several years, we have compiled a list of

words used on fourth- and fifth-grade playgrounds to describe
boys who are perceived as *not* behaving in an acceptable masculine, or *manly* fashion:

> *sissy, pussy, wussy, wuss, scaredy, scaredy cat, chicken,*
> *chicken shit, gutless, nutless, ball-less, wimp, geek, dweeb,*
> *dork, fag, queer, homo, gay, lezzie, limp wrist, fudge packer,*
> *gq fag, baby, cry baby, momma's boy, girl, woman*

There is rarely a male who has not been called one of these
names or has seen some other boy called one of these names. It is
one of the most common occurrences for boys in grade school, a
form of peer pressure that often borders on torture. When males
are asked what *must* happen next, the answer is nearly unan-
imous: He must fight. He does not have to win the fight, but in
order to "prove" his masculinity, and to avoid this happening
every day—*over two hundred times each year,* as Tony Avicolli
described— the effort *must* be made.

What Is Taught

Institutional discrimination, or heterosexism, can be seen in
other ways. For example, in 1993 the Utah State Board of Education rejected any textbooks that accepted or advocated homosexuality as a "desirable or healthy lifestyle." Many would not
find fault with this prohibition, particularly within elementary-
and secondary-school textbooks. But beneath this relatively benign exterior, a rigid and biased heterosexist agenda exists. For
instance, teachers are not prohibited from discussing homosexuality in the classroom, as long as they do not advocate it. But
according to Bonnie Morgan, director of curriculum for Utah's
public schools, "What you'd have to be doing to be *advocating* is
saying it doesn't matter what a person's sexual orientation is"
(Autman, 1993, p. B2). According to this definition, unless a
teacher is openly against homosexuals and homosexuality, then
that teacher is "advocating" it—a clear example of discrimination
against homosexuals, or institutional heterosexism. If this litmus

test were applied to religion, there would be a major uproar—and rightfully so—because *no one* would agree that saying "It doesn't matter what religion a person is" *advocates* religion (for those who are members of a religion to be tolerated, accepted, treated with respect, and understood).

In an additional example, when a fifth-grader in Colorado's Shaffer Elementary School's sex-education class asked how gays have intercourse, a teacher matter-of-factly described homosexual sex. Colorado for Family Values, a Colorado Spring–based group that pushed the antigay Amendment 2 in the 1992 state election, attacked Denver's public school curriculum as "homosexual indoctrination" (Herrick, 1993, p. 36A).

In 1993, New York City School Chancellor Joseph Fernandez tried to confront institutionalized heterosexism and triggered a near revolt. He urged the adoption of the "Rainbow Curriculum" by all New York City schools. This program suggested courses aimed at reducing prejudice and intolerance. The problem was not the inclusion and tolerance of ethnic, racial, and gender diversity, but textbooks that portrayed lesbians and gays "as real people to be respected and appreciated." One school board refused to adopt the new curriculum, describing it as "gay and lesbian propaganda" (Lacayo, 1993, p. 52). For Fernandez's courage, he was fired. Unfortunately, school districts across the country are doing nothing to reduce prejudice against and hatred of lesbians and gays.

As with racism, some of the most damaging aspects of heterosexism (discrimination against gays, lesbians, and bisexuals) and homophobia (fear of and prejudice against homosexuals) are the internalization of cultural prejudice. Many adolescent homosexuals experience self-loathing and profound loneliness:

> School was one of the more painful experiences of my youth. The neighborhood bullies could be avoided . . . by staying in my room. But school was something I had to face day after day for some two hundred mornings a year. I had few friends in school. I was a pariah. Some kids would talk to me, but few wanted to be known as my close friend.

Afraid of labels, if I was a sissy, then he had to be a sissy, too.
I was condemned to loneliness. (Avicolli, 1988, p. 203)

The level of loneliness, alienation, and isolation can have dramatic consequences for many gay, lesbian, and bisexual children. Homosexual adolescents are over three times more likely to attempt suicide than heterosexual adolescents. It is also estimated that, of all teenage suicides, which are the second leading cause of death among all adolescents, one-third are related to questions about sexuality and sexual orientation ("Organizing for Equality," 1990, p. 4).

Even though some of the consequences can be deadly, schools play their part in reflecting society's fear of and hatred toward gays and lesbians.

We have used only the *family* and *education* to illustrate how prejudice is learned, but as noted at the beginning of this chapter, the legal system, the media, the economy, and religion are institutions that could also be examined. We must remember that prejudice and discrimination do not exist in a social vacuum; they are part of the very fabric of U.S. society. These ways of unequally valuing and treating Americans based on their social class, race, gender, or sexual orientation are reinforced every day of our lives by fundamental social institutions.

Chapter 6

Prejudice and Hate
A Personal Face

Social scientist C. Wright Mills convincingly argued that to adequately understand why people do the things they do, we must examine how individual "personal troubles" are intimately connected to broader "public issues." He warned that to focus only on individual problems, even tragedies, without tracing connections to and consequences in the wider society offers little understanding of the social factors that often provoke personal troubles.

Mills and other social commentators have offered this warning because U.S. society too often remains caught in dramatic individual stories and fails to see wider implications. For example, the U.S. media were in a frenzy over the Lorena and John Bobbitt case. Lost in the titillation and snickers were more substantial social issues of intimate abuse, the latent hostility of many women toward men, and even issues about overall media coverage.

This book takes Mills's warning to heart. In fact, most of our approach is from the direction of public issues. This chapter presents again the issues of prejudice and discrimination, only this time from the personal troubles direction. To fully understand the implications and consequences of continuing prejudice, it is important to hear individuals' personal experiences. These are often rough, verbatim accounts of six people's encounters with U.S. prejudice that put a more personal face on troubling public issues.

ANA DITTMAR

Ms. Ana Dittmar, forty-five, was born and raised in a white ethnic area of Philadelphia. A single mother of two, she attended college after her children were born. She has been a professional dancer, a university professor, and a yoga instructor and is currently working in an AIDS hospice.

AUTHOR: When can you remember the first time that you realized that you were being treated unfairly because you were female?
ANA: I probably didn't see it as unfair, just being treated differently. I grew up in a family where I was the only girl. I mean I had a mother, but I had brothers, so a lot of the time I did boy things without realizing the distinction. I had no sisters. It was a boy house. My mother was very "girly." She had tea parties and all those girly kinds of things. But the house definitely was a boy house, a rough-and-tumble kind of boy house. I was probably a tomboy-type girl. I didn't really want to be associated with the kind of femininity that my mother always exhibited.
AUTHOR: Do you know why?
ANA: Maybe I saw the limitations. She was limited because she was a woman and I didn't want to identify with it. Her world seemed limited to inside the house, and that was about it. She is a very kind, loving, nurturing type of a woman, but I think it kind of frightened me that she couldn't go past the house. Compared with the other women in the neighborhood, she was very independent. But compared to what I wanted or felt comfortable with, I just distinguished myself from her. I knew that I wasn't like her. We had very different personalities.

AUTHOR: When did your evaluation change from being treated differently to being treated unfairly?

ANA: Very, very late. When the rest of the country did that, like in the 1970s, like when I was almost of marriageable age. When I was little and was treated differently there was *shame* attached to it. "You can't do that, you can't go in there, you can't because you are a girl." I internalized it right away. Oh, of course, silly me.

AUTHOR: Like where, like what?

ANA: I grew up Catholic, ethnically Catholic, not just a religion. We are talking about a whole culture: food, the language, and everything. The church had a lot to do with it. The altar boy phenomenon was a position that I could never have. By that time I realized there wasn't any point in me asking a question about "could I." So only the boys were allowed into the sacred parts of the church. The girls could only watch. There were other things, like paper boys. Girls weren't allowed to have paper routes. So how could you earn any extra money?

AUTHOR: Any other things you were denied?

ANA: Having to wear dresses was kind of restrictive, too. I wanted to do cartwheels and somersaults and things like that on the front lawn, and if you had a dress on, you couldn't do that. It was so subconscious and so built in, but there was *shame* attached to it. It was like you can't do that because there is something wrong with you.

AUTHOR: When did you sense the shame?

ANA: When I was an adult. All of these things were so second-nature and knee-jerk that it wasn't until the rest of the country started talking about it and I heard about it from the outside world, outside my family, outside the sources that had oppressed me. Even in graduate school, there was discrimination against women. I got my Ph.D. in 1983, so male faculty and administrators were still sleeping with their female students back then. There was nothing a woman could do. In fact, women so accepted it that if one of these men didn't want to sleep with you, you would have some problems. You would have to accept that you would have a harder route.

AUTHOR: Was it generally accepted that if a woman graduate student had a relationship with one of the professors then it was an easier route?

ANA: Oh, yeah, absolutely. I was a married woman at the time and not open to fooling around, and so no one asked me once. They just said, "Oh, well, keep your hands off her, she's married, very married." So I had to make it on my own. Making it on your own was a real disadvantage. But then before I was in graduate school, I had been a ballet dancer. The wonderful world of dance is even worse in terms of having to sleep your way around. I guess that was back in the 1960s. I was about fifteen. Like date rape or something, you don't know that you are doing it because you are being coerced. You don't have a clue.

AUTHOR: There was a lot of that going on in the ballet world?

ANA: Yeah, real bad. Women were nothing. They were meat. But then again the whole concept of the body in the dance world was different, because your body was an instrument. But getting back to getting discriminated against, I didn't know that it was going on until the 1970s. Then there were words to use for it. Then you could describe it and discuss it because there was something to call it.

AUTHOR: So what happened after that? How did you deal with the gender world after you had some awareness?

ANA: I felt angry. I was angry the way other women were in the 1970s until I had children. Then it really became obvious that things were unfair. Not just separate but unfair. I got stuck with the responsibility and was expected to be like a man and earn money and be equal, and if you're not, then it must be your fault. I remember a scene when I first got married back in the late 1960s. My husband was in his first year of college, and I was working at a rock 'n roll record shop. We would get up early in the morning and go on the subway. We lived in a big city, and his college was about two blocks from the record shop where I worked. He went to classes, and he had a pretty easy schedule, rolled into class and rolled out. It wasn't very pressing for him. I worked as a cashier all day, and it was a very busy shop. I was constantly running around. At the end of the day I was totally exhausted. We would get on the subway and ride back home, and my husband would sit at the dinner table and wait for his dinner to come. I would run around the kitchen making it. I was totally exhausted and bitchy, and I didn't know what was wrong. I remember he would say, "What's wrong with you?" He literally one time sat holding the knife and fork and the dish on the table waiting patiently. He said, "What's wrong with you? You are acting up." I said, "I don't know." I was so exhausted; that's what it was. I was so exhausted. I hated myself for feeling grumpy, for being tired, for not being able to make it, not being able to do everything that was expected of me. I also, for one fleeting moment—now, this is back in the end of the 1960s when there were no words to talk about this—for one moment I thought, "There is something wrong. There is definitely something wrong with this picture. But what could it possibly be?" I forgot about the whole thing after that because I had no concepts, no words, and neither did he.

AUTHOR: Where do you think this culture is going in terms of gender relationships?

ANA: I'm probably a living example of the classic stereotype American baby-boomer woman in some ways. And that is I went through the sound-asleep era. Then I woke up and went through the wake-up era and was angry for maybe eight to ten years. After that I realized you can't just walk around pissed off all your life because nobody's going to like you. I didn't want to not be liked, and I was getting tired of being angry. When you get to the point when you realize that the anger is pointless and drop that, then you still have to deal with the realities. That's where I am today. That's where I think women are today. I think it's the same thing that's happening to blacks. They still feel discriminated against. They still feel that there's more pressure on them. All things being equal, there's more pressure on them just because they are different. I don't know if there's anything I can do about it. I try to—and this is probably what many people are doing now—is try to work on myself.

AUTHOR: Where do you think we will be in thirty years as a culture? Any guesses?

ANA: Well, I think we are at a crossroads right now. I think it could go many different ways. Things have got better since the 1969 era, when I didn't know what was wrong with the picture. But it's not anywhere near equal, that's for sure.

AUTHOR: Do you it ever will be?

ANA: No, I don't think it will. On one hand, one of my fantasies is that the globe is changing, the world is changing, the universe is changing and that female attributes will become more valued. Like this total-quality-management stuff, that's an effort of male management to soften, to bring inside their very male-dominated organization, to bring female quality into it. Because male qualities have dried up things. And if it were only female qualities, that would dry things up, too. You need both.

AUTHOR: So you are saying we need to change how we evaluate what's feminine?

ANA: To *value* the things that are seen as feminine things. To allow males and females to exhibit or experience these things. Without that balance, there is no hope.

AUTHOR: OK, thanks, Ana.

ANDRE WHITE

A twenty-seven-year-old self-described "black man," Mr. Andre White was born and raised in an African-American section of Oakland, California. A single father of two, Mr. White is currently paying his way through college by playing football. In less than a year he will attend graduate school in social work.

AUTHOR: Andre, will you describe in your own words your racial or ethnic background.

ANDRE: I would call myself a black man. I don't consider myself African American, just a black man. The reason is that being called an African American and all, I guess white people from America aren't called Euro-Americans. I have a problem with that, and so I'm a black man. I'm twenty-seven years old, I feel old.

AUTHOR: Where are you from?

ANDRE: I'm from Oakland, California. I was born and raised there.

AUTHOR: Can you tell us something about your family background.

ANDRE: I come from a dysfunctional family. My father was hardly ever around. He spent a lot of time in jail or away, and I was raised primarily by my mother and my grandmother. Even when my father was around, it wasn't considered by me to be a family. When I was younger and he wasn't there, I would watch TV and look at the *Brady Bunch,* and I thought that was the way things were supposed to be, and I had wishes and just hoped it would be like that when I got to spend time with my father, but it never worked out that way.

AUTHOR: What did your father do for a living?

ANDRE: He was into everything from drugs to bad checks, all kinds of stuff. He went to jail, I'm sure it was for writing bad checks. He went to jail and spent a lot of time in prison. My father and I never got a chance to know each other. Even to this day, I know where he lives, but I don't want any contact with him, because I guess you could say that I'm still angry. I try not to think about it, just let it go, because I have got to live my life. I wish I could have had a father, but it just didn't work out that way.

AUTHOR: I want to ask you about incidents of racism, discrimination, and prejudice that you may have experienced, that may have been directed at you. Can you tell some stories about things like that?

ANDRE: This is weird because I experienced so much and I kind of let it go. I experienced racism and prejudice all my life. I don't know if it's just ignorance, white people not knowing about black people, or not dealing with them or what, but the most recent one I had was about a week ago. I was in a car accident. They searched my car; they searched me. I told them I had a history. I had been in trouble before. But we weren't dealing with that, we were dealing with the accident, so I couldn't understand why they would search my car. They just tore my car up. I had a TV and a VCR, and they opened those up and looked all in there. I explained my history. I was being honest with them. I told them they could search all they wanted.

AUTHOR: Who is "them"?

ANDRE: Utah Highway Patrol.

AUTHOR: White officers?

ANDRE: Yes. First it was just one highway patrolman. Then about three or four other cars came. They searched the hillside off the side of the freeway, looking for stuff, thinking maybe I threw something out.

AUTHOR: What did you think they thought?

ANDRE: I'm pretty sure they thought I had drugs. I just laughed. I said, "Why are you searching my car? What's the big deal?"

"Well, you have a history." "Yeah, I have a history, but I didn't have to tell you about my history. I'm not on probation. I'm not a criminal. It was something I did when I was younger. Let's deal with the situation at hand. This is an accident here." They were just real rude, basically just treated me like I was a black man, a black man they looked at as a criminal, a stereotype. I had a nice truck, coming from California, on my way back to school. I knew it was coming. Just like the time in LA, where I guess they got a report that a guy was waving a gun at a girl or whatever in a black BMW—my BMW is blue. It was like, suddenly, cops came out of nowhere. I was at the gas station pumping gas, and they drew shotguns and everything else. They tied me and handcuffed me, and I didn't know what was going on. The white officers were real rude. We got on the subject of Rodney King. I can't remember exactly what was said, but an officer said Rodney King got what he deserved. Just little comments. Even here, going to school, trying to get financial aid, trying to get into school. They are not as apt to help you out. They tell you what you need to do. You can sit back and watch, and you see a white student, and they roll out the red carpet and say let's get this together, you need this and you need that. It's like pretty much basically you are on your own here. It's hard, real hard. It's emotional to talk about. It's hard to deal with.

AUTHOR: How does it make you feel?

ANDRE: It upsets me. It really upsets me. I don't understand what the difference is between me and a white student.

AUTHOR: When you say you feel upset, can you be more specific? Does it make your stomach hurt? Tell me about it.

ANDRE: I just feel like I want to cry. I am so angry. I just want to cry and let it out. It's hard being strong here at an all-white school. The reason I came is I had a football scholarship. It's just been real hard. Even like the financial aid officer, and it's not just me but a lot of my friends. We get together and talk about it. Some of the people that work in the financial aid office, they seem upset because we are getting aid. One of my friends was talking to me and said he got his check, and the lady questioned him like, "How did you get all that money? How did you pull that off?" He was like, "It's none of your business." Why would you ask him that? He is going to school.

AUTHOR: Can you remember as a kid the first time you were consciously aware that you were the victim of prejudice or bias? What's the first thing you remember in your life?

ANDRE: That's a tough one. I would probably have to go back to elementary school. It was a primarily black school, but we had a majority of white teachers. This was in the heart of the ghetto near Oakland Coliseum. I was playing sports. I was very good in sports, and there was this one teacher that hated everything. I played everything. Everyone always wanted me to be on their team. This white teacher, he had it in for me. I don't know what it was exactly, but something was said, and we got into an argument. Sports to me were everything. All we had was sports. I played basketball, volleyball, softball, football, and we got into an argument. The next day he took me off basketball, football, and softball. I don't know why. I told my mother, and she went to talk to him. I don't know what was said, but then I was back on the team. I don't really know how it got started. That was my first real experience. This was a guy I looked up to because he was real athletic and he worked with some of the kids, and I wondered why he would treat me like this and talk to me like this. What did I do? I was a pretty good student. I didn't get in trouble. I just couldn't understand. That was in the fifth grade.

AUTHOR: He said something about your race?

ANDRE: Yeah, that I was black. I couldn't understand why, because I hadn't done anything. I felt as if he was picking on me. I looked up to him. I liked what he was doing. I didn't do anything to get in trouble. I couldn't understand it, just that I was black. That was my first real thing with prejudice. Sometimes

I just try not to think about it. In California it's not as blatant as it is here. In California if you feel they don't like you, it's like I don't want to be bothered with you. It's like a subtle way. But here it's as if you know right off the bat if they like you. I kind of like that.

AUTHOR: Here in Utah?

ANDRE: Yeah, Utah. I kind of like that because you know whether or not you can go up and talk to them or keep your distance. I would rather know if someone likes me than not know where they are coming from. I think prejudice and racism come from being ignorant, not willing to learn or know about a different race. My roommate has a white girlfriend. This past weekend she talked to me at least two hours about how her parents wanted to wash their hands of her: "What are you doing with a black guy?" And she told them he had taught her a lot about life: "What can he teach you? How to make babies and live in the ghetto?" This is here in Utah; they are from Panguitch. They don't want to help her with school now. They want to stop helping her with school. Her grandfather asked her to go to school in Arizona, and he would pay for it just to get her away from my roommate. This is 1994 and she is only nineteen, and her parents can't be more than thirty-five or forty—forty-five at the most. It is ignorant. I don't see how people still have a bias or prejudice just because of someone's color. I can't understand.

AUTHOR: So what do you think is wrong with the United States?

ANDRE: I just think ignorance. Ignorance as far as AIDS, igno rance as far as racism, prejudice, gender. It's just a lot of ignorance. People are not willing to learn about what's really going on.

AUTHOR: Why do you think that is? Why is there so much ignorance?

ANDRE: I would say lack of education. Parents not teaching their kids or their parents not teaching them. It's really hard to say. My parents never taught me to be racist or prejudiced. They never taught me to dislike people because of the way they dress, the way they look, or their color. I was just thinking that it starts with your parents, how you are brought up. A lot of people nowadays are being brought up wrong. I give my mom all the credit because she is the one who raised me. My father was never around. My mother used to spank me. I didn't consider I was being abused. If I was doing something wrong, she let me know. I wouldn't do it anymore. I think she did a good job. I give her all the credit in the world for raising me. I made mistakes, but I learned from my mistakes. I don't make the same mistakes twice. I think people need to be educated. Some people don't want to be educated. Some people don't want anything to do with black people just because of their color. It's hard for me to understand. I can't understand it at all.

AUTHOR: Where do you think this country is going to go in terms of race relations?

ANDRE: Nowhere, really. We're making very, very, very, very little progress. Economically black people still have it hard. I don't see anything good happening. I just don't see it. You have to be lucky or in the right place at the right time to be able to succeed. I consider myself lucky because I have been in trouble. I was locked up for eighteen months. I consider myself lucky. I say my prayers and have faith and try to do the right thing and that's it. The world is going crazy. I just can't see anything good happening. If it is, it's very little progress here and there. The world is crazy. Personally I am just trying to do the best I can for me. I got two kids. Show them the right way. Give them a little something to work with, a little foundation so they won't have to go through the things I went through. I had to pay my way through school. The only way I got into college was my scholarship, and that was for just one year until I got in trouble, and then I had to come back and pay for it myself. Then I got a scholarship. Without a foundation, especially being black it's real hard. If you have no foundation, its going to be rough for you.

AUTHOR: Thank you.

BRENDA BENALLY

A twenty-eight-year-old Navajo woman and the mother of four, Ms. Brenda Benally was born and raised in Sheepsprings, New Mexico, on the Navajo reservation. She is of the Towering House Clan. She is currently a resident of St. George, Utah.

AUTHOR: Can you describe to me in your own words how you perceive or define yourself in an ethnic or racial sense?

BRENDA: First of all, I come as a Native American. I am a Navajo, and I grew up in the Navajo tribe. That's where my roots start out. It's taken me a few years to take a lot of pride in being Native American, in spite of the things I was taught when I was growing up. I grew up in a very structured way of life.

AUTHOR: What is the name of the reservation you grew up on, and where is it located?

BRENDA: It is the Navajo reservation. I grew up in the Four Corners area right on Highway 666. The place I grew up is Sheep Springs, New Mexico, so we were kind of on the interstate. We grew up with a lot of livestock—sheep and cows. My parents were not educated. There are eleven of us. I grew up at the tail end of the trading-post system, when they were still known to people. Now you can't really find a trading post anymore that gives credit. I have been off the reservation for about fifteen years now. When I go home now, I see a big difference. I am living in St. George, Utah. I've seen St. George grow from a small farming community to a very commercialized community.

AUTHOR: In your fifteen years of living in St. George, what experiences have you had living in what is essentially a white community that may have been prejudice toward you as a Native American?

BRENDA: Oh yeah. I got it all the time on the bus. The secretary's son in our high school and I were in the same grade, and the minute I got on the bus, he would start making "Hollywood-style" Indian yells. He tried to imitate an Indian. I got in a fight

with him, and I made sure I put him on his butt, and I got kicked off the bus and he didn't. I had to listen to this from the beginning of the school. He would make comments about the way I talk, he would make fun of how I would wait at the bus early, because Indians are always supposed to be late, and I was always the first one there. He would always just make comments. It was just this one particular kid. No one else stood up for me on the bus even though I knew everybody on the bus. He and I were both at Dixie College. We took courses together, and he still remembers, but this time he has more respect for me. At least he will open the door, or have a "do-you-need-a-ride-home?" kind of attitude. To me that was a good win.

AUTHOR: You mentioned changes on the reservation. Is there an alcoholism problem among Navajo people? Or is it just certain individuals?

BRENDA: The majority of men are alcoholics on the reservation. It's prohibited on the reservation, so anybody who's going to drink, of course, has to drive far distances to drink, and a lot of the men end up in jail because they have to drive.

AUTHOR: Do you have any ideas or theories—and this is just your opinion—why so many Navajo men abuse alcohol?

BRENDA: Well, in my family, all of my brothers are alcoholics. There's not one that isn't. But none of the girls drink because I think we've all made choices when we were growing up that that was one thing we didn't want to be a part of our lives. The things I've seen my brothers go through are enough not to let anybody drink. My father drank all of his life.

AUTHOR: Why do you think this drinking is happening?

BRENDA: As far as my father, I think a lot of it was pressure. There are so many things expected from the male. Navajo men cannot represent themselves as the American father. My father has worked all his life—labor work—and today he doesn't have a penny to show for it. I remember his going to the railroad, getting laid off two weeks before he was to retire from the railroad. None of the benefits were given to him. He went on to another job at the sawmill, worked for twenty-one years at the same place, and then he got laid off about three months before he was to retire again and never got any benefits. He is barely getting by with Social Security today. He really never had a mainstream job. He was always the cook, the cleanup; he was put in the laundry. He can tell me stories about how hard he had to work sometimes, and then the next day some of the guys would spill the laundry and he would have to do it over again. He worked really hard, and a lot of times we never saw him, so we kind of grew up with no father image. The father image was mainly substitute fathers from my brothers. A lot more pressure was put on them because they were still trying to get through school, and it was really hard for them. I can see a lot of problems.

AUTHOR: You mentioned your brothers have a drinking problem. Does it have something or anything to do with the same kind of pressures that may have contributed to your father's drinking?

BRENDA: No, I don't think my brothers were under the same kind of pressures as my dad was under. My dad was under far. Even before a lot of the black people were even fighting for their rights, he was in there before minorities were even considering to have rights. When people started to get rights, he was allowed to sleep in the same sleeping quarters on the train. Before that, he had to sleep outside. He went through all of that, so he, in a sense, tried to keep his sanity by drinking because that is a lot of pressure. As far as my brothers are concerned, a lot of teachers on the reservation were Caucasian teachers. So compared to what we grew up with and what they wanted us to understand, there was no one in between telling us what they were trying to explain to us. In our family, we all spoke Navajo, period. We were brought into a boarding-school setting, and we were told not to, but there was a law that got passed when I was in the boarding school that we could speak our language, so that's the only reason why we were allowed to speak Navajo. But other than that, we were so structured: "This is the way the white man lives. This is how you are going to learn it." We were trained. We had to learn dining room style, how to set up a plate, how to eat, how to walk, how to dress. That was a lot of pressure just right there by itself. We had to learn how to finish a sentence just to go get a drink of water. We had a certain way.

AUTHOR: Do you feel in any way that your Navajo culture was being denied or oppressed because these white teachers wanted to make you like them?

BRENDA: Oh, yeah. There is no doubt about that. One white teacher, for one instance, in eighth grade, her name was Mrs. Keller. Mrs. Keller used to carry a cross on her, and she used to tell us every morning, "I'm praying for you. I lit a candle for you today. We are really going to learn today." When I think back on that, I wouldn't even hire a teacher like that.

AUTHOR: Why was she praying for you?

BRENDA: She was praying for us because she wanted us to learn what she wanted us to learn.

AUTHOR: She felt sorry for you?

BRENDA: Oh, yeah. She felt like she owed us something, to teach us how to live in the dominant society, which was the Anglo way of living. But then she didn't stop to think that we were the dominant society on our own reservation, which was never picked up because our school was run by Anglos. Nobody ever questioned what kind of feelings these teachers had toward minorities. Nobody ever questioned if they even knew what Navajo was. They never knew the clan structure. A lot of the kids in class were brothers and sisters through clan. If one person got into trouble, the next person got into trouble, because, clanwise, we were related and the clan kids stuck together. Those are the things the teachers didn't understand. Teachers did not understand that, yes, we want to be a part of the main society, but please, just teach us what we need to know academically to move on. But they were too busy trying to socialize us, trying to dress us, trying to fix our hair a certain way. They were too busy on these types of things, instead of trying to teach us how to read. They spent less time trying to teach us how to spell. These are the things that should be taught in school.

AUTHOR: How about the way the whites treat your people today. Do you feel that you and your people are treated as equals in all ways?

BRENDA: Not in all ways. The way we're looked at in the public view, such as *Time* magazine did a television show from the reservation about five or six years ago in Gallup, on how alcoholism was overcoming the reservation. They picked the right town, of course. Gallup is the biggest drunken area you will find. But the thing is nobody stops to look at other things. We have two masters of social work who work right in St. George. We have an Indian legal service in St. George. There are a lot of programs that are being opened up to Native Americans, but we're too busy thinking alcoholism—*Indian* and *alcoholism* go in one sentence. Nobody stops to question me, has anyone ever asked me if I'm a drunk? The Navajo reservation is going through a big change right now, and nobody cares except people that have lived there. We have a big gap compared to when my parents never had any education.

AUTHOR: The last area I want to discuss is your thoughts about the future. Where do you think the Navajo nation is going? What kind of condition? Are things going to get better?

BRENDA: What I see is, we are a few years behind where the African-American people are. We are going to be in their same shoes when we get enough educated, when we get enough seniority, when we get enough stability where we want to be known. That's where we are. We're a few years behind. Also, another thing is the Navajo culture is so strong, it will never die out either, so people will have to interact somehow to meet our needs as Native Americans. We are not going to give up our culture, our values, and our morals. These were embedded in us as young kids. Little kids are taught stories and songs. For an example, I grew up with these and then all of a sudden just forgot it. My first grade to maybe twelfth grade, I never sang a song. Then all of a sudden one day I'll be walking down the street and a song hits my head and it just comes out. This is because these songs were sung to me when I was little. These are songs that are always going to be inside me no matter what I've been taught. No matter how society says this is how you are supposed to be, this is what you're supposed to be, this is what we want you to be, these things will not be taken away. If I was ever asked to choose, I would rather have my values and my tradition and my morals as a Navajo.

AUTHOR: That's a good note to end on.

CURTIS LOYD

Also a self-described "black person," Mr. Curtis Loyd is a twenty-four-year-old father of two girls. Raised in an all-black area of Dallas, he graduated from college in 1994. He, his white wife, and their children live in Europe, where Mr. Loyd plays professional basketball.

AUTHOR: Curtis, how would you describe your racial or ethnic background? How would you describe it to someone from Sweden?

CURTIS: I would just say that I'm black. Because everyone puts everything black or white, then I guess I'm the black person.

AUTHOR: You don't consider yourself African American?

CURTIS: No.

AUTHOR: Any particular reason?

CURTIS: Well, I wasn't born in Africa. If you're going to get like that, then I'm a black American.

AUTHOR: Tell me something about your family background, parents, siblings.

CURTIS: Well, it's just me and my mom. I never had a father. It's mostly girls in my family. We weren't blessed with a lot of men. Being a family with all girls and stuff, the women really stick together on trying to emphasize a family structure—something that I never had, but they emphasized it. That's what I'm trying to do with my family, trying to give them family structure, even though I'm not used to it. I don't know the first thing on being a father, because I never had a father, so I'm just going day by day.

AUTHOR: Anything else you can tell me about your family setup when you were in Dallas?

CURTIS: My mom worked at a bank ever since I was born. As soon as I graduate from college, she can retire. It will be twenty-four years that she has worked there.

AUTHOR: Why can she retire when you graduate?

CURTIS: She has put me through school. It's been me, me, me and her, and she just wants to rest and I don't blame her.

AUTHOR: Try to describe for me the most obvious case of prejudice that you've encountered.

CURTIS: Well, mostly if you're black, if you're tall, if you look athletic, you're an athlete. That's right off. You could dress all dapper and still go to class, but somebody eventually will ask,

"Well, how's the team doing this year?" For some reason, I couldn't get over that statement. Do I look like an athlete that much? If I wear a coat and tie the whole year, how many people would come up to me and still say "Well, how's the team this year?" And especially when you're going up to a majority white school.

AUTHOR: Have you had any kinds of interactions with people where you've been made very aware that you were black?

CURTIS: Yeah, we were in my beat-up car, we were just cruisin' on the highway, and we were by ourselves, me and my wife and my little girl. The cop, I didn't see him, but we weren't going fast. But the cop turns on his lights as soon as we made eye contact; I mean he just whooped around there.

AUTHOR: He was going the other way?

CURTIS: No, he was just in the median. I didn't give him the pleasure of chasing me. Right when he turned around, I pulled over to the side. He went on my wife's side and asked me for my license and all that kind of stuff. I asked him, "What's the problem, Officer?" and he said, "Well, I got two readings clocked here, two readings going eighty-five miles per hour." So right then, I have the liberty in seeing the radar, so I got out. As soon as I hopped out, "Well, sir, what's the deal? What's going on?" I said. Then he pulled his gun out.

AUTHOR: Pulled his gun out?

CURTIS: Yeah.

AUTHOR: Do you think that this was racially motivated?

CURTIS: I don't know. There's so much of that, you know, black people use that word so much these days: "If I don't get this, then it's racism." They're using it as a grudge.

AUTHOR: Were you going eighty-five?

CURTIS: No. We were like barely going fifty. I told you my car won't—if I go eighty-five, I won't have it long.

AUTHOR: How did you feel when he pulled his gun?

CURTIS: It kind of shocked me because I didn't have a threatening motion. I was just talking to him in my normal voice.

AUTHOR: Where do you see yourself in this society as a young black male?

CURTIS: Dangerous. I'm dangerous right now. I'm dangerous because I'm in school, and I'm getting an education. Once I get an education, no matter how far I go, I can talk shit. 'Cause there's one thing you cannot take away from me is my education.

AUTHOR: Why does that make you dangerous?

CURTIS: To society it makes me dangerous because you know a black man with an education—well, look at the black men in our history with an education. So if I get too much power, then I know I'll be gone. It depends on how far society wants me to go.

AUTHOR: How far do you think society wants you to go?

CURTIS: Right now it depends on where I'm at. If I'm in my own environment, I can excel.

AUTHOR: In general, where do you think young black men are in this society?

CURTIS: In general, they are on the top of the endangered species list. That's where they are. We kill ourselves, perfect example. We kill ourselves. With all I have, I'll give it to them before I'll give it to you. This is the way I was taught. White people, they can get theirs, but black people, they are going to need some help. I have to help my own kind before I help you. That's the way I was taught.

AUTHOR: What do you think is wrong with the United States in terms of race?

CURTIS: In terms of race, I think it is really ignorance. I am not that evil. I am not that bad.

AUTHOR: What evidence do you have that society in general thinks you're evil?

CURTIS: Do you have a dictionary? In Webster's dictionary look up *black* and look up white.

AUTHOR: Yeah, I see your point. Where do you think the ignorance comes from? Is it intentional?

CURTIS: When slavery was here, it had to be intentional because the master had to keep control. I think now it is more of a norm: how you treat black people, where we need to park, where we need to sit. That's the same way with us. If I get on the bus, the first thing I go to is the back.

AUTHOR: Seriously?

CURTIS: Go to Dallas right now. If I'm walking down the hall, white people are the aggressor. You know they got you pinned all the way up against the wall. What you got to do is walk all the way around. This is anywhere. This is on campus. If I'm trying to get to the front door, and a white person is right there, I bet you I will alter my step. It's nothing but etiquette now.

AUTHOR: What do you think the ignorance is based on? How do we end the ignorance?

CURTIS: Do people want to end it? Does society want to end it?

AUTHOR: What do you think?

CURTIS: How would society look if now I'm equal to you? I don't think so. If black people and white people are all-of-a-sudden equal, then it's just one big race, and a lot more people are going to get hurt than what it is now. Sometimes you keep us happy, when you sign Charles Barkley to a TV contract, but that's Charles Barkley, that's just one black man.

AUTHOR: One more question. Where do you think we are going?

CURTIS: That's tough. That is tough. If society keeps going as it is, the true nature, the true *color* will come out. I don't want to answer that.

AUTHOR: What are you going to tell your daughters?

CURTIS: First I'm going to tell them, right off, since they were born they are in a position where they are less than I am. Because right now nothing is worse than being mixed, black and white. Because they look at you, and you can be called every name in the book now. Your parents couldn't stay with their own color or their own kind, so you don't even have a place. I'll tell them that you are black and you're proud. Whatever you are, whatever you want to be, you're proud. I am. I'm proud to be black. Now the stuff that goes on with it, I'm not proud of it, but I'm proud to be black. I want to instill in them to be proud.

AUTHOR: What do you think their world is going to be like?

CURTIS: Because they are between, I want them to experience both worlds: her mother and her family and where I come from. My mom would tell it like it is, and that is how I am. If you want to know, then ask me, and I'll tell you.

AUTHOR: Thank you, Curtis.

STEVE SUSOEFF

Mr. Steve Susoeff, forty-two, was born and raised in Tolleson, Arizona, a small farming community that was racially mixed, comprised of whites, Latinos, and Native Americans. He has been a lawyer and a clinical therapist. He is currently a writer and a counselor at a drug and alcohol rehabilitation home.

AUTHOR: How would you characterize your childhood if you were writing some sort of essay or describing what it was like?

STEVE: I guess I was lonely a lot. I felt like escaping a lot. I didn't really have a plan to escape until I was about twelve. I knew I wanted to get as far away as I could by the time I was about five, probably.

AUTHOR: Why?

STEVE: I don't know if it was something about me as much as feeling the reactions of people to me. People just seemed to think I was a strange kid. It's not that other kids didn't play with me, because they did. It's hard to describe. There was just a difference. I could write about this. This is just hard to talk about.

AUTHOR: At age five or six, when you realized that you didn't want to be there, did you have any idea that your sexuality was going to be different from most people's?

STEVE: Probably. I had it figured out by the time I was seven or eight.

AUTHOR: How old were you when you were first called "queer"?

STEVE: Grade school, probably six.

AUTHOR: What did it mean to you?

STEVE: I had no idea. Something bad, but I really didn't know what it was. I knew what homosexuals were because my mother talked about them.

AUTHOR: How did you feel when kids called you queer?

STEVE: Alienated, pushed away. I remember at some point when I was a kid, about eight, watching some chicks that had hatched, and there was one that was very weak. I think the horse had stepped on it and it limped around, and the other chicks ganged up on it and pecked at it all the time and finally killed it. I remember feeling like that, thinking that was pretty much what was happening to me and that I needed to get away from that.

AUTHOR: How old do you think you were when you realized that words like *queer* were the same as *homosexual*?

STEVE: I guess I had that figured out by eight.

AUTHOR: When was the first time you remember someone treating you differently because you were queer or whatever?

STEVE: In high school it started pretty early. I had been in school about a week. When I was twelve, a senior who was seventeen said, "Hey, queer," and he was sitting on the grass with some other seniors, and something in me said if I let him get away with it, then it would never stop. So I hit him. I went over and punched him and broke his nose and broke a couple of his teeth and got suspended from school. But it was definitely worth it because I think it slowed it down. It didn't stop it, but it slowed it down a little bit.

AUTHOR: So you get verbally harassed from six to twelve, go to high school, and verbal harassment is still going on. When did you first experience physical harassment?

STEVE: Thirteen. Four guys shoved a bar of soap up my ass in the shower. In the gym after school.

AUTHOR: What did you think?

STEVE: I thought that I needed to get out as soon as possible, that they were going to kill me if they could. I also thought afterward that up until then I had been really fighting what they saw in me and trying to pretend as if I was like everybody else, and then it became clear that whatever I was doing wasn't working, that they knew more about me than I did, and also, the bar of soap was painful and very humiliating, but if that was the worst they had to offer, they weren't going to kill me doing that, and I'd be better off not pretending than pretending because they obviously saw through the pretense. What finally dawned on me was that the more I hid from people, the more they would have to hurt me with. I think from that day on I was more-or-less out of the closet in terms of not pretending anymore. I still didn't know what I was pretending not to be, but I wasn't going to pretend anymore, I knew that.

AUTHOR: This is an incredibly general question, but how would you describe our cultural attitudes toward gays and lesbians?

STEVE: I think the most dominant thing is that people even with benign attitudes don't want to have to hear about it or think about it. I think it is embarrassing to them. It's like everything else that's sexual. It's offensive to people to have to hear about what somebody does in bed. I find it kind of offensive. I don't want to know everything about other people's private lives. There's something about the way gayness is presented that makes it all about sex.

AUTHOR: What sorts of pressures do you think gays and lesbians have that maybe they didn't have a few years ago?

STEVE: Actually, I think a lot of people today think gay and lesbian people are under a kind of pressure to be emissaries to the straight world, that we're supposed to be setting some kind of example, and we had better lead exemplary lives and not be too sexual and not be too political and not be too outrageous be-cause then straight people won't like us. To me, they never liked us and they never will like us, just because we do things a certain way. So why bother? This recently came up in a discussion about using the word *lover* to describe one's life-mate, and my point about that is if that's the person who loves me, then that's my lover, and I don't really care what people think of that name. If they assume that it's only a sexual rela-tionship because that's what that word has come to mean in straight society among people who are married and take lovers on the side, that's too bad. They're are missing out on the use of a beautiful word. I can't worry about what they think. I'm not going to come up with some name for a loved one in my life just to please heterosexual society, because I don't think I can please them anyway. As long as I'm looking to them for valida-tion, I am always going to be in trouble. I think that's what's changed since the 1930s or even since the 1960s—that gay people look to themselves and to their own community for validation now.

AUTHOR: Where do you think gays and lesbians are as a group, in terms of how they respond to straight culture, how they respond to each other?

STEVE: I think the pendulum swings back and forth. I think we are in a phase where it has been realized by the dominant culture that we're a force to be reckoned with, especially economically, of course. When it was recognized that divorced women could still hold jobs and be credit-worthy, they were finally able to get credit in their own names. For years and years, a divorced woman could not get credit. But when it was recognized that she was still buying a car and a house and participating in the economy, then she got to have credit. I think businesses recognize that gay people are a huge, sometimes untapped, market for travel money, for every kind of money, because we participate at every level of the economy. They are being targeted now in advertising and marketing efforts in a way that they used to be shunned. Coors advertises every two weeks on the back of *Christopher Street*, a gay literary magazine, a full-page cover ad.

AUTHOR: Do you see in some ways a breaking down of the prejudice?

STEVE: I think at other levels. People have more serious things to worry about for one thing. We've reached a saturation point with exposure where there is no turning back.

AUTHOR: What do you mean?

STEVE: I mean when everyone figured that Rock Hudson was gay, and that he got AIDS through homosexual activity. That broke a lot of denial for a lot of people, I think. Here's this icon of American manhood, and he's gay as a goose. He's taking it up the butt, and yet people got to see his loneliness and his isolation because, even in the last days of his life, he wasn't able to be who he really was.

AUTHOR: So you think sexual orientation is going to become less and less important as we go along?

STEVE: Yeah, I think so. In general, we're getting used to people talking about such personal things. We're used to gay people being around and being visible. They never have been before. Not in this society.

AUTHOR: That's what you mean about Rock Hudson?

STEVE: Yes. He became visible. I'm hopeful, when I see high school kids now forming gay groups and having gay friends. I think it's a different world. I'm not saying it's completely easy or without risks or fear, but I think it's better than it was.

AUTHOR: If you had access to the print media and people would actually come to you and ask you these questions, what would you say to society?

STEVE: I guess I would just want to remind them that, whether or not they acknowledge gay people around them, they are everywhere. You deal with us everyday. Nothing too terrible has happened to anyone yet. Just to remember that we are people just like you are.

AUTHOR: That's good. Thanks, Steve.

TINA FREDERICK

A twenty-nine-year-old single woman, Ms. Tina Frederick was born and raised in Rochester, New York. She has always been intellectually inclined and is currently a professor of psychology at a small western university.

AUTHOR: Describe a recent situation where you felt some form of discrimination because of your sex.

TINA: This past fall I had a student in my class who was an older man, and he was fairly uneducated and had very few social skills. He was very much like an antisocial personality, a Vietnam vet, and was from the deep, deep South. He put on the good-old-boy attitude. At first I thought he would be a challenge in class because people had told me that he was very antisocial and would have lots of strange behaviors in class. They didn't tell me the extent of what this guy would do. What I found out later was that this guy really hates women. The last day of the class he came up and told me that he hated women.

AUTHOR: What did he say?

TINA: He said, "I really enjoyed this class," or "I really learned a lot in this class." I'm not sure he used the word *"enjoyed."* Then he said as he was still shaking my hand, "Of course, you know I hate women." My response was "Yes, I know you hate women, and it must have been very difficult for you to get through this class, but I think I've seen some change in you"—trying to tone it positively on his way out the door. Of course he said, "I'll never change." I said, "Well, if you don't change, you die." But throughout the class he challenged me. In fact, later I found out that students who had been with him in other classes felt that he challenged me more than he challenged any of the male professors. He would challenge and confront me just to be confrontational. Some of the students felt that it really disrupted the class. There were times when I would say, "We're not going to talk about that; it's irrelevant," and really forcefully put him in his place. It worked. He would shut up and just sit and glare at me through the class, but it was not a pleasant feeling. He would use intimidation by trying to glare at me. Or he would wear a knife on his belt to class.

AUTHOR: That's relatively intimidating.

TINA: Yes, that's relatively intimidating. I'm glad it wasn't a gun. Then, when he was being angry at me and sitting there glaring at me in class, he would all of a sudden get up and leave the room, and I never knew whether I should shut the door and lock it, whether he was going out to get his gun to kill us all. Because I certainly think he had that capability.

AUTHOR: Were you ever physically afraid?

TINA: There were a couple of times when he really got in my face after class, when he just wouldn't leave an argument alone. The physical signs were there as well as the verbal signs. He was on

the verge of being out of control. His lips would quiver; he
would start shaking. I knew that at some point I could have
pushed him over the edge. In fact, someone said, "If you want
to get him out of there, why don't you just push him over the
edge?" A male colleague said, "Why don't you push him over
the edge, and then if he gets physically violent toward you at
least some of your students may step in and help you." I'm not
even sure the person said it in jest. I think he was half serious.
AUTHOR: What was the result of this guy? What did you do?

TINA: What I did was file a complaint with the dean of students along with other women on campus whom he had stalked and harassed.

AUTHOR: Were you afraid he would stalk and harass you?

TINA: I felt like he already *had* harassed me. Even telling me that he hated women was enough.

AUTHOR: With a knife on his belt.

TINA: Yeah. To indicate that he was harassing me. I felt as if he should not have been at a university at all. He was very antisocial, and certainly I felt we could not give him a psychology major. That would have been malpractice on our part to allow this guy to be a psychology major. The dean of students, interestingly enough, for all their talk on sexual harassment on this campus and harassment in general, felt that there wasn't evidence, objective evidence. I don't know what objective evidence is needed to put this guy before a disciplinary committee. That's when I said that was ridiculous because the dean of students hadn't talked to me about him yet. He had no idea what evidence I had. So I had to march myself over to the dean's office. He said, "The only way you can get him out of your class is to say that he is a threat to you," so I said, "Well, he is a threat to me."

AUTHOR: What was the dean's response to that?

TINA: I think he probably thought I was overreacting. But I also think he had no idea what the other women were going through. They were going through so much, much worse than I was. They were getting phone calls, they were being stalked, and they had been physically harassed. They just went through much more than I did, and because he wasn't going to take it seriously, I felt that I had to do something.

AUTHOR: Anything come of it?

TINA: Yes, after I talked to the dean of students, they decided to send him to a disciplinary committee, which is made up of faculty, students, and staff. When he found that out, he withdrew from school.

AUTHOR: Were you worried after that?

TINA: Oh, yeah. This guy is violent. I mean he would tell us stories in class about how he tried to kill his mother. In personality theories class, he would bring his dreams in, and they were all violent, involving guns and being violent toward women. I would double-lock my doors at night and make sure my windows were locked and have the phone by my bed. This went on for two or three weeks, and then he finally ended up leaving town. The police were kind of monitoring him, and they knew that he could be a threat to any of the women who had filed the complaint. Until he left town, I was a little more cautious than I normally am.

AUTHOR: You mentioned the fact that other women were involved. Do you think this is widespread? Not with this fellow, but in general, this sort of behavior?

TINA: He was an extreme case, but I think it occurs all the time. Milder, more subtle forms of it. I was talking to a student, a perfectly nice person, and we were talking about sexual harassment. He said something like "Well, if I want to hug you, then I want to hug you." I said, "You know, you can't always just do that. Some people would find that harassing. Some women would find that that's not what you can do and that's not appropriate." He got kind of upset about it, and we had this big, long discussion about appropriate touching behavior in the workplace. I've also found it even with a student who worked for me. My class and I went to lunch or to breakfast recently at the Market Grill. It was our last day of class, so it was to kind of sum up and rehash and stuff, and he came in and put his hands on my shoulders and said, "Hi, Tina, how are you doing?" I don't feel that offended by that, but certainly I'm a professor, I'm a woman, I'm sitting down; it's a power play. I don't think he even knew that it might not be appropriate behavior. I think things like that go on all the time. I don't know if it is discrimination, but it's definitely control. I mean, it was clear that he was the big guy standing up, and when he came over, I was the only one he put his hands on.

AUTHOR: Where do you think gender relations are in general?

TINA: I think no one knows how to relate to anybody anymore. I think that political correctness is gone way over the edge. But it has a point. Awareness has to be there, but what sometimes happens is there is no naturalness in a relationship anymore; it's all guarded, which isn't good either. I have to monitor every single word I say, for fear of offending anyone. So the relations become unnatural.

AUTHOR: Why do you think they are unnatural?

TINA: Because I think we are all questioning what we do. I think things will eventually even out and will go back to some kind of status quo or some kind of steady state. But right now I think it is real difficult.

AUTHOR: If you had to pick between this difficult stage, the uncertainty and unnaturalness of it, and the way it was, say, twenty years ago?

TINA: Oh, I would take this any day. At least there is awareness, and people are trying and recognizing the issues. I would definitely pick this.

AUTHOR: Where do you think this is going?

TINA: Hopefully, to some better place. Hopefully, to someplace where people are treated as human beings and not as men versus women. *Versus* is the key word there, I think. Where we are treated more as equal beings and less as one gender or the other. I think that some of the old generation—the old boys' club if you want to call them that—I don't think there is that much hope for them. I think there is a superficial awareness, and they offer this great sexual harassment training, so they offer us conflict management or workshops on how to relate to other people, but it's all just words. But I think the hope is for the younger generation: people going through school now, people in their thirties or forties, hopefully. They are not at a point where this is just words, but they are really thinking about these issues.

AUTHOR: What do you see when you look at teenagers and how they relate to each other in terms of gender? Does it look better?

TINA: Where I came from in New York, I think it looks better. I think you see a lot more coed groups hanging out together. I think that younger people are doing much better. I like to see it when high school kids are in coed groups and they are relating to each other as human beings—based on, maybe, interests or activities, rather than dating situations.

AUTHOR: How do you think we can promote that, for instance, in high school or grade school? Coed groups where boys and girls can see each other as equals?

TINA: I think that probably the best way is to get them to work on activities together. Cooperative learning is great, where you mix these groups with diverse kids in the class and each person in the group has to learn a segment for the whole group to be able to learn the whole thing. I think that way of interacting is very helpful. But it's hard, especially in the teenage years and adolescent years, in a natural way and not forced.

AUTHOR: This is a good place to end. Thank you, Tina.

Chapter 7

Prejudice in the Criminal Justice System

RACISM IN U.S. JUSTICE

Scholarship on the U.S. criminal justice system (CJS) offers clear evidence of a long history of racial, cultural, and class-group biases in its administration. The experiences of the racial, cultural, and class-group minorities within the CJS are marked by victimization by the nation's courts, police departments, correctional agencies, and other structures. Indeed, the current struggles of racial, cultural, and class-group minorities against dominant-group ethnocentrism and prejudice, as well as institutional racism and class-group oppression, are played out in the nation's courtrooms and judges' chambers, police stations, jails, and penitentiaries, as horrendously as anywhere in the United States today. The blatant injustices against minorities of racist-motivated arrests, sentencings, and incarceration, as well as those against America's poor and low-income, have significantly diminished their chances for a life of liberty, happiness, freedom, and contentment.

America's CJS has its foundations in the early embracement of "scientific racism" and other oppressive ideologies that have dominated U.S. thought and social practices for two hundred to three hundred years. The scientific racism of the eighteenth and nineteenth centuries preached social and racial inferiority of the world's peoples of color. Southern whites embraced this ideology during the nineteenth century and used it to justify plantation slave labor after the international slave trade collapsed in the early 1800s. Southern laws, courts, religion, and other "moral-inducing" southern institutions during the mid-nineteenth century quickly seized and advocated scientific racism to neutralize the world's tilt toward humanitarianism. By aggressively attaching southern race relations and the southern way of life to a public ideology based on African Americans as socially and mentally inferior, the South, with the strong backing of its CJS, sought to halt any direct challenges to white privilege and power in the region at the time (Burns, 1973).

With slavery's demise in the late nineteenth century, whites engaged in an aggressive policy and campaign of violence against African Americans to reestablish their authority. Lynchings, violent assaults, and murders became instruments of brutal oppression against African Americans in the seventy-five-year period following the abolition of slavery. The South was not alone in its terrorism against early-twentieth-century African Americans. Law enforcement, criminal courts, and other institutions of northern criminal justice were major players in the orchestrated campaigns of violence against the African Americans in the early 1900s. Police incited and encouraged white mob violence against African Americans in the towns and cities north of the Mason–Dixon line. In a white riot in 1900 in New York City, a mostly Irish-American police force encouraged working-class whites to attack African-American men, women, and children wherever they could be found (Feagin and Feagin, 1993). In the 1919 Chicago race riots, police not only did not stop white violence against African Americans by refusing to arrest most white rioters, but also rearmed whites who were arrested, with the rioters' own ammunition, and with the understanding that the weapons were to be used against blacks (White, 1919). The U.S. court system has applied and continues to apply capital punishment, imprisonment, and other criminal sanctions in a racist and socially discriminatory way. Its role as a facilitator and sponsor of dominant-group interests in applying U.S. criminal justice has been effective in its reproducing racism (Marable, 1983). Most disturbing in the U.S. CJS's oppressive history against racial, cultural, and class minorities is its role in continuing the current structures of power and influence in U.S. social and political life. This oppression forces racial, cultural, and class minorities to be subordinated by the very agencies and authorities of justice. The inequalities of the U.S. CJS contribute to the low status and position of racial minorities and the poor in the United States. Police relationships with the rich and the powerful have been extensively studied: Police present themselves as representatives of the interests of the power structure. The "power-maintenance" police role has ominous implications for those groups and individuals who are targets of the power structure's opposition and retaliation (Yates, 1984). This role ties local civilian police politically to the local power structure, cancels their objectivity in enforcing the nation's laws, and seriously jeopardizes the integrity of U.S. law enforcement.

The history, preoccupation, and structured role of the criminal justice system, for adults and juveniles, has ensured the political, social, and economic subordination of this nation's racial, cultural, and class minorities. These and other acknowledged inequalities reveal the bias against groups and interests outside the sources of power, privilege, and influence in the contemporary United States.

PREJUDICE IN U.S. CRIME

The influence of privilege, position, and power on the CJS is obvious in the legal and popular concepts of crime. What legally defines crime in the United States, its enforcement and judiciary sanctions, and public perception is extremely political. As a concept in legal and popular discourse, crime is the biased nature of criminal events. Crime is significantly related to the prejudices and interests of America's privileged, powerful, and influential (Quinney, 1977).

What a society considers or describes as criminal events must be seen beyond legal codes, as it indicates how aggressively or passively sanctions are enforced. This invites the notion of "criminal events" not existing in the absence of unassociated activities, or a "vacuum." Crime is defined by how prohibited behavior is pursued by the system of criminal justice authorities and sanctions and includes active pursuit by law enforcement agencies and the courts. It also includes an aggressiveness of criminal as opposed to civil code violations, which are associated with the most punitive sanctions and, most importantly, are successfully drilled into the public consciousness and attitudes as being crime. This dichotomy of active versus passive law enforcement and judiciary sanctions is nowhere more apparent than in the different treatment applied to the poor and to the well-to-do.

"Street" Crime versus "White-Collar" Crime

Comparing the pursuit of and sanctions against "street" crime with "white-collar" crime illustrates the bias of America's CJS. The criminal events of most interest to America's police and courts are the offenses typically associated with the powerless, including the poor, the working class, racial minorities, and the young. On the other hand, the offenses of the rich and affluent rank lowest in the criminal justice system's priorities, interest, and punishment (Pfohl, 1994).

The concepts of street crime versus white-collar crime remain unambiguous in this context. Street crimes are the offenses against persons and property that strike with stunning immediacy in the streets and homes of everyday Americans. They are popularized as offenses serious enough so that police give them special attention and often combine them to form a "crime index": murder, forcible rape, robbery, aggravated assault, auto theft, larceny, burglary, and arson. Street crimes are also the crimes most actively pursued by the more than sixteen thousand local police agencies. These statistics make up the FBI's *Uniform Crime Reports* and are the standard for popular images of crime in America. Limiting the *Uniform Crime Reports* to these eight crimes further establishes the most "official" crime problem in America.

White-collar crime is, however, much more complex to define. It is linked to occupationally related offenses, including corporate and government crime and its associated activities. In contrast to street crime, white-collar crime is rarely pursued by local police and the FBI. Unlike street crime, where there is severe and nearly certain punishment, the punishment for white-collar crimes is generally lenient and without imprisonment (Clinard and Yeager, 1980).

These patterns of different treatment are not lost in the distinct ideologies that govern the popular conception and enforcement of crime in the United States. Crime here is mostly associated with the offenses of the poor and of racial minorities. Civilian police widely ignore white-collar lawbreakers. These include "routine," occupation-related crimes committed by persons of high social status like bankers, physicians, and corporate executives. Their crimes are likely to involve embezzling by the banker, Medicare fraud by the physician, or toxic waste dumping by the corporate official (Reid, 1991). These crimes are not pursued by U.S. criminal justice with the vigor or the vengeance with which it pursues the crimes of the poor and racial minorities. The *Uniform Crime Reports* (UCR), overemphasizing the offenses of the poor and underemphasizing the offenses of the rich, reflect the racial and cultural prejudice of crime in the United States.

Further, any real merit for maintaining this dichotomy of street crime versus white-collar crime is not self-evident in measures traditionally used to decide criminal policies and pursuits. Stephen Pfohl's insight into white-collar crime is representative of researchers' opinions:

> [White-collar] crime is generally committed by highly calculating individuals in the rational pursuit of illegal profit.

It is, moreover, among the most costly forms of lawbreaking to society as a whole. The annual economic toll of corporate crime totals billions of dollars, far exceeding that from any form of conventional or street crime. Yet the punishments for such crime remain among the lowest and most lenient. (p. 84)

Researchers have calculated that the costs to society of corporate crime are tremendously greater than those of conventional street crime. Austin and Irwin (1987) estimated the total cost of all street crimes at $11 billion a year, compared to $175 billion to $231 billion a year for white-collar crime. More recent FBI data show that the total take for all robberies reported to the police in the United States in 1991 was $562 million. This included cash or property worth an average of $817 per incident, bank robberies netting $3,177 per incident, and convenience store robberies netting $387 per incident (Goode, 1994, p. 336). By comparison, in 1989, President George Bush announced that the savings-and-loan fiasco would cost U.S. taxpayers $200 billion over the next decade, and a total of $360 billion over three decades (Pizzo, Fricker, and Muolo, 1992). Less than a dozen men have gone to prison for this massive fraud.

Rather than recall the Pinto to correct its defective fuel tanks, Ford executives calculated that the cost of insurance claims would total less than repairing the autos. They estimated that Ford would pay less than $50 million for the deaths of approximately two hundred people from Pintos exploding during rear-end collisions. The minor adjustment to repair the gas tanks, at $11 per vehicle, would have cost Ford $137 million. Ford executives saved stockholders nearly $100 million, but they killed two hundred people. Not a single Ford official spent a single night in jail (Dowie, 1977).

Researchers have estimated the number of human lives lost because of white-collar criminals. According to Bohm (1986):

Conservative estimates show that each year at least 10,000 lives are lost due to unnecessary surgeries, 20,000 to errors in prescribing drugs, 20,000 to doctors spreading diseases in hospitals, 100,000 to industrial disease, 14,000 to industrial accidents, 200,000 to environmentally caused cancer, and an unknown number to lethal industrial products. (p. 195)

These startling figures contrast sharply with the roughly 24,000 criminal homicides occurring each year in the United States. Most researchers do not yet count smoking deaths as a form of corporate crime, but the day when these deaths, now estimated at over 400,000 per year, will be counted as criminal is rapidly approaching.

With white-collar crime's high cost to society financially and in lives lost, it is difficult to ignore the political nature of what constitutes crime and criminal sanctions in the United States. Historically the criminal courts have exercised little jurisdiction, instead deferring oversight and punishment to administrative agencies. Thus white-collar crimes are not real crimes, and the typical upper-socioeconomic-class perpetrators are not real criminals. Instead, the crimes are infractions of administrative rules, a distinction that allows the affluent to go unpunished and avoid the liability.

Changes in public opinion since the middle 1970s in seeing corporate offenders as criminal have increased courts' interests in pursuing and punishing white-collar offenders (Wheeler, Mann, and Sarat, 1988). Some of the changes are illustrated by the successful prosecution and four-year jail sentence of Paul Thayer, former chair of LTV, for perjury related to insider trading activities; similar prosecutions of executives at E. F. Hutton, who confessed to a multi-billion-dollar check-kiting scheme; and the prosecution of top executives at General Electric, who defrauded the Pentagon. However, the continued lenient punishment of white-collar criminals compared to street criminals means maintaining this dichotomy of social-class prejudice and racist behavior in U.S. criminal law and justice. Considering the administrative law and its sanctions on white-collar crime, and criminal law and its sanctions on street crime, the institutionalized oppression, racism, and class bias of street crime versus white-collar crime will continue.

PREJUDICE IN THE U.S. JUVENILE
DELINQUENCY SYSTEM

The biases and pervasive differences in treatment within America's juvenile justice (JJ) system have been consistently linked to gender, race, and class. Juvenile arrest patterns have shown racial, gender, and class discrimination by the police, and among court, probation, and parole officials.

Police also tend to see lower-class boys as substantially more involved in delinquent behavior than both middle- and upper-class boys, and they act on these prejudices (Staples, 1987). Police regard parental neglect of lower-class juveniles as much more common than among upper-class parents. Police believe the irresponsibility of lower-class parents helps explain the disproportionate incidence of lower-class delinquency. Similarly, African-American teenagers are labeled as delinquent by the police and referred to the juvenile court disproportionately more than white teenagers when engaging in the same or similar behavior (Huizinga and Elliott, 1987). This is especially true of serious offenses and offenders. An African-American youth charged with a *violent* and/or *abusive offense* has an almost 25 percent greater chance of being arrested than a white youth charged with a similar offense.

Also, an African-American youth charged with a *property offense,* such as theft, burglary, or vandalism, faces an almost 20 percent greater chance of being arrested than a white youth. Studies in Philadelphia in 1972, updated in 1985, found that African-American youth were at much higher risk of arrest than white youth. Among non-Index offenders, including truants, runaways, and vandals, African-American youth were seven times more likely than white youth to be arrested. Among Index offenders, such as thieves, burglars, robbers, arsonists, murderers, and rapists, African-American youth were two times more likely than white youth to be arrested (Wolfgang, Tracy, and Figlio, 1985).

African-American children also face substantially higher arrest chances than white children for most minor offenses. The highly punitive response by the police to the minor infractions by African-American youth is attributed to police patrolling inner-city neighborhoods more intensively and their harsh responses to the "antiauthority demeanor" of black youth (Gibbs, 1984, pp. 8–9).

These patterns of police prejudice also apply to gender groups. Historically research shows that female adolescents have a much narrower range of acceptable behavior. Integrating the traditions of male "paternalism and chivalry" into a gender-biased framework for applying the nation's juvenile justice laws, Chesney-Lind (1973, p. 54) observed that even minor deviance by girls may be seen as a substantial challenge to the authority of the family, the viability of the double standard, and the maintenance of the present system of gender inequality. What is clear in the arrests of female juveniles is that a much higher percentage of adolescent females than males is referred to the juvenile court for committing relatively minor offenses. For example, in Honolulu, running away from home and sex offenses, referred to as "status offenses," accounted for 60 percent of all female referrals to the juvenile court; male status offenders accounted for fewer than 30 percent.

The nation's juvenile detention centers and training schools also promote and maintain the racism, sexism, and class discrimination institutionalized in the outcomes of the juvenile court process for females, African Americans, Latinos, Native Americans, Asians, the poor, and others of the powerless in the United States. Members of these groups are more likely to be placed in detention because of their race or because they are female. In Tampa, Florida, African-American youth—although much less deviant than white youth in alcohol and illicit drug use, problem behavior at home and school, and emotional and psychological maladjustment—were still more likely to be put in detention than white youth (Dembo, 1986).

For minor offenses adolescent girls are treated more punitively by juvenile justice authorities than adolescent boys. Once referred to the juvenile court, teenage girls face a higher risk of detention than boys, are more likely to be put in detention after arrests, are more likely to face detention for status crimes, and traditionally remain in detention for a longer period.

For serious crimes both gender and race affect juvenile arrests. Social scientists Horowitz and Pottieger (1988) found both female and African-American male property offenders more likely to be arrested than white male property offenders. Many researchers believe that JJ system bias against girls continues despite efforts to deemphasize the official processing of youth arrested for noncriminal, status offenses. Such infractions still account for about a fourth of girls' arrests and less than a tenth of boys' arrests (Federal Bureau of Investigation, 1989).

The 1990 Children in Custody Annual Report shows the disturbing trend among American JJ authorities of unfairly committing African-American and other racial minority youth to detention centers, training schools, jails, and other facilities. The proportion of African Americans in public juvenile facilities grew 9 percent from 1985 to 1989 (from 33 percent to 42 percent). Latino youth experienced a 4 percent increase in their proportion in public facilities during the same period (from 12 percent to 16 percent). The numbers of white youth in public juvenile facilities, on the other hand, dropped from 53 percent to 40 percent. In 1989, for the first time, minorities accounted for more than half (52 percent) of all juveniles in public and private facilities.

Minority youth who were charged with a delinquent-category offense were much more likely to be placed in juvenile detention than white youth charged with a delinquent offense. Table 7.1 shows how detention varied depending on sex, race, and age. Twenty-eight percent of the delinquency cases involving nonwhite youth resulted in detention compared to only seventeen percent of those involving white youth. The variation in the

Table 7.1. Variation in the Use of Detention in Delinquency Cases by Sex, Race, and Age at Court Referral (Percentage of Cases Detained), 1988

	Total delinquency	Person	Property	Drugs	Public order
Offense	21	24	17	33	26
Sex					
Male	21	26	18	34	25
Female	17	18	12	26	27
Race					
White	17	20	14	21	24
Nonwhite	28	29	22	51	30
Age at court referral					
10	5	7	4	*	5
11	8	12	7	14	12
12	12	15	10	29	19
13	17	20	14	29	25
14	20	24	17	32	27
15	23	26	19	34	29
16	24	28	20	34	28
17	23	28	19	32	23

*Too few cases to obtain a reliable percentage.
Note: Youth of Latino ethnicity were generally included in the white racial category.
Source: National Center for Juvenile Justice, Juvenile Court Statistics, 1988.

use of detention was present across all offense groups. Minority youth are particularly singled out when charged with a drug offense. The greatest racial variation in the use of detention was for youth charged with a drug law violation; 51 percent of non-whites were detained, compared to 21 percent of white youth (*Children in Custody,* 1990). The 1990 custody reports also prove true for 1991. The *Children in Custody Annual Report* for 1991 indicated that racial minorities, males, and older adolescent juveniles were treated more punitively by JJ authorities (see Table 7.2).

PREJUDICE IN THE TREATMENT OF GANGS

Gangs, as a deviant aspect of social structure, have been the subject of social research for at least seventy years. Thrasher's

Table 7.2. Variation in the Use of Detention in Delinquency Cases by Sex, Race, and Age at Court Referral (Percentage of Cases Detained), 1989

	Total delinquency	Person	Property	Drugs	Public order
Offense	22	26	17	37	26
Sex					
Male	23	27	18	38	27
Female	18	20	13	28	26
Race					
White	19	22	15	23	26
Nonwhite	28	31	23	55	30
Age at court referral					
10	6	10	5	*	8
11	10	14	8	31	13
12	13	17	10	29	21
13	18	21	15	33	26
14	22	26	18	35	29
15	25	28	21	38	39
16	25	30	21	37	28
17	25	30	20	37	26

*Too few cases to obtain a reliable percentage.
Note: Youth of Latino ethnicity were generally included in the white racial category.
Source: National Center for Juvenile Justice, special analysis of 1989 data from the National Juvenile Court Data Archive.

(1927) early insights on juvenile gangs in the early twentieth century not only provided a successful framework for studying these groups but also helped stir public policy debate, social curiosity, and broad academic interest in the phenomenon of gangs. Gangs today have evolved to an unprecedented level and range. The early "near-groups" of gang structure, which defined most of the groups Thrasher studied, have given way to much more complex social structures within gangs. The institutionalized structures of urban gangs have a level of group dimension that would be hardly recognizable to the early writers on urban-centered social gangs.

U.S. criminal justice policy today remains uneven in the pressures it exerts on gang structures in the United States. Street "gangs," mostly of young African Americans and Latinos, are the targets of the most intense and persistent law-enforcement efforts. Rich, powerful "Mafia" and organized crime "gangs," on the other hand, have been generally given a kind of immunity from intense police aggression in its wars against criminal gangs (Simon and Eitzen, 1990). U.S. law-enforcement and criminal-court policy toward gangs represents a double standard of horrendous proportions. The power and wealth of organized syndicate gangs have been critical in shaping current CJS policies *away* from interrupting their financial interests and activities. Organized crime has infiltrated legitimate industries, including construction, waste removal, the wholesale and retail distribution of goods, hotel and restaurant operations, liquor sales, motor vehicle repairs, real estate, and banking. One report estimated that organized crime's infiltration of the U.S. construction industry alone nets organized crime more than $45 billion in annual income (Organized Crime Commission, 1986).

The tremendous financial power of organized crime groups allows them to purchase freedom from the "burdens" of aggressive law enforcement. Organized crime groups are often protected by corrupt officials in government and the private sector. Social research has shown the police to be in collusion with organized gangs to control and suppress racial minorities and union workers. Police allegedly use organized crime to control ghettos by creating a "small army of heroin addicts," whose energies are deflected from challenging the otherwise miserable conditions of their existence. Organized criminal gangs have also been protected by criminal court judges, attorneys, and the police. Few organized crime leaders are ever arrested, and gang underlings, who may on occasion be apprehended, are released (Reid, 1994).

Well known to the public are the aggressive tactics of police "gang" sweeps into racial and ethnic neighborhoods, as well as the tough court punishment of members of racial and ethnic minority gangs. Central to gang treatment within this society has been the pervasiveness of racism. Minority gangs and white organized crime share capital accumulation, competitiveness, managed business, inventive entrepreneurship, and other interests and goals that have been linked to the social structures of gangs (Jankowski, 1991). The desire and drive to accumulate money, material possessions, status, power, and respect are experiences that organized crime and inner-city minority gangs share.

While social scientists see little distinction between these groups as outlaw social structures, the ways in which law enforcement and the courts have responded to these two groups illustrate severe and troubling differences. While police routinely raid racial minority gangs, these same kinds of raids are almost unheard of against organized crime groups. Organized crime has been given considerable latitude with which to operate in this country. Criminal activities in bank transactions, real estate sales, and transfers of funds to foreign banks show organized crime operating with little attention from U.S. police and courts. These and other continuing differences in the application of "justice" spotlight a criminal justice system that is deeply prejudiced.

RACISM AND THE DRUG WAR

The emphasis today on "just desserts" and "tough justice" as the prevailing model of crime control is well illustrated by how aggressively the police and the courts pursue drug offenders. The politically popular war on drugs significantly contributed to the rise in the U.S. prison population, which soared from 300,000 in 1980 to 925,000 in 1994. In that period, adult arrests for the sale or manufacture of drugs increased by 293 percent, and for drug possession, 128 percent. The proportion of federal drug offenders rose from 25 percent of all prisoners in 1981 to 53 percent in 1991. Narcotics offenders alone occupied 61 percent of the beds in federal prisons in 1994 (Smolowe, 1994). In state prisons, drug offenders rose from 6 percent of all prisoners in 1979, to 22 percent in 1991.

The current U.S. drug war, fought by both civilian and national forces, is not a neutral war: It is a war on the poor and minorities. The police's drug enforcement measures are directed at the inner city, poor neighborhoods, and African-American and Latino drug users. Drug enforcement policies are biased. While African Americans make up only 12 percent of the regular drug-user population and 16 percent for cocaine, more than 48 percent of those arrested for heroin or cocaine drug charges in 1988 were African American (Meddis, 1989). This bias is also evident in juvenile arrests and prosecutions. Courts are much more likely to suspend drug offense cases involving white youth charged with illegal possession than minority children (*Juveniles Taken into Custody Annual Report*, 1990). Between 1984 and 1988, youth drug offenses of whites retained for court review declined by 2 percent, while they increased more than 260 percent for minority youth.

Minorities continue to make up an increasingly large percentage of the arrests for drug crimes. African-American arrests rose from 30 percent of all drug arrests in 1984 to 41 percent in 1989. Michigan is an excellent example. While overall drug arrests in Michigan doubled from 1985 to 1990, for African Americans they tripled (Mitchell, 1990).

The war on drugs is sadly void of solutions outside law enforcement. The U.S. Attorney General estimated that the enforcement of the drug war alone cost taxpayers over $12 billion in fiscal year 1990 (U.S. Attorneys and the Attorney General of the U.S., 1989). This money targeted at treatment instead of enforcement would be more successful in removing violence and crime from our communities. The police and the court system are in the poorest position to turn a drug-oriented society around. Solving the illegal drug problem of this country lies not in a biased war on the poor and minorities, but in a well-financed system of treatment, education, job training and creation, and other programs of hope that are painfully absent in drug policies today.

PREJUDICE IN U.S. PRISONS

The racial and class injustices of federal, state, county, and local prisons or jail placements strongly illustrate the gross inequities of the courts toward minorities and the poor. Historically these groups have been overrepresented in U.S. prisons. In 1988, African Americans and Latinos accounted for nearly 70 percent of state prison admissions. Minorities were nearly 60 percent of the federal and state male prisoners in 1988; Latino males, 12.2 percent, and African Americans (the largest percentage of prisoners), 46.1 percent. Latinos have the highest federal incarceration rate, at 25.8 percent in 1988, more than doubling the state rate of Latino incarceration. In 1990, Native Americans were only slightly above their 0.6 percent of the general population in state prisons, but they made up a disturbing 1.8 percent of federal prisoners in 1988 (Correctional Populations in the United States, 1988, 1992).

A majority of 1988 state prison admissions—63.5 percent—were of people with less than a high school education (Perkins and Gilliard, 1992). And minority prisoners are more likely than white prisoners to have been impoverished at the time of their arrest, to have less education, and to have a lower occupational status.

Local jails are not free of bias. By 1988, racial minorities constituted 58 percent of the nation's jail population. Racial minorities are more likely to be jailed than whites regardless of the offense. And as is true of the social-class backgrounds of minority prisoners, minority jail inmates tend to be mostly from poor neighborhoods, and to have experienced disadvantaged educational and occupational histories.

Besides disproportionate incarceration rates, racial minorities and the poor as offenders are disproportionately on death row. Racial minorities make up more than half of the prisoners under sentence of death; African Americans alone constitute 40 percent. These groups are also far more likely than whites under similar sentence to have their executions actually carried out. Data on capital punishment between 1930 and 1967 revealed that, of those sentenced to death, between 10 and 20 percent more African-American prisoners were executed than whites, and worse, a majority of the murders in that time had been committed by whites (Wolfgang and Reidel, 1973).

POLICE BIAS IN THE UNITED STATES

Striking examples of police bias are found in citizens' perception of the police. Studies show that minorities, the poor, the young, and other powerless group persons feel greater hostility toward the police and perceive them more negatively than whites. African Americans evaluate police effectiveness more negatively than whites, and many Latinos feel hostility toward the police, who are perceived as enemies who protect only the white power structure. Latino leaders feel more isolated from the police than African-American leaders. The negative attitudes that Latinos feel toward the police have been linked to, among other things, the frequency of Latino encounters with police (Carter, 1985).

The critical questions that must be asked are how police bias and prejudice affect police decisions to arrest suspects, and how they influence police decisions that result in brutality. In fact, police decisions to arrest suspects are broadly anchored in police prejudice. The impulsive behavior and comments of police officers in one study did reveal a considerable amount of prejudice. In this investigation, 75 percent of the officers were described as "very" or "considerably" prejudiced against blacks (Conklin, 1986).

Most studies that examine the influence of racial or class discrimination on police arrests have focused on police encounters with juveniles. Racial bias by the police is evident when the arrested youth's disposition is considered: It increases the chances of a minority youth's having a police record that then affects future police and court actions involving the youth. Racial bias affected the police in Tampa, Florida: Their decisions to arrest youth and place them in local detention was much higher for male African Americans, relative to arrests and detention, than for white males (Dembo, 1988). It has been shown that police bias is tied more to an individual's socioeconomic status than his or her race (Hollinger, 1984). But along with class, race is important, since minority groups are overrepresented in the lower classes. And police discrimination against racial, ethnic, religious, and lifestyle group minorities is based, in part, on deeply rooted prejudice acquired through a lifetime of cultural and occupational socialization, the latter usually occurring on patrol and in contact with minorities. Unfortunately, the U.S. Supreme Court sanctioned racial discrimination by allowing race to satisfy probable cause requirements in searches for illegal aliens and for highway drug couriers (Johnson, 1983).

Rodney King and Police Brutality

The Rodney King incident alerted the nation to the brutal police violence inflicted on the poor and racial minorities and helped erase the innocence that middle- and upper-class white communities have about police. What the poor and minorities already knew when viewing the Rodney King video—that extreme violence at the hands of the police is all too common—sent shock waves throughout the nation and the world. Particularly embarrassing to the Los Angeles Police Department were the racial slurs made by the police at the King beating, including references to *Gorillas in the Mist*, *Mandingo*, and other racist allusions. Unfortunately, the beating and the abusive language that King endured that night is common among Los Angeles police officers responding to suspects who initially flee pursuing police.

The Rodney King incident conveyed the fact that police brutality is far from rare in the United States. Just as in 1968 the National Advisory Commission on Civil Disorders reported that African Americans witnessed police brutality constantly in their communities, so the U.S. Commission on Civil Rights reported in 1991 that police brutality is a serious problem. Studies show that police favor using excessive force (Barker, 1986), and that excessive force is sometimes necessary, if not a right in retaliation against those who use force against the officer (Carter, 1985).

Deadly Force and the Police

Police using deadly force has been linked to the race and class of their victims. Both African Americans and Latinos are more likely to be shot by the police than whites. Since 1949, almost half of all citizens killed by the police have been African American. While more restrictive rules in using deadly force were instituted in the 1970s, minorities are still at greater risk of being shot and killed by the police. While police shootings of minorities have declined by some estimates, African Americans and Latinos tragically continue to be disproportionately shot by police (Weagel, 1984).

COURT BIAS IN THE U.S. JUSTICE SYSTEM

Substantial evidence shows that race, class, and gender influence the treatment received from the nation's courts and jurists in criminal case processing, criminal sentencing, decisions to incarcerate, plea bargaining outcomes, and capital case sentencing. Unequal treatment remains even when all other objective conditions, such as prior record, severity of the offense, and mitigating circumstances, have been accounted for (Blumstein, 1982). What reflects U.S. court inequality most may be found in the early stages of exposure to the system, and in cases in which African-American drug offenders have a greater risk of arrest and prosecution than whites under the same circumstances. Thus the courts are not the first oppressors. That troublesome title belongs with those responsible for arrests and prosecutions—the very agencies assigned to the criminal courts.

There is no doubt, however, of the courts' dubious history of oppression. Sentencing that is more severe for African Americans than for whites has been and remains pervasive in this country. African Americans, for instance, are more likely than whites to be sentenced to death for capital crimes. Racism is also very clear in the capital sentencing in rape convictions. Eighty percent of the studies on death penalty impositions showed that race was a significant factor in the death penalty decision (Kleck, 1981). Even the death sentences of white capital offenders are more likely to be commuted to life in prison than the death sentences of African Americans, who are disproportionately, among those sentenced to death, actually executed. The race of both offender and victim—specifically the African-American-offender–white-victim combination—in a likely capital case strongly influences which cases prosecutors will seek the death penalty in, and which cases judges or juries will impose the death penalty in (Amnesty International, 1987).

Racist practices in plea bargaining increasingly appear as a component of "get tough" policies on drug offenders, and the outcomes of federal mandatory sentencing statutes in drug-related and other federal crimes are influenced by race. Prosecutors plea-bargain below the mandatory minimum sentence in a way that appears related to the race of the defendant (Mandatory Minimum Penalties, 1991).

Besides obvious and established bias, there is an inherent

lack of objectivity in the courts. African Americans, Latinos, Native Americans, and Asians, especially those in inner-city ghettos and barrios, and on reservations, are at risk of unfair and unequal justice because their culture remains uniquely separate from the norms governing U.S. criminal court processing, litigation, and decision making. The U.S. court system operates through white, middle-class, Protestant norms and values that make those outside of these racial, cultural, and class-group traditions endure injustice.

The cultural gap between the poor and the affluent is not helped by a racist jury selection that disproportionately keeps minorities off U.S. juries. This is especially true where the minority defendant is of the same race as the potential juror. The U.S. Supreme Court has reduced the number of peremptory challenges attorneys can use to dismiss potential jurors; these challenges mean that attorneys can dismiss a prospective juror without cause. The Supreme Court's failure to ban excluding racial minority members from meaningful representation on the nation's criminal court juries causes alarm and distress to those concerned about these injustices. It also sends a discouraging message about the criminal justice system's true values with respect to this nation's racial minorities and poor.

CONCLUSIONS

The U.S. criminal-justice-system biases, deeply rooted historically in early "scientific racism," have been discussed throughout this chapter. This racism not only extended the plantation slave labor during the eighteenth and nineteenth centuries but served as a pretext for institutionalized racial and ethnic oppression through law enforcement, the criminal courts, and the corrections system. The turn-of-the-century South was not alone in its terror against early-twentieth-century African Americans. Northern law enforcement, courts, and other institutions of criminal justice were major players in the suppression of African-

American progress. Late-twentieth-century criminal justice continues to suppress racial and ethnic minorities.

The influence of privilege and power is evident in the enforcement of legal and popular concepts of crime. Crime in the United States relates to the prejudices and interests of the privileged, powerful, and influential. The dichotomy of "harsh" street-crime pursuit and sanctions and the "leniency" on white-collar crime illustrates the biases against racial and ethnic minorities and the poor. Crimes by the powerful have an unparalleled impact in costs to taxpayers and, more importantly, in human lives lost through white-collar fraud and other criminal activities.

The nation's juvenile detention centers, training schools, police, and courts have sponsored and maintained patterns of racism, as well as gender and class discrimination. African Americans and Latinos, especially, are at much higher risk than whites of being placed in detention because of their race, and female minor property and status offenders at much higher risk than males, because of their gender.

Policies toward gangs are unjust. Street gangs, made up mostly of young African Americans and Latinos, are targets of intense law enforcement efforts, while rich, powerful "Mafia" gangs remain largely immune from police and court pursuit. The tremendous financial power of organized criminal gangs has allowed them to purchase freedom from the "burdens" of criminal-gang law enforcement today.

Federal and state penitentiary placements provide poignant illustrations of the gross inequities in punishment. Racial minorities and the poor are overrepresented in U.S. prisons compared to white offenders. Death sentences are also influenced by racism, and the African-American-offender–white-victim combination significantly affects whether the death penalty will be chosen by juries.

Police decisions to arrest racial-minority-group members and the poor are broadly anchored in their own prejudice. The Rodney King incident alerted the nation and the world to the history of police violence toward the poor and racial minorities. This incident helped erode the middle- and upper-class white community's innocence about the police. Police use of deadly force has also been linked to race and class.

Finally, substantial evidence exposes the biases of the U.S. court system. Being a member of a minority, poor, or female in the juvenile court system can negatively affect criminal case processing and sentencing, decisions to incarcerate, plea-bargaining outcomes, and other court decisions.

Chapter 8

How the United States Hates Girls and Women

Americans pride themselves on fairness. We insist that each American has equal opportunity; although we may have different talents, interests, and skills, we begin at the same place in the competition for the "good stuff" of our society. Yet this book has illustrated that people of color, people of different social classes, and people with different sexual orientations are not treated equally. For many, the "ladder of success" has broken rungs. These ladders are difficult to climb.

The women's movement showed the broken rungs that girls and women in our society cope with, and until then, Americans generally believed that the "real" differences between girls and boys, women and men, did not constitute inequality. Even today, most Americans argue that they are not prejudiced and do not discriminate because of a person's gender. The evidence suggests otherwise.

In 1993, *Primetime* conducted a videotaped experiment where a young man and a young woman went separately to purchase a car, and to sign up for tee time at a public golf course. The young woman was told that there were no tee times available; the young man was given one. The young man was offered a lower car price without negotiation than the young woman got after negotiation, and she was not allowed to drive the car off the car lot because of "insurance requirements," though the young man was told of no such requirement and was allowed a test drive. When both young people applied for the same job, she was directed toward a secretarial job, whereas he was directed toward a possible managerial position.

Prejudice against women is discriminatory, and it is found in looking at the different layers of society: in face-to-face interactions of people, in institutional settings, and in the cultural norms, values, and traditions of our society. But of all the ways that prejudice and sex discrimination are manifested in our society, the most harmful form is violence directed toward women by men.

SEX *OR* GENDER:
WHAT MAKES THE DIFFERENCE?

People assume it is easy to tell whether someone is a woman or a man by looking. If people can't see, they become anxious, because they do not know how to interact. When a baby is born, it is immediately reported to the parents whether the child is a girl or a boy. Although all a newborn needs is warmth, the usual procedure is to color-code the infant's wear: blue for boys and pink for girls. Since it doesn't make any difference to the child, this "dress code" must be for the hospital staff, and for the parents, family, and friends: a quick sex identification that allows for "sex-appropriate" comments.

An infant's genitalia are difficult to identify only very rarely, but when there are confusing signs, such as both male and female sex organs, or when tests are inconclusive, the doctor usually makes the final determination. Recently, a pair of Siamese twins were born in Canada joined at the abdomen. Although the two children could be separated, they shared a penis. Since only one of the children could have the penis, the doctors said the other child should receive a surgically constructed vagina. But how should it be decided which infant would get the penis? The surgeons thought the more "active" of the two children should have the penis. But how active can infants be? How active can Siamese twins be? What behaviors define "activity"? Is there any indication that male infants are more "active" than females? Would a tossed coin have made just as good a decision as one based on stereotypes of how girls and boys behave? These questions were not asked, the surgery was done, and irrevocable life decisions were made for these two children.

While surgeons don't ask such questions, social scientists do. Any person can identify girls that are more physically active (if that was the criterion used to define active) than some boys. Still, most people believe that males and females are different solely because of their different genitalia and reproductive organs. There is little scientific evidence to support this. A person's sex is biologically based; that is, usually there is physical evidence that can be observed to determine whether a person is a woman or a man. But no similar physical evidence exists to determine whether a person is feminine or masculine, because these are social categories. Biology is only a very small determinant of who women and men are; what primarily shapes our identity and how we behave is social expectations. Social scientists call this *gender*.

When a woman loves to work with cars, enjoys very physical sports, and dislikes child care, is she any less feminine? When a man loves to write poetry, enjoys the opera, and dislikes car maintenance, is he any less masculine? Most Americans would answer no. Masculinity and femininity are social notions of what men and women *should* stereotypically be like. Even so, there is a wide range of behaviors, attitudes, and beliefs which are, if not actively encouraged, not discouraged for women and for men. Some, however, are actively discouraged for both sexes and are often featured on afternoon talk shows. For example, women on *Oprah* or *Donahue* are usually portrayed as needing love, whereas men need sex. Heterosexual cross-dressers and gays and lesbians explain what "normal" lives they live, presumably to combat the gendered norms of who women and men are. But many social scientists argue that there are *no* characteristics completely dictated by one's sex, that almost everything we as a society define as masculine and feminine is socially derived, not biologically based. Gender, then, is the social construction of masculinity and femininity and plays a major role in shaping and forming behavior, attitudes, personality characteristics, and even body shapes.

How is this possible? Through interaction with our parents, with other family members and friends, and with other members of society, we learn how to be a woman or a man. Through socialization at school and at church, at work and in leisuretime activities, we develop a gender identity. Some parents tell their little boys that to be a big boy, they must not cry. Some parents would never give their daughters toys that they would give their sons, like trucks, GI Joes, and water guns. Many parents encourage their boys to defend themselves physically, but they discourage their girls from doing the same. In such subtle and not so subtle interpersonal ways, children are given "gender lessons" about how to act and think and what to value. Teachers, clergy, and even clerks in stores enforce appropriate gender behavior. Teachers in public schools often say they prefer to teach girls, but research shows that they pay more attention to boys (Goodman, 1994). In most religious settings, God is represented as and referred to as male. Most clergy are men, although statistics indicate that more women than men are active in church work (Lindsey, 1994). At work, women often receive less pay than men doing the same job or are segregated into jobs where only women need apply (like secretarial work). Sports are usually segregated by gender, sometimes for physical reasons, but not always. On February 15, 1994, Ila Borders became the first woman to pitch in a men's NCAA (National Collegiate Athletic Association) baseball game and struck out two men ("First Woman Pitcher," 1994). Baseball may be one of those sports in which women and men can compete equally.

Interpersonal interactions and institutional settings encourage one thing for boys and another for girls because our cultural norms, values, and traditions are "gendered." One of the most difficult assignments that can be given to students on gender roles is to ask students to violate a gender norm, that is, to do something in public that is not typical of their gender. For instance, men might knit in public, or dance with another man, or wear women's clothes, whereas women might spit or scratch their crotch in public, play football, or make explicit sexual comments to a guy. Students always report that their norm violations attract attention and often elicit sanctions from observers, like dirty looks, disapproving comments, and even shunning. Even more interesting is that students report how extremely uncomfortable they are violating gender norms. Some students would rather receive a failing grade for the assignment than violate any cultural gender expectation, no matter how insignificant. This exercise illustrates how pervasive gender norms, values, and traditions are in our society and what powerful shapers they are of women's and men's identity and their behavior.

So biology does not determine destiny. So nurture wins over nature in the age-old debate. The problem is what this outcome causes for women and girls in our society, because prejudice occurs when learned attitudes of dislike and even hate are expressed. Some claim that the two genders play complementary roles in society, and that, although they are expected to do different things, behave differently, and even have different attitudes and values, they are still valued equally. Some people argue that women have an "edge" in our society because they are more valued than men. This seems unlikely. Though men and boys may be significantly harmed by sex discrimination, it is women whose lives are shattered by prejudice and discrimination, particularly when it includes violence. While violence against women occurs in interpersonal interactions, it is the end result of our cultural norms, values, and traditions. When personal examples of prejudice and discrimination are examined individually, they may appear insignificant, but they are not. What follows are examples of how everyday occurrences have tremendous social consequences.

INTERPERSONAL PREJUDICE AND DISCRIMINATION

In one of the authors' neighborhoods lives the typical nuclear family: a father, a mother, and two children. The parents are high school teachers, and the father is also a high school football coach. Their two children are bright, beautiful, very active daughters. When the first daughter was born, family and friends alike were excited; however, when the second daughter was born, these same family and friends began to make comments, particularly to the father, like "Don't you wish she were a boy?" or "Will you try again, so you can have a son?" or "Don't you wish you had a son to play football with?" The father was deeply hurt by these comments because he was delighted that he and his wife's two children were daughters. Unfortunately he is unusual: Preferring male children is common in our society and in societies around the world.

In most cultures, sons have more "value": They usually carry on the family name, inherit family property, and may be expected to take over the family business. In the United States sons do not always receive these particular benefits, but we still have a subtle preference for boys. This manifests itself in interesting and sometimes contradictory ways. For example, higher expectations of sons may contribute to men's health problems, including heart attacks caused by stress. Parental expectations of sons to be tough and strong in every social setting may cause some men to have difficulty in achieving intimacy in interpersonal relationships. Interestingly, when girls are expected to be as successful as their brothers (so that they are often more successful than their female peers), they may be susceptible to the same stress-related disorders (Lindsey, 1994). But, when sons are valued more highly and have different expectations placed on them than girls, daughters may feel unaccepted and have low self-esteem. Evidence suggests that women with low self-esteem are more likely to be in abusive relationships (Lindsey, 1994). A seemingly simple thing like a cultural preference for boys over girls can have far-reaching social ramifications.

Consequences of the social construction of gender are complex and often harmful. For instance, jokes and humor can ease tension and break social barriers; they can also be smoke screens for hate and prejudice. In every generation, a joke has singled out a group as less bright than another group. Polish jokes were common in the 1950s and 1960s; today, the jokes are about blond *females*. More serious is the "shock humor" used by people such as Howard Stern, who targets lesbians, and Rush Limbaugh, who attacks women who pursue equal rights, calling them "femi-Nazis." Radio disc jockeys across the country also use this type of humor to boost ratings, arguing that they are just "poking fun."

Where is the line between poking fun and verbal abuse? Verbal abuse occurs when humor or name-calling puts down a member of a group for the purpose of gaining control. When humor is used to gain power by elevating the self over another person or group, then it is abusive. People who use humor in this way may say they are only teasing, just as those who call another person a name may say they are only kidding. But verbal abuse is an insidious form of social control with consequences far beyond the targeted individual. Verbal abuse, while damaging a person's psychological well-being, also enforces harmful gender norms and expectations. Stern's "jokes" about lesbians create a social climate where heterosexuality is socially enforced. Limbaugh's "jokingly" comparing feminists to Nazis labels unfairly women who actively campaign for equal rights and puts all women on notice that politics are not for them. In other words, this kind of humor intimidates.

The most vicious name-calling maintains gender boundaries. While gender is only socially constructed, it is not easily changed, particularly when it is maintained through intimidation like name-calling. It is interesting that both women's and men's gender roles are maintained through references to their sexuality. Women are called sluts, whores, bitches, and cunts, and men are called studs and hunks; in either case, there is a quantitative and qualitative difference. Research indicates that there are many more such names used for women than for men, and that both

women and men think that being a stud is valuable while being
called a cunt or a bitch is disparaging. Also, women are supposed
to be "honored" when told they act like men, whereas men are
disparaged when they are told that they act like women. For
instance, parents often tell small boys to quit crying and "stop
acting like a girl"; young boys call each other a girl, a sissy, and
a wimp; young men who falter in military boot camp may be
called women (Kokopeli and Lakey, 1992). Being called a woman
is the worst verbal abuse a man can receive. The horrendous
association is that to be a woman is terrible because to be like one
is to be degraded, and to *be* a woman means you are "worthy" of
degradation. In all of these ways and more, societal norms, values, and behavior are enforced in face-to-face, interpersonal interactions.

It is not our intention to minimize the pain boys and men feel
who are verbally abused and ostracized for their body shape,
mannerisms, attitudes, and behavior, for being different from the
generally accepted norm for men. But verbal abuse is a common,
everyday occurrence for females: girls and women are constantly
told they are too fat, too thin, too pushy, too passive, too sexy, or
not sexy enough. These contradictory messages bombard girls
and women at home, school, and work and during play through
advertisements and popular magazines and books and, of course,
on TV. These messages are prejudicial and discriminatory because images of what women should be are usually based on male
beliefs and attitudes about masculinity and femininity, and because they help maintain men's control over women. Whether
they are used consciously or unconsciously, the social consequences for women are the same: Advantages and privileges for
men are maintained, and women are second-class citizens.

INSTITUTIONAL DISCRIMINATION

An entire library of books has been written on discrimination
against women in the family, in the workplace, and in religious,

educational, political, and legal institutions. We give only a brief overview of the subject and identify several important issues. These issues are equitable pay for women at work, equal treatment of women in the family and at work, sexual harassment, and gender bias in the classroom. The concept that most helps us to understand these issues is *gender roles*. Gender roles come from where we are located in the social structure; that is, our social location, such as race, age, sex, and class, shapes and prepares us for how we are to behave and shapes societal expectations of the ways in which we will interact. This forms what social scientists call *roles*.

An example explains this concept. A woman named Debbie has a child and a job, and is a member of First Methodist Church. All three roles have different societal expectations.

Debbie receives a phone call at work from her minister reminding her that she has volunteered to help sort Christmas gifts for needy children that evening. Debbie's boss might expect her to work late because a big project is underway. Debbie has also to pick up her child on time from day care and buy numerous Christmas gifts. Debbie is expected in one evening to be a responsible church member, employee, mother, and family enabler. Debbie might also need to add the roles of wife, daughter-in-law, friend, and citizen.

Both women and men have to make decisions about which roles are more important at any particular time. But for women, there are also gender expectations based on the various roles. For instance, most members of society expect that Debbie will do more housework and child care than her husband, as well as more volunteer work in her community and at her church than her male counterparts at work. Because of power relations at work, Debbie, a secretary, is expected to be at work eight hours a day (although her female boss may skip out to attend her child's school holiday program), and to be available for overtime. Her male co-workers expect her to make coffee, to listen to their problems with their wives and girlfriends, and to be goodhearted when they joke about her large breasts. Besides all of these things, Debbie is paid less than the guy who sweeps the floor at night!

TREATMENT OF WOMEN IN THE FAMILY AND AT WORK

Debbie's story illustrates not only gender roles but also institutional discrimination against women in the family, at work, and at school. Like Debbie, almost 60 percent of all women over the age of sixteen work outside the home at least part time, and like Debbie, most of those women also do the majority of the housework. In fact, most working women do double duty: they work eight hours at a job and work another four to eight hours at home, cooking, meeting the emotional needs of their children and their spouses, doing laundry, counseling friends, cleaning, and much more. There is a widespread notion in our society that husbands "help out" more when their wives work, but there is little supportive evidence. Most families in our society have a rigid division of labor by gender. Women do all the things described above, and men do car and lawn maintenance (Lindsey, 1994, p. 167). Interestingly many women and most men do not question these gender arrangements, expecting to do what their mothers and fathers did, an expectation that is also supported by gender arrangements among their friends, in schools, in books, and on television. Many readers will say, "Yes, but times have changed; yes, but things are different in the younger generation; yes, but *my* male friends are different." Young women's lives *are* different from their mothers'; they now have two jobs instead of one. Equality in family life has not been achieved.

EQUITABLE PAY FOR WOMEN

Besides doing double duty, women have two additional problems when they work outside the home. First, women are rarely given financial compensation that is comparable to that of men, and second, women's lower pay seems justified to many people, because women are not "equally distributed throughout the occupational structure" (Christie, 1994, p. 187). Let's consider each of these institutional discriminatory practices and how they relate to gender roles.

Most people in the United States now know that women make about 60 cents for every dollar men make, so is pay inequity between women and men really decreasing? Not really! In 1994, for every dollar a man earned, a woman earned sixty-four cents; that percentage has remained unchanged since the mid-1970s (Christie, 1994). This wage gap between women's and men's salaries is not altered by factoring in "ethnic or minority group status, educational achievement or experience" (p. 244). This astonishing fact must be carefully considered. For Debbie this fact means that it does not matter if she is white, black, or Latino; has a high-school or a college degree; has been employed nine months or nine years—she will still make only sixty-four cents for every dollar made by men in her company doing comparable work. If Debbie is not married, she is probably unable to support her daughter, requires some kind of social assistance, and can't afford the same quality of merchandise as the men she works with. Debbie can't pursue her leisuretime interests as aggressively as her male friends, because she has less disposable income. She is less likely to return to school to upgrade her skills, because she cannot afford either the money or the time. Simply, women's wages are inequitable compared to men's, and this circumstance has wide-ranging social and personal ramifications.

Many people argue that women are paid less because of the jobs they choose, for example, teacher, day care worker, secretary, social worker, and salesclerk. Many people believe that gender roles reflect basic innate differences between women and men, and that women are better at "nurturing" jobs than men, although most social scientists disagree. They argue that unequal pay and jobs that are female-dominated are caused by women's not being equally distributed throughout the occupational structure. Sex-typed occupations, like elementary-school teacher, waitress, and stewardess, are mostly held by women, while mechanics, waiters, and electricians are mostly men. These are all sex-typed occupations. If you are sighing with a big "So what?" consider how sex-typed occupations cost women money. In the United States, generally, women are very underrepresented in high-status occupations and largely overrepresented in the lowest-status jobs, which receive the lowest wages. Social scientists call this sex discrimination in the workplace, and it is not coincidental or accidental. In fact, women in a job *equals* lower pay. As an example, librarians know this firsthand. When librarianship was a female-dominated profession, the pay was comparable to that of teachers and social workers. As more men became librarians, salaries began to climb, particularly in management, where there were more men than women.

SEXUAL HARASSMENT

Further plaguing women are the constant sexual jokes, innuendoes, and propositions that they encounter in their day-to-day work life. *Sexual harassment* is the legal term for this common experience of women, and it came to national attention with the confirmation to the U.S. Supreme Court of Clarence Thomas. On live TV, Anita Hill accused Thomas of sexually harassing her by using inappropriate sexual talk in her presence and by touching her in inappropriate ways. This case brought many of the issues of sexual harassment—inappropriate sexual behavior in the workplace—to the forefront. Although sexual harassment can occur wherever women and men congregate, legally it is defined as repeated *unwanted* physical or verbal sexual behavior that makes the workplace a *hostile* environment.

We will briefly discuss this topic because it is so prejudicial and discriminatory against women. Although the definition of sexual harassment seems straightforward, there are common cultural misunderstandings about its meaning. Many people wonder what is inappropriate sexual behavior between employer and employee, between professor and student. When does joking, for instance, become hostile rather than just annoying, and why don't women just leave any job or school in which they are uncomfortable with their bosses' or professors' sexual behavior? Underlying these questions is the misunderstanding that sex could be or should be eliminated from the workplace. However, this potential elimination ignores the fact that mutual sex is not discriminatory and does not fall within sexual discrimination policy. The key word is *unwanted* sex, and the key indicator is whether there is a power difference between the two parties. If employees believe there will be repercussions for refusing sexual overtures, like losing their jobs, then sexual harassment has occurred. Inappropriate sexual behavior is behavior that is *unwanted* by the person in a lower power position.

The newest Justice of the U.S. Supreme Court, Ruth Bader Ginsburg, said it best: "Why can't there be a simple standard for wrongdoing: conduct that, on the basis of sex, makes it more difficult for one employee [or student] than another to do a job? Is it really more complex?" (Ingrassia, 1993, p. 57). Complexities do occur, however, because different people have different interpretations of what conduct makes it difficult for a person to do her job.

Overt sexual aggressiveness, like women being chased around their bosses' desks or being slapped on the butt, is not easily misinterpreted. But most sexual harassment is more subtle than that. Debbie, for instance, does not want the constant comments about her large breasts; her embarrassment definitely interferes with her work. Some women might enjoy the attention. Some women object to and are distracted by pin-ups of naked women in their office, while other women are not annoyed by such pictures. Many men do not understand how sexual comments, *Playboy* posters, or a "friendly" pass could be interpreted by women as either annoying or hostile. So how does one make sense of these conflicting perceptions between women and men and between women themselves? What is unwanted sexual behavior in the workplace? When does it become a "hostile" environment? These are legitimate questions, and the answers will become clearer as more women step forward to assert their right to a "user-friendly" work environment.

It is difficult to remedy the situation. Most women find it difficult to leave a hostile environment, whether it be a job or a school, for personal and/or financial reasons. Many women are justifiably fearful of reprisals if they do report incidents of sexual harassment. The personnel responsible for receiving the reports may not take women seriously or may actually try to dissuade them from reporting. Women have been fired or given lesser responsibilities for reporting. Even though 70 percent of the women who serve in the military, 50 percent who work in congressional offices, and 40 percent who work for federal agencies had experienced sexual harassment ("Sexual Harassment," 1991), it is not surprising that only 26 percent of women who are sexually harassed actually report it (Ingrassia, 1993). Even when it is reported, women may be victimized further by the legal proceedings. Court cases are extremely costly and usually lengthy, causing impossible burdens for most working women. Women who sue may be attacked in court, and conviction rates are very low. Changes have made universities and businesses more worker-friendly for women, yet sexual harassment is still a major problem.

GENDER PREJUDICE IN THE CLASSROOM

There is growing public consciousness of the problem of sexual harassment, including a desire to protect not only women but also young girls in schools. *Newsweek* (Ingrassia, 1993) recently reported an incident that is commonplace for many young girls; verbal sexual abuse in the schoolyard:

> [A] 12-year-old girl at Kennilworth Junior High in Petaluma,
> CA began to be teased by two pubescent boys. "I hear you

have a hot dog in your pants," they'd say. The taunts soon
came from girls, too. Even the haven of the classroom was
punctured when a boy asked, "Did you have sex with a hot
dog?" After two years, the girl's parents sent her to another
school, but the ugly joke followed. Now she attends a private
high school—and she's suing the Petaluma school district
for $1 million. A federal judge has ruled that taunting is
peer-to-peer harassment if it creates a "hostile environment," but he also said that to win damages, the girl would
have to prove "discriminatory intent" by officials. (p. 58)

Some would argue that this is an age-old problem; we have already discussed how any child may become the target of aggressive language when other children perceive him or her as
different. The new question about this old problem is: Are girls
discriminated against by this behavior, and is it the responsibility
of public and private schools to provide a safe environment for
girls on the playground and in the classroom?

We think so, and educational experts agree. Laura Border, at
the University of Colorado, says that studies indicate that "All
teachers, regardless of gender and ethnicity, [are] biased *toward*
White male students" (our italics) ("Gender Bias," 1993, p. 22).
Gender roles again can help us to understand why there is a bias
toward male students and discrimination against female students
in the classroom.

Gender roles become one of the "lenses" teachers use when
they see children in their classrooms, and the consequence is that
teachers treat boys and girls differently. Myra and David Sadker
have spent years researching gender discrimination in the classroom. Their findings include: "Teachers interact with boys eight
times more frequently than with girls. Boys are called on more
often. Girls are given less time to answer. Boys are rewarded for
being smart. Girls are rewarded for being neat, pretty, compliant,
nice. Teachers help girls by doing things for them. They help boys
by teaching them to do it themselves" (Goodman, 1994, p. 6). As
a result, boys tend to develop a knowledge base and a confidence
that make it appear that they are smarter. But Border argues that

teachers can be trained to change their "ingrained" gender bias. She suggests asking probing questions of all students and encouraging each student to analyze the issues ("Gender Bias," 1993, p. 22). Sadker and Sadker (1994) agree, and they also suggest other possibilities: Teachers must encourage girls to speak up, textbooks need to be monitored, seating arrangements need to be flexible, and maybe coeducation doesn't work for girls.

Without these considerations, school is harmful and discriminatory for all girls, but it is particularly harmful to gifted and academically talented girls. Silverman (1993) argues persuasively that our gifted girls are "disappearing." Presumably an equal number of gifted girls and gifted boys are born, but as they get older and enter school, gifted girls "mysteriously disappear: there is a gradual, relentless decline in the number of [identified] gifted girls and women" (p. 299). Silverman recounts several ways in which this happens. In preschool, gifted boys are identified by teachers as "natural leaders," whereas gifted girls exhibiting the same characteristics may be labeled "bossy." It is said that gifted girls are often particularly adept at conforming to societal expectations. They conform to the expectations of their teachers and their peer group: they don't stand out and are not too smart or too bossy. They work quietly at their desks and don't cause problems. This can already be observed by the fourth grade among early-identified gifted girls. By middle school, many gifted girls' grade-point averages, previously consistently higher than those of boys, begin to drop dramatically. Most gifted girls have disappeared by high school, choosing conformity over achievement.

SEXISM

What we call *institutional discrimination* in this section is also called *sexism* by social scientists. Unlike interpersonal prejudice and discrimination, which is individualistic and thus sporadic, inconsistent, and unsystematic, sexism and institutional discrimination are systematic and consistent discrimination against women.

We have painted a bleak picture. Of course, there are positive signs of change, but powerful sexist beliefs, values, and traditions remain to be overcome.

Sexist Beliefs, Values, and Traditions

Culture is defined by social scientists as beliefs, values, and traditions that are held in common by a group of people. Culture is sexist when there are different expectations of women and men, and when these different expectations are discriminatory. Usually sexist beliefs, values, and traditions are "taken for granted" and are thought of as being the "way life is"; men do some things, women do other things and neither recognize that these customs were created historically and are maintained today. Most of us do not notice how sexist culture is until a belief, or a value, or a tradition is violated. These examples are drawn from actual experiences.

Beliefs. Stacey shaved her head on a whim and was unaware she had violated a sexist belief about women's hair. She quickly knew "something" was wrong, though, because she received stares and uncomplimentary comments from strangers, as well as lectures on "being a lady" from her family and friends. A customer at the store where Stacey works told her she would never shop there again until Stacey grew her hair back. Eventually, she did allow her hair to grow back to a "normal" length, but not before learning her own role in complying with social expectations.

Values. Sherry, who is overweight, violates a sexist value by being fat. Although she has lost weight on numerous diets, she regains it again quickly. Sherry knows, as do all women in our culture, that "a woman can't be too thin or too rich." Yet, for Sherry and most women—thinness is not an option; body shape and size are largely genetically determined. Sherry, too, receives stares and uncomplimentary com-

ments from strangers, lectures on "controlling" her eating
from family and friends, and discrimination when she applies for a job.

Traditions. Susie is a writer of computer software, a male-
dominated profession. She is the only woman in her department and regularly receives performance awards. Each year
the company picture generates chuckles among her friends,
because the men in the picture are wearing tuxedos, and
Susie is wearing her "basic black" dress, the only time it's
worn all year. The one year she also wore a tuxedo, she
received critical comments from her boss and veiled threats
that she might not receive promotions.

Why do women and men wear different hairstyles, different
clothes, and different makeup and jewelry? Gender beliefs, values, and traditions. Why were Stacey, Sherry, and Susie sanctioned for their "inappropriate" behavior? Because many gender
beliefs, values, and traditions discriminate against girls and wom-
en; they are sexist.

Gender beliefs, values, and traditions are apparent very early
in the lives of children. The first question asked new parents is "Is
it a girl or a boy?" Immediately infant boys and girls are dressed
differently; new parents tie a pink ribbon around the head of their
newborn daughter. Why? So friends and family and strangers can
respond in a gender-appropriate way, for instance, giving gifts to
the new child that are gender-specific. Children soon learn what
their parents and other adults think the appropriate beliefs, values, and traditions are for their gender; children not only conform
to but soon insist on gender-appropriate behavior. We have already seen how sanctions against violations of gender-appropriate behavior by adult women cause them distress, so it is not
surprising that most children refuse to violate cultural gender
expectations. Gender beliefs, values, and traditions often seem
insignificant. But the fact that any member of our society could
readily identify blue, football, and GI Joes as "boy things" and
pink, ballet, tea parties, and Barbies as "girl things" means that
almost everything that children do is gendered.

Both children and adults violate cultural expectations when they dress like the other sex, except on occasions like Halloween or Mardi Gras. Maybe readers can imagine their own uncomfortable feelings as well as the social sanctions, like stares, ridicule, and other forms of verbal abuse, that they would receive if they cross-dressed. These reactions are certainly not insignificant; that is why almost all of us conform to these gender rules.

So what's the problem for women? The problem is that, when they *conform* to gender expectations like appropriate dress, discrimination occurs. This may seem untrue, or even ridiculous, to the reader. Does wearing a bra or high-heeled shoes or even a skirt constitute discrimination? Maybe asking the question differently will clarify the answer. Are there social consequences when women do not conform to societal expectations of their dress? Clearly, the answer is yes. Are there social consequences when women conform to societal expectations of their dress? Although the answer is less obvious, it is still yes. Consider Gerda Brantenberg's book *Egalia's Daughters* (1985), in which she completely reverses our expected gender roles and illustrates very concretely what the social consequences are.

In Egalia, women wear very comfortable, functional clothes. The men, however, are required to dress for women's pleasure: They shave all their body hair, wear low-cut shirts, short skirts, and high heels. As if this isn't bad enough, men are also required to wear a contraption that envelops their penis and keeps it in an erect position at all times. This contraption is called a *pehoe*, physically uncomfortable, of course, but it also prevents the men in Egalia from working in certain jobs. For instance, only women can be deep-sea fisherwomen, the main occupation of Egalia, because Egalians believe that men are just not psychologically suited for such a physically demanding job. Besides, the wet suit required for the job could not possibly accommodate a pehoe. One young man wants to fish, and his mother supports equal rights for men, but it is very difficult to find someone who will make a wet suit with a pehoe. No one thinks of the possibility of not wearing one. Once this young man goes into training for this nontraditional job, he is treated with disrespect by other trainees and the teachers and shunned by his friends, and he eventually drops out of the program. After reading this book, many people better understand why women feel confined by their clothing and discriminated against by beauty regimens. Bras, hairstyles, and makeup may seem insignificant, but they have an important impact on the everyday lives of women.

Another common everyday life experience of women is eating, seemingly a simple activity, but also a good illustration of how sexist cultural expectations have an impact on women's lives. Eating disorders afflict women at ten times the rate that they afflict men and are an increasing health problem for many young women. When women try to conform to cultural expectations of how they should look, eating disorders like anorexia and/or bulimia may occur. Anorexia is eating such small amounts of food that body muscle rather than fat is lost, whereas bulimia is consuming normal amounts of food or binge eating and then vomiting after eating. Both eating disorders can cause severe health problems. The social costs of young women's desire to conform to the cultural and sexist standards of beauty in our society are much too high.

For most women, conformity to standards of beauty does not usually take such an extreme form. Even so, there are consequences for individual women and for society at large when women, more than men, are in a constant state of dieting; when women, more than men, exercise 2 to 3 times a day so they can eat a candy bar; and when women, more than men, surgically take "nips and tucks" from their bodies in order to be more beautiful. Goodman (1994b) argues that "We [women] alternate between thinking we should love it—fat—and being sure we should lose it. Between rejecting the imposed ideal of a thin woman and trying to conform to it" (p. 6). Educators, parents, and experts say that, because of their infatuation, most women are always on a diet, even girls as young as seven or eight ("Preteens Developing Fat Phobia," 1993, p. A15).

Are women just "naturally" obsessive about their looks? Why

do most women attempt to comply with standards of beauty even when they are doomed to fail? Socialization, as we have already seen, is a powerful force. Parents, teachers, friends, and strangers send messages that women who look like models are more valued. An aura created by television, movies, and advertising surrounds the beautiful *and* thin woman. If readers are unconvinced, then take more than a cursory look at *People* magazine, or *Women's Home Companion*, or the infamous swimsuit edition of *Sports Illustrated.* The hottest model of 1994, Kate Moss, looks like a preteen waif, and if dirt were applied to her face rather than makeup, it would not be hard to imagine her as a "pinup" for the poor and homeless. Why do women *believe* that they must be thin to be *valued?* Sexist messages throughout society socialize them to believe things that are probably not in their best interests. Sexist messages are supported by ideologies that deny the right to be fully human.

VIOLENCE AGAINST WOMEN: PREJUDICE AND DISCRIMINATION HURT!

Intimate Violence as a Social Problem

Prior to the mid-1970s the term *wife abuse* did not exist, academics rarely studied intimate violence, and most people believed that assaults on women by intimate partners were "rare, not serious, and somehow caused by the women themselves" (Loseke, 1992, p. 191). In 1994, by comparison, most Americans believe that wife abuse is common, and undeserved, and that women in violent relationships need social assistance.

Intimate Violence as Discrimination

Intimate violence is harmful to girls and women. No disagreement. It is also harmful when it happens to boys and men. No disagreement. But is it discriminatory? We believe that the answer is yes. In domestic violence, even if women and men participate equally in the use of physical force, as Straus and Gelles argue (1990), women are injured in a violent incident more often than are men. This is discriminatory.

Although violent events in intimate relationships appear in near-epidemic proportions, they do not happen in isolation. They must be analyzed in the context of family structure and the social forces impinging on family life. Feminists believe that wife abuse, as well as other forms of intimate violence, is caused by three factors: sexism, the glorification of male violence in our male-dominated society, and the use of violence by men in relationships to maintain their dominance. First, the family is embedded in a sexist society, and traditional sex roles contribute to wife abuse (Yllo and Straus, 1990). As women struggle to liberate themselves in the family, their male partners use violence to maintain the traditional family structure. Second, male-dominated institutions like the church, the state, and sports condone and even glorify male violence and, as a result, do not effectively sanction its use against women (Shupe et al., 1987). Third, the intended and unintended consequence of sexism and the glorification of male violence is that, in our society, men are not adequately discouraged from using violence to control their female partners.

The O. J. Simpson murder trial, which has garnered unprecedented media coverage, highlights the interplay of these three factors. Because men bring more status and power with them into intimate relationships, their ability to control girls and women is enhanced. Control comes in many forms. Psychological control is nondiscriminatory because it may be used equally by both women and men. Physical control is discriminatory because it cannot be used as successfully by women as by men (Hubbard, 1993).

We agree that prejudice against women, institutional discrimination, and sexist beliefs, values, and traditions strongly shape the abusive practices of men against women in intimate relationships. Intimate family relationships do not occur in isolation; they are informed by the beliefs, the values, and the traditions of the culture. When the culture is sexist or, more strongly, when Americans hate girls and women, violence against them is the consequence.

IS CHANGE POSSIBLE?

We could illustrate at length the changes in U.S. society that are a direct result of the feminist movement that began when women started demanding their right to vote in the 1850s and again in the 1960s when women demanded equal opportunity in the political, religious, and social life of our nation. Many young women coming of age in the 1990s prefer not to call themselves feminists. They believe that the label has negative connotations, even though they ascribe to most of the feminist agenda. The activism of the feminist movement needs no apologies. We only point to the rights achieved by feminists and the changes made in American life that contribute to respect for women and girls, instead of hatred, sexism, and discrimination.

But the battle, military terminology notwithstanding, is not won. We have tried to illustrate dramatically how deeply sexist beliefs, values, and traditions are embedded in our society and how prevalent discrimination against girls and women remains. Although we firmly believe that the social reality in which girls and women are devalued was created and therefore can be changed, we also firmly believe that it is not easy to do so. Maintaining gender discrimination is more often than not economically profitable, politically astute, religiously enforced, and socially acceptable. But maintaining gender discrimination also has its social costs; women and girls have much to contribute to American life. Americans want to be fair; what is fair is for women and girls to have the same ladders to climb as the most advantaged in our society.

Chapter 9

Prejudice in the 1990s

To the Editor:

Dec. 7, 1941 was the beginning of World War II. I was a patient in a sanitarium with a communicable disease and even though I desired very much to join the armed forces, I was denied entry because my sickness. I was declared a 4F.

The reason I was in this sanitarium was because I could spread the sickness to others, so I did not rebel and claim my "rights" were being violated. I stayed isolated until I was declared safe to the public. Even though I was ready to serve my country, I was a detriment to others serving. I could never be as good as the best because I had this weakness!

We want our armed forces to be healthy mentally and physically. We want the best army in the world with the healthiest men possible. This will not only be safer for us, but will also be safer for each healthy soldier in the armed forces.

We all know homosexuality is an aberration of the mind. There are only a minuscule number of people who are born physically impaired and even then they are not necessarily homosexual. This is not a matter of rights or privacy, it is a matter of keeping our armed forces clean, healthy and strong—physically and mentally.

CONRAD H. CAMPOS, Hurricane, Utah
(Letters to the Editor, 1993, p. 5)

The letter above was written during the early weeks of the Clinton administration when there was a national dispute over President Clinton's proposal to permit gays and lesbians into the U.S. armed forces. This letter is an example of the prejudgment of the condition and behavior of gays and lesbians.

Visitors to the Beit Hashoah-Museum of Tolerance in Los Angeles are greeted as they enter the museum through automated sound speakers with the following taunts: "Talkin' to you, Nigger," a voice hisses as the visitor walks through the gloomy passageway. "Faggot," taunts another. With every step comes a whispered insult, a mean murmur: "Loudmouthed kike! Lousy gook! Dumb Polack! Camel jockey! Redneck bastard! Sexist pig! Goddam beaner! Get whitey!" A wolf whistle rings out, and a leering voice calls, "Hey, baby." And with every message of hate, the feeling of alarm grows: "What you gonna do about it, Jew boy?" (Willwerth, 1993, p. 54).

Rabbi Marvin Hier, a founder of the museum, hopes the displays of racist and cultural hatred, which range from exhibits of Nazi concentration camps to videos of the Los Angeles riots of 1992, will contribute to "the eradication of hatred" (Willwerth, 1993, p. 54).

Time magazine's story on the museum was entitled "A Museum of Hate." The hatred that often flows out of prejudice is so pervasive in the United States that now we are even erecting museums to document it.

On the thirtieth anniversary of the civil rights march on Washington, D.C., in which Dr. Martin Luther King gave his famous "I Have a Dream" speech, an Associated Press poll (August 27, 1993) reported, "Most Americans believe equal justice still is more a dream than reality for minorities in this country." When asked, "Do minorities generally get equal justice in this country today, or is getting equal justice still a major problem for minorities?" 54 percent responded that "justice is still a problem."

The AP report went on to compare the social and economic status of African Americans and other minorities with that of whites for the years 1960 and 1990.

According to the Harvard Project on School Desegregation study, racial segregation in the 1990s is spreading in public schools to an extent not seen since the 1960s ("Study: Racial Segregation Spreading," 1993). The study found "that two of every three African American children attended schools where blacks were more than half of the student population during the 1991–92 school term" (p. A3). For Hispanics, the situation is just as bad. Seventy-three percent of Hispanic children "attended minority-dominated schools in 1992" (p. A3).

Gary Orfield, the Harvard Project director, stated, "The civil rights impulse from the 1960's is dead in the water and the ship is floating backward toward the shoals of racial segregation." Orfield blames these patterns of school segregation on increases in segregated housing patterns. Orfield urges that the federal government "restore aid to school systems with successful integration strategies and step up enforcement of civil rights laws" ("Study: Racial Segregation Spreading," 1993).

An investigative report in *Time* magazine entitled "Do Teachers Punish According to Race?" (Hull, 1994) reported:

> In the basement of Dater Junior High, just next to the boiler room and marked off by thick prison bars, school officials have crafted a fate worse than algebra class. Teachers at the school, part of the Cincinnati, Ohio, public school district, simply call it "the dungeon." Students have more descriptive—if unprintable—names for the small windowless cell. Though the prison bars are just painted on the cinder-block entrance, the punishment is real. Delinquent students must remain in the room—absolutely quiet—all day. (p. 30)

This dungeon punishment cell is a controversy in and of itself, but the issue is much bigger than just the dungeon. It turns out that African-American students are twice as likely to be sent to the dungeon than are white students. Indeed, in the entire Cincinnati school system, African-American students are at twice the risk of being disciplined of white students. The Cincinnati Board of Education seeks to remedy this situation by tracking the race of the teachers and of the students disciplined to determine if prejudice and racism are influencing the disciplinary process. One white teacher complained, "We're very worried. . . . Do we have to start thinking about race now every time we discipline a student?" (Hull, 1994, p. 30).

Attempting to explain the disproportionate number of African-American students disciplined, Cincinnati school superintendent J. Michael Brandt stated, "Blacks tend to be more boisterous." John Concannon, an attorney for the school system, said, "Some black males are more physical" (Hull, 1994, p. 30). Persistent prejudice and racism have led to continuing hatred and violence in U.S. society. For instance, in a different AP story the headline read "Racism Drives Massacre" (1993): Colin Ferguson, a thirty-five-year-old African-American man, had used a 9-millimeter handgun, with fifteen-round clips, to kill five people and wound eighteen others on a Long Island Rail Road train on December 7, 1993.

According to the AP story, "Ferguson, police and witnesses said, walked silently up and down the third car of the train, shooting people in the head, the neck, the arms, the buttocks." When Ferguson sat down to reload for the third time, three passengers jumped him and held him down. Attempting to analyze his motives, *Time* (Toufexis, 1993, p. 25) blamed it on "black rage." *Time* pointed out that in 1990, when Ferguson was a student at Adelphi University, he had often gotten into hostile confrontations with white students and called African-American student activists "Uncle Toms." Ferguson had once interrupted a lecture by yelling "Kill everybody white!" (Toufexis, 1993, p. 30). He had also often talked of violent race wars and revolution. Was Ferguson's killing spree simply the result of one individual's mental illness? Or were real social factors pressuring Ferguson that contributed to his horrendous behavior?

In another racial incident the same year, Christopher Wilson, an African-American tourist visiting West Palm Beach, Florida, was soaked with gasoline and then told by his white assailants, who used racial slurs, that he was about to die. Wilson described his ordeal to the jury at the trial of the attackers, stating, "It was like when you're lighting a stove . . . you feel this tremendous heat . . . I can't even describe it . . . you feel pain all over. You hurt so much . . . I felt like my whole body was on fire . . . I never did anything to anybody . . . why are you doing this to me?" ("Tourist Describes Burning," 1993, p. A3).

However, despite all the evidence of the persistence of racism and hatred in the United States there are occasional instances of goodwill. For example, in 1974, Bobby Powers, a white man, participated in a physical attack on Ted Landsmark, an African-American attorney, during a school busing demonstration. This physical attack was documented in a dramatic Pulitzer Prize–winning photo that pictured a white assailant hitting Ted Landsmark with an American flag and its flagpole. After twenty years, Powers, one of the attackers, apologized to Ted Landsmark, indicating that he could no longer carry the guilt and shame of his past behavior.

PERSISTENT SYMBOLS OF PREJUDICE, HATRED, AND VIOLENCE: THE CONFEDERATE "STARS AND BARS" FLAG

In addition to overt and subtle racist and prejudicial behavior, symbols of racism and prejudice play a powerful role in perpetuating prejudicial behavior and attitudes. In most parts of the world the Nazi swastika symbolizes hatred, violence, genocide, and racism. For many Americans the Confederate Stars and Bars flag also evokes strong reactions and emotions.

Max Weber, the German social scientist, defined power as the ability to achieve personal ends despite opposition. Another way of putting it is that power is getting others to do what they might not do voluntarily. An important dimension of power is how it is manifested symbolically through myth, mystical symbols, ritual, and even irrational symbols. Power is often manifested through symbolic or physical sanctions. The locus of power may be in symbols, personalities, ideologies, economic or property ownership, political institutions, and social organizations. And there are various forms of power: individual, collective, institutional, cultural, religious, kinship, economic, ideological, and legal, to name a few.

Although political and military violence and economic sanctions are obvious and understandable examples of the use of power, an important question is to consider the way cultural (i.e., symbolic, normative, mystical, ideological, ritual, and even irrational) factors can force people to think and behave in certain ways. Other types of symbolic (noncontractual) behavior is evident in state ceremonials, sports and drinking behavior, to name a few examples. Bizarre and mystical patterns of symbolic actions are not the result of cultural lag; they play important roles in modern society. The continuities of customs exist, but their functions change.

For example, *The Chronicle of Higher Education* reported on the 1993 battle over symbols at the University of Mississippi in an article entitled "Old Times Not Forgotten" (Lederman, 1993). The article began:

> As the ball carrier sprints across the goal line for a touchdown, thousands of University of Mississippi students erupt in cheers.
>
> They thrust their arms to the sky, many holding flags aloft, as the band breaks into a stirring song. Backs are slapped, high fives exchanged. It is one of those magical moments that bring classmates together and unify a community.
>
> But not one of the university's 700 black undergraduates is seated among the thousands in the students' section. Most blacks say they don't feel at home there, in part because the flags the students are waving are those of the Confederacy, and the song is the Southern anthem, "Dixie." (p. A51)

In the spring of 1992 African-American student band members refused to play "Dixie," and many other students as well as some faculty members believed it inappropriate for Ole Miss, with an African-American student population of 35 percent, to continue to permit the display of the Confederate flag and the use of the Dixie anthem. L. Williams, an Ole Miss alumnus, felt, "We do not see these as racist symbols. Just because you're proud to be a Southerner doesn't mean you don't like blacks. They're our friends. We work with them. We live with them" (Lederman, 1993, p. A51). However, the Confederate flag and the Dixie anthem were adopted by the university only in 1948 as a defiant act of opposition to integration. Charles W. Eagles, a history professor at Ole Miss, believes "The symbols are seen as a real burden for the University of Mississippi" (p. A51).

In another case regarding the Confederate flag, the flying of the Georgia state flag, which includes the Stars and Bars of the Confederate flag, at the January 1994 Super Bowl game held at the "Georgia Dome" ignited a controversy. Reverend Tim McDonald stated at the time, "We see this Super Bowl as a prelude to the 1996 Olympics, and it would be a shame and a disgrace to stand under this flag when the world comes to Atlanta" ("Flag Battle at Georgia Dome," 1994, p. 1A). The governor of Georgia, Zell Miller, had attempted the year before to have the Georgia legislature change the flag because "those who find the flag offensive view its Confederate insignia as a symbol of Deep South racism" (p. 1A). Indeed, the Georgia state legislature "added the Confederate symbol in 1956 in a gesture of defiance over the U.S. Supreme Court's school desegregation ruling" (p. 1A).

Reverend McDonald added, "The [Super Bowl] players must understand that whether they want to be or not, they are being used to support a racist past" (p. 1A). Bruce Smith, an African-American member of one of the teams, the Buffalo Bills, indicated he didn't like the idea of playing under the Confederate symbol and stated, "Racism exists, period. It's unfortunate. It's ignorance. It offends me" (p. 1A).

A related issue was debated on a Sally Jessy Raphael talk show that aired on February 7, 1994, entitled "Teen Racism." A white mother (Debbie) and her teenage son (Scott) explained the problems the son had wearing a T-shirt at school with the Confederate flag on it. The verbal exchange on the show went as follows:

DEBBIE (SCOTT'S MOTHER): Well, the school, first of all, the school situation last thing that happened that kind of put the icing on the cake for him, I think, was a situation that was handled poorly, in the school system, it was a bad judgment call. The shirt—Actually, the shirt that he's wearing now is the incident that happened at school. It is a Confederate flag, which that doesn't mean anything about race. He was asked to remove the shirt at school, along with the flag that he has on his truck that he drove, and he said, "Why?" He said, "I feel—" the dean, or the principal, I believe it was, said, "I feel that that's a racial T-shirt," and he said, "It has nothing to do with race."

SALLY: So, you think this threw him further over into that category which, by the way, you don't agree with?

DEBBIE: No, I don't agree with it.

SALLY: Are you afraid that he will, in some way, affect your other children?

DEBBIE: Yes, I am. I'm happy that he speaks his mind and he's not influenced or afraid to, but I do not agree. I am not prejudiced at all. He was not raised that way. I fear for him sometimes. I mean, he's a big kid, and he isn't one that someone will go up and pick on, but I have two other children, a seven-year-old and a 13-year-old. They do not show any signs of prejudice. He does not influence them at all, but just hearing him talk to his friends, or whatever, speaking—

SALLY: Being the older brother, I would think that would influence the kids, and it worries you?

DEBBIE: The situation, I'm sorry to interrupt, but the situation that happened at school was with the T-shirt. There was a young man, child, that had a Malcolm X shirt on. Malcolm X was a racist. He's very racist. He told—Scott said, "I'll take this shirt off, or inside it out, but what about the black kids? Why don't you tell them to inside out their T-shirts?" He says, "No."

"Why?" and he says, "Oh, I don't want to start any problems."
That's wrong. OK, he's afraid to tell the black kid to take that
racist shirt off, but my son had on a Confederate shirt which has
absolutely nothing to do—I have Confederate shirts, so it's
nothing to do with black or white.
SCOTT: But why is it if I have white pride, why does it automatically demean them?
AUDIENCE MEMBER: When you walk around with the Confederate
flag—
SCOTT: What is a Confederate flag? What is that?
AUDIENCE MEMBER: What you're saying is that slavery was OK,
because that's what happened.
SCOTT: I'm not saying—No, no, no, see, that's where it's all wrong
here. I don't agree with beating up blacks. I do not agree with
this. I do not agree with that at all, but there's so many problems
today, and the problems are caused by the black community
where I've seen. Maybe it's different up here. Where I live, that
is the problem. (Multimedia Entertainment, Inc. 1994, pp. 5–6)

A related controversy over the Confederate flag took place in
the authors' home state of Utah. The city of St. George (population
about thirty thousand), located at the extreme south end of the
state of Utah, near the Arizona and Nevada state borders, has the
nickname of "Dixie."

The nickname originated from the historical fact that in 1857
Brigham Young, president of the Church of Latter-Day Saints
(LDS), or the Mormon church, sent a band of LDS pioneers on a
"cotton mission." The LDS thought southern Utah, as well as
parts of what is now Nevada, would be well suited for growing
cotton, a commodity that would be especially desirable if a Civil
War in the United States began.

Until 1994 Dixie College, a two-year community college in
St. George, Utah, had as its symbolic mascot a Confederate rebel,
named Rodney Rebel, holding a Confederate flag (see Figure 9.1).
The college bookstore sold Confederate memorabilia, rebel hats,
Confederate flags, and so on.

Figure 9.1. Dixie College mascot "Rodney Rebel." (Photo credit: *Daily Spectrum*.)

In the wake of a campus pipe bombing on October 2, 1993, believed to be racially motivated, the college's Student Executive Council voted to abolish the flag as the college symbol, claiming it to be a racist symbol. According to a story in a local newspaper, Dixie College dean of students Bill Fowler stated, "I had never equated it as a racially discriminatory symbol until about two or three years ago," remembering when a skinhead tried to buy one from him. Fowler was in Las Vegas on a recruiting trip: "I had it draped over the table at our display, and a guy came up and said, 'Hey, man, I want to buy that flag. It's our symbol.'" The kid was a white supremacist, and a black man later told Fowler, "You're not going to get many black students to visit Dixie College with that thing there" (Graff, 1993, p. A5).

Local opinions about discarding the Confederate flag differed sharply and serve as an excellent example of the public perception of and sensitivity to racism. On October 31, 1993, the regional newspaper, *The Daily Spectrum*, printed an editorial that stated in part,

> the Confederate battle flag is a tradition that not only has outlived its time, but is one that should be offensive in a Christian community. . . . Over time, it is easy to become desensitized to what a symbol means, especially when you've grown up in a community that has historically not been racially diverse. But that doesn't take the meaning away. The swastika is historically a Sanskrit symbol meaning well-being and blessing. But using it today for that purpose would not overshadow its more prominent use: a symbol of the Nazis and the atrocities they committed in the name of anti-Semitism. . . . To understand the reality of it, one only has to see the rifle decked rear window of a pickup truck plastered with the Stars and Bars and the slogan "The South Shall Rise Again," or see white-sheeted Ku Klux Klan members marching with burning crosses and Confederate flags, or look into the frightened eyes of a child—white or black—thrown into a situation of hatred and violence.
>
> These are scenes not from the last century, or from three decades ago. These scenes are still being played out today.
>
> These scenes make it reprehensible for that symbol of violence and oppression—the Confederate battle flag—to represent an institution of higher learning. (*The Daily Spectrum*, 1993, p. D1)

The Daily Spectrum also featured various pro and con statements by its readers regarding the flag. Some of these reader comments are instructive regarding the level of sensitivity to racism in U.S. society. For example, one reader, Maureen Booth, wrote:

> The flag is a tradition of Dixie College that has become the one icon the college has which represents its spirit, its past, and is a symbol of Dixie College. It is not a "racist" symbol

as it has been made out to be. Nor was it instituted years ago
to cause problems or degrade. It is merely a symbol of what
we in Dixie call the "Dixie Spirit." Nothing more, nothing
less. You can't take away my flag!!! . . . This kind of mentality has to stop somewhere or else our whole lives can be
dictated by the whims of the society in which we live. As for
me, I will fight to keep the Rebel flag flying at the college.
(*The Daily Spectrum*, 1994, pp. D1–D2)

Other readers, however, had a different point of view, which
recognized the Confederate flag as a symbol of racism and hatred.
For example, reader Tim Anderson wrote:

To many visitors to our area, however, the display of the
Confederate flag seems strange and inconsistent. The Flag is
suggestive of racism, slavery, rebellion against just causes,
and a general affront to minorities. For such reasons, it is
regularly displayed in other parts of the country at marches
and demonstrations by the Ku Klux Klan and the American
Nazi Party, and other anti-minority rallies in which the attempt is made to draw a powerful statement from a darker
part of our nation's history. It is, in effect, an icon with a
symbolism which in many parts of our country is akin to
that of the swastika in Europe. (Anderson, 1993)

Much of the success of Dixie College on the basketball court
and the football field can be attributed squarely to young men
whose forebears suffered the hideous crime of slavery. To allow
symbols of the past that infer any disrespect to that segment of
students, or to any other persons in the community who felt a
concern, was a wrong that needed correction.

It is noteworthy that the University of Utah changed its mascot from the Redskins to the Utes out of respect for any Native
Americans who might be concerned. More recently, Southern
Utah University altered its thunderbird logo from a Native American god of war to a more traditional illustration of a bird. The
Stars and Bars flags have been banned by many educational institutions in the South (*The Daily Spectrum*, 1994, pp. D1–D2).

A related issue that has been completely overlooked in this

Figure 9.2. First author with Southern Utah monument to the Confederacy. (Photo credit: Rich Gilmore.)

controversy is the life-sized statue of a mounted Confederate soldier holding a Stars and Bars flag in one hand while attempting to lift a wounded comrade up onto the horse with the other hand. This statue stands in front of the "Dixie Center," a college and public convention center in St. George, Utah (see Figure 9.2). Although it is a magnificent piece of art, entitled *Brothers* by artist Jerry Anderson, not a word has been spoken or printed regarding the racist implications of this statue.

By January 29, 1994, the Dixie College Board of Trustees had chosen a "new" flag to represent the college after retiring the Confederate flag as its official banner. Alumni President Clayton Ramsey said "It should please alumni because it resembles the old flag that is a beloved tradition to former students" (Graff, 1994, pp. A1, A8). It is highly questionable whether the new flag

Figure 9.3. The "revised" Dixie College flag. (Photo credit: *Daily Spectrum.*)

(see Figure 9.3) is not itself still symbolic of hatred and racism. The Stars and Bars and colors of the original Confederate battle flag are still present, just rearranged. Unfortunately, the use of such symbols will probably continue to promote and legitimize racism and prejudice well into the twenty-first century.

Chapter 10

Political Racism

The homeless, the poor, the working class, the middle class, racial minorities, and women were worse off at the end of the Reagan–Bush administrations than before. During the twelve years of Republican control, changes in social and economic policy crippled a great majority of Americans. The poor minorities were the most adversely affected, but the middle class suffered as well.

The mid-1990s have seen the twelve years of the social and economic policies of Ronald Reagan and George Bush evaluated. With Clinton's defeat of Bush in the 1992 presidential elections, it was hoped that the conservative challenge to post–New Deal democratic liberalism would come to an end. However, given the election results of 1994, the conservative challenge is alive and well. A number of critical reviews have appeared of the Reagan–Bush years, and not surprisingly, most are unflattering to these two men. Scholarship on the new urban homeless, for instance, warned the nation of the connections between the plight of the homeless in this country and the domestic policies of the Reagan–Bush administration. This research showed the highly partisan and destructive nature of the Reagan–Bush housing programs of the early and mid-1980s (Ropers, 1988). Other writers who examined housing policies in the late 1980s and early 1990s also tied the state of the homeless to the partisan politics of the

249

Reagan–Bush years. The devastation of housing policies is clearly illustrated by the federal government's failure to invest substantially in permanent housing for those with low incomes. Marginally improving the worst aspects of the homeless situation today—shelters, single-room occupancies, transitional programs—made housing policies of the late 1980s reflect the general climate of inept leadership and elitist politics of the Reagan–Bush White House (Rubin et al., 1992).

As damaging to the nation's psyche as the economic and social losses of those twelve years were the oppressive policies that caused large-scale racial, class, and gender polarization. It is more than ironic that the resurgence of the Ku Klux Klan, and the emergence of other racist groups, including the White Aryan Resistance (WAR), the Aryan Nations, and the overtly racist Christian Identity Movement, paralleled the Reagan–Bush years. The rhetoric of an antiminority, antipoor, antiwoman, antiwelfare campaign and presidential agenda in the 1980s inspired those who hate to tear away their systematically placed controls. Given tacit encouragement by the empathy shown to individuals and groups committed to racial and ethnic violence, the atmosphere of the Reagan–Bush years revived the hate movement in this country unlike that of any administration since the White House years of Andrew Johnson and Andrew Jackson (Feagin and Feagin, 1993).

In 1992 some 346 hate groups—ranging from "skinheads" to a variety of neo-Nazi and white-supremacy groups—were found to be active. Michael Donald's lynching in 1981 was the first of a man by an emboldened Ku Klux Klan in modern times. These violent legacies have continued into the 1990s. In 1991 alone, some twenty-five hate-motivated murders of minority persons by whites were recorded in the United States, triple what the number had been just one year earlier.

Some researchers warn that hate violence has expanded beyond anti-African-American and anti-Jewish activities, to taxes, immigration, foreign aid, crime rates, the farm crisis, and antigay violence in conjunction with the AIDS epidemic. At the same time, white supremacists have garnered an unusual amount of media attention, allowing some, like David Duke of Louisiana, to become elected to public office. Hate groups take their cue from the racism of government personnel and policies, and the Reagan–Bush years saw sizable increases in racist policies.

THE POLITICS OF RACISM

The history of political life in the United States is that the traditions of racist ideology are and have been central to the policies and actions of federal, state, and local governments. Early federal government support of slavery vividly attests to its record of racist ideology as a dynamic of political life in this country. Nineteenth- and twentieth-century restrictive immigration laws based on race and imprisoning Japanese-Americans during World War II are merely two of a host of examples that illustrate racist ideology as part of the U.S. political experience. It is difficult to separate racist politics and racist economics in any intellectual analysis of the issues of race and social policy. Contemporary class-centered perspectives on racial injustice and prejudice anchor such dynamics within the interaction of class and race stratification. This view of power and stratification in the United States offers racial minorities' subordination as the product of capitalist class exploitation (Barrera, 1979).

African-American scholar Oliver Cox has emphasized the role of the capitalist class in racial exploitation. He proposed that the slave trade recruited labor to exploit the great natural resources of America (Cox, 1948). African slaves were chosen because they were the best workers to be found for the heavy labor in the mines and plantations across the Atlantic. While a search for cheap labor by a profit-oriented capitalist class led to a system of racial subordination, racial prejudice emerged later to rationalize this oppression of African Americans.

Racial minorities must currently endure the results of past economic and social exploitation. Contemporary internal colonialism ties African-American, Latino, and Native American subordination to a history of racially motivated colonial oppression. In the peculiar classic colonial oppression, the urban ghetto of today exists as the spatial home of the modern-day colony. The message of internal colonialism is very clear: Today's oppression of minority groups is played out in the politics and the economics of racism. The black ghetto exists precisely to maintain elite white exploitation, domination, manipulation, and control of the resources, peoples, lands, and property inside the oppressed community's invisible walls (Blauner, 1972).

The political and economic elite have exploited their positions of power and the social definitions of race and racist ideology in contemporary American life. The politics of racism is shown in how government ignores the inner cities and minority constituencies when it allocates public dollars. Particularly ignored are young African-American males. National policies have failed to ensure them a quality education, employment and skill development training, decent housing, and a generally broad outlook for the future. This segment of America's population has been described as "endangered." Their tragically high homicide rates, unemployment, imprisonment, delinquency, crime, and suicide are the bitter harvest for the African-American community of decades of national policy neglect of young black men (Gibbs, 1988).

Rather than investing in these young men's future as productive citizens and contributing taxpayers, national spending policies have favored building jails, detention centers, and prisons, and financing their incarceration in these same facilities. Most of these young men don't belong in prison, while many others are kept longer than necessary. The politics of racism rears its ugly head as politicians vie for votes from a paranoid and anxious public. Criminal-justice-system officials oversee the public's financial interests in the hysteria of the prison system buildup in this nation today.

The federal government's eroded support of civil rights legislation affecting racial and ethnic minorities is also evidence of a *new* political racism. The Reagan and Bush presidencies were less supportive of the civil rights agenda than previous presidential administrations. What they stood for departed from the traditions of moral leadership and democratic principles most Americans associated with the White House. Cutbacks in programs for the poor and the unwillingness of Reagan and Bush to enforce civil rights laws brought a measure of contempt to their office, not seen in other presidencies.

With the cooperation of many Democrats, the Reagan–Bush administrations dismantled the civil rights programs that had underpinned racial accords since the 1960s. Reagan and Bush equated affirmative action with quotas and reverse discrimination, destroyed the budgets of civil rights enforcement agencies, and appointed civil rights opponents to the Civil Rights Commission and the U.S. Supreme Court (Chambers, 1987).

In 1990 Bush vetoed the Civil Rights Act that tried to redress some past wrongs. In 1991 Bush replaced the retiring pillar of social justice, Thurgood Marshall, with Clarence Thomas, a conservative African American opposed to affirmative action.

Reagan and Bush created a climate that reversed the gains of inner-city minority residents in education, housing, and employment. Government grants went to the suburbs or overseas, rather than to the central cities—a stark illustration of the politics of racism. While cities such as Detroit, Atlanta, and Baltimore were written off by federal agencies and state legislatures, these same agencies poured billions of dollars into suburbia, with tax rebates to rich white corporations and wealthy white businesspeople. At the heart of this policy disparity was the politics of race. Analysts say that the power of white capital both controls the distribution of resources and keeps white communities from being seen in a racial context. These two factors help establish the inequality in public investment between wealthier white communities and minority communities and neighborhoods (Hacker, 1992).

REAGAN AND BUSH:
TWELVE YEARS OF DECLINE

Reagan and Bush have been subject to unflattering analyses of their moral and leadership credentials. Far from economic and social improvement in most U.S. families, Reagan and Bush presided over the sharpest increase in inequality since well before the Great Depression of the 1930s. Much of this increase was tied to Reagan–Bush policies that transferred public money to the rich. Cuts in the income maintenance programs that served the poor, direct and indirect cash subsidies to the affluent, trade and budget advantages to big business, tax loopholes, and other similar vehicles of welfare to the rich resulted in, indeed, the rich becoming richer (Yates and Pillai, 1992). Besides severely widening the distance between the affluent and the poor, Reagan and Bush left a trail of wreckage and devastation in people's lives and futures that only a thousand stories could more thoroughly convey.

A plethora of dashed hopes, retrenchment, setbacks, and losses for the marginally secure of this nation characterizes the Reagan–Bush legacy. There is no shortage of outrageous, self-centered interest in their policies. Budget wars launched against the working poor, children, prenatal mothers, the homeless, the elderly, the disabled, and the inner-city unemployed of the central cities barely describe their legacy. While Reagan and Bush actively sought to cut child nutrition programs, prenatal care, medical care, and other established low-income health and social welfare maintenance programs during their years in office, they simultaneously favored budget windfalls for the highest-income earners, big business, defense contractors, private insurers, and other substantially well-off groups. The empirical evidence tells a story of severe retrenchment in the 1980s from the successes of the 1970s.

There is a human toll from Reagan's and Bush's removing medical and nutritional services for many infants, children, and mothers during the 1980s: Cuts in Reagan's 1981 budget for Aid to Families with Dependent Children (AFDC) removed nearly 600,000 women and children from needed aid. This cut automatically meant that this same number was removed from Medicaid, and thus these women lost their health insurance as well. Because of Reagan–Bush cuts in AFDC, the gains that low-income, high-risk pregnant minority women had made in getting access to prenatal care in the 1970s declined.

Cuts of 18 percent from community health centers meant that 725,000 persons were denied services; 64 percent were children or women of childbearing age. Early in their terms, Reagan and Bush significantly reduced federal dollars for the Special Supplemental Nutrition Program for Women, Infants, and Children (WIC). The WIC program had to absorb a 33 percent cut in inflation-adjusted dollars.

Reagan–Bush policies also constituted a radical shift from the commitment to the working poor that was a staple of the Carter presidency. Equally true, the Reagan years shifted concern and resources away from children and toward the elderly. The 1980s were thus characterized by an increasing number of children in poverty, contrasted with a decreasing incidence of poverty among the elderly (Combs-Orme and Guyer, 1992).

Poverty in the 1980s affected a larger percentage of Americans than in any year since before 1968, reaching 15.2 percent in 1983, the highest rate since 1965. By the end of Reagan's term, poverty had declined only slightly, just 2.2 percent to 13 percent, a rate higher than any year from 1968 to 1979, and equal to the 1980 rate. By 1989, the poverty rate was 12.8 percent, the same as in 1968, with some 31.5 million persons—3.2 million more than in 1980—being officially poor (Plotnick, 1992).

Only the elderly made strides against poverty. Children, on the other hand, soared in their rates of poverty, reaching more than 22 percent in 1983, and almost 20 percent in 1988. The poverty rate for children in 1988 was 5.6 percent greater than in 1969, the year when child poverty was lowest, and 1.2 percent greater than in 1980. Poverty among African Americans, 31.3 percent in 1988, was no lower than it had been throughout most of the 1970s; Latino poverty climbed slightly to nearly 27 percent between 1980 and 1988.

The cutbacks in welfare programs we described earlier were particularly devastating to single-parent families. The cutbacks in AFDC and food stamps, especially, pushed more than 1.1 million single-parent families below the poverty line—a 3.9 percent increase by 1988. Cutbacks in the income-maintenance programs that served the poor meant that most states decreased the number of recipients of AFDC benefits (Plotnick, 1992).

Also reversed during the Reagan–Bush presidencies was a half century of federal aid to cities. Without question, the failure to fashion a coherent urban policy meant the emergence of an American underclass. Moreover, absolving the federal government of its responsibility for social problems while assigning the tasks to subordinate levels of government (federalism), and to nongovernmental providers (privatization), accomplished the Reagan–Bush strategy of shifting the focus away from urban communities.

Federal housing dollars to cities and municipalities, a staple of assistance since the New Deal, dropped considerably. For example, funding for housing decreased from $27.9 billion to $9.7 billion from 1980 to 1988, and the result was a net loss of 2.8 million low-rent units for low-income families between 1974 and 1985 (Stoesz, 1992). The budget cuts affected new appropriations over the same period. For example, from fiscal 1981 to fiscal 1988, housing units for those with low income fell from 280,000 to 88,000. The Farmers Home Administration (FHA), which assists low-income housing programs in rural areas, saw the number of new units for poor rural families drop from 360,000 in 1979 to 70,000 in 1987 (Yates and Pillai, 1992).

Federal grants to cities also declined sharply during the Reagan–Bush era. While federal aid to local governments for community development increased from $38 million to $3.9 billion during the Ford and Carter years, 1975–1980, by 1987 it had dropped to $3.3 billion. Similarly, federal grants for community services decreased from $557 million in 1980 to $354 million in

1986. The Housing and Urban Development (HUD) budget declined from a high of $57 billion in 1978 to a low of $9 billion in 1989. The connection between HUD and the federal funding of local government has been, perhaps, closer and more direct than local government's connection with any other cabinet agency.

The Bush administration's record, then, appears particularly belligerent toward the cities, as this administration actively pursued an additional 4.2 percent cut in 1991. The Bush administration's hostility toward the cities included reducing federal community-development dollars from $3.3 billion in 1987 to $2.7 billion in 1991 and community-service support from the $354 million approved by Reagan to only $42 million (Stoesz, 1992).

Perhaps the biggest shortcoming shown by Reagan and Bush toward the cities was their failure to address shifts in the cities' population and in capital flight from U.S. cities: Millions of Americans abandoned the older, industrial cities for the Sunbelt; industries were deregulated; and tax policies favored the rich. What resulted was that now-cash-heavy industry left the central cities. Tragically, nothing was put in place by either Reagan or Bush to make up for the shortfall. The economic base of the cities, which once included the opportunity for secure work and meaningful jobs, has fallen victim to an urban policy heavily favoring high-income, suburban corporations.

It is ironic that, while low- and very-low-income consumers experienced diminishing federal support of their housing needs during the 1980s, other forms of housing assistance, such as federal tax expenditures for homeowners, increased. Tax deductions for mortgage interest and property tax payments totaled more than $40 billion in fiscal year 1987. These same subsidies jumped from $32 billion in 1981 to nearly $50 billion by 1986 (Yates and Pillai, 1992).

The Tax Reform Act of 1986 tried to rid the current tax laws of some of their most visible abuses. However, the wealthy continued to benefit from the tax laws. The income disparity between the rich and the poor widened throughout the 1980s. For example, between 1980 and 1990, the federal tax burden for the richest 20 percent decreased 5.5 percent, while the taxes of the poorest 20 percent increased 16.1 percent (Karger, 1992).

By 1989 the massive tax cuts for the wealthy during the 1980s had created an income gap between the poor and the wealthy that is wider than at any point since such data were first collected in 1947. This incremental increase in social-class inequality, combined with the savings-and-loan (S&L) scandal caused by Reagan–Bush deregulation, is the most injurious legacy of the Reagan–Bush era. The deregulation, especially, hurt those most in need of federal health and medical, social, charitable, and supportive services. U.S. taxpayers are obligated to repay S&L depositors an estimated $300 billion to $500 billion in ten years.

Because the S&L losses occurred mostly in institutions in the economically expanding states of the West and the South, the federal bailout is essentially a transfer of public funds from the Northeast and the Midwest regions to regions currently experiencing rapid economic growth. The obvious losers in this transfer of funds are central cities of the Northeast and the Midwest and their minority, low-income, working-class populations, as well as others whose benefits are likely to be negatively affected by the nation's debt and economic woes resulting from the S&L debacle. While preaching the evils of deficit spending, Reagan increased the nation's debt from $78.9 billion to $155 billion. Many analysts of the Reagan–Bush legacy openly worry about the profound impact the deficits have had and will have on the national government's ability to meet the health needs of the poor and other social services traditionally provided by the federal government (Combs-Orme and Guyer, 1992).

NEW PROMISES: CLINTON AND THE RACE ISSUE

President Clinton and Vice President Gore have brought hope that the nation will reverse the erosion of rights, programs, services, and opportunities affecting minorities and the poor stripped away by the Reagan–Bush era. Clinton and Gore sent a clear message that they meant to reverse the inept leadership and biased policy that the United States had endured in its federal government administration, particularly its executive arm. One thing seems certain: that the impact of the federal deficit, as well as the S&L scandal left by Reagan and Bush, will hamper the early economic efforts of Clinton and Gore. Because future dollars are already obligated to this debt, the current administration entered its role handicapped and burdened, without the economic resources normally accorded newly elected administrations. This handicap will have an impact on the economic revitalization projects likely to win support in Congress, even with an aggressive campaign for their passage by a skillful and effective president and vice president.

There is some evidence that Clinton is sincere in leading the country out of regressive policy and leadership doldrums. In his first State of the Union Address, Clinton pledged to enforce all civil rights laws and tied the nation's recovery to giving *all* Americans the education, training, and skills they need to seize the opportunities of tomorrow. This is a major shift in White House policy toward civil rights. This policy has already been put into action with Clinton's very aggressive move against discrimination in home mortgage lending. The Office of the United States Currency has new procedures to detect discrimination in residential lending by the country's 250 national banks (U.S. Office of Consumer Affairs, 1994).

An equally clear demonstration of leadership on minority issues is the Clinton administration's commitment to improving educational standards. Clinton and Gore made "Goal 2000" a cornerstone of their current education policy and actively called for and supported a minimum skills level for the secondary and primary grades. The recent congressional appropriation, endorsed by Clinton, of $105 million to help the states decide the minimum knowledge and skills levels for their schools demonstrates a commitment to minority educational concerns ("National New Standards Can Improve Schools," 1994).

The reemployment of America's working and underclass is

also a very clear goal. As part of Clinton's "Re-employment Act," sent to Congress recently, he pledged at least $13 billion to reemploy the nation's workers permanently displaced because of, among other things, shifts in the economy. Part of this money will be used to retrain workers and assist in job placement afterward (Manegold, 1994).

High joblessness and underemployment in minority neighborhoods defined the economic crisis of families, workers, and individuals residing in the nation's central and inner cities during the 1980s. A current favorite of mayors to revitalize their central cities and the harsh conditions of their residents—the minority "underclass"—is the economic initiatives associated with public entrepreneurship.

As a strategy for economic revitalization, urban leaders today seek innovative relationships with foundations and businesses to create public projects of an entrepreneurial nature. Public entrepreneurship draws from private foundations, business, and community groups in creating opportunities for profitable investments. The profits, then, can be reinvested in the community to fund housing developments for the poor and job training for the underskilled, to initiate construction and other job projects in the central cities, and to contribute to revitalizing the central cities and their residents. To succeed, these projects will ideally require a capital and political commitment beyond the initial startup, government investment. Popular models of public entrepreneurship call for the comprehensive development organizations that are tailored to the local community, as well as for significant resources for both economic and social problems. Investments are the primary activity of the organizations, and their primary goal is building the capacity of local people and institutions (Osborne, 1988).

The other touted comprehensive economic program for the central cities debated in Congress has been the conservative-backed urban-enterprise-zone (UEZ) concept. These projects offer business special considerations, such as tax rebates, a reduced minimum wage, and exemptions from certain occupational and health protections to entice firms to relocate in poor areas (Stoesz, 1992). This project's best chances of passage came during the first four years of the Reagan administration. Its poor chances of support today make it no longer politically viable.

The current plethora of policies and initiatives for urban areas already taken by the Clinton administration suggests an expanded public entrepreneurship policy for the nation's cities. Promising urban revitalization, Clinton believes that the federal government can effectively empower the African-American community by allying with local governments, private industry, small businesses, and organizations to provide African Americans and black-owned enterprises with the means to economically empower themselves:

> We cannot create a larger black-owned business sector overnight. But we can work as partners with existing African American businesses, entrepreneurs and organizations to create an environment that facilitates African-American enterprise. (Brown, 1993)

Equally encouraging is the present administration's concern about minority children's welfare. Commerce Secretary Riley announced the administration's "new-ethic-of-learning" initiative, which encourages schools to design school-to-work transition programs, and to link education to local social services (Riley, 1993).

U.S. Attorney General Janet Reno supported the administration's position that the nation must invest in our children now, or pay a higher price later. Reno observed that if the United States is to restore its greatness, to achieve racial justice, and to move progressively into the twenty-first century, then the United States must first reweave the fabric of society around children and their families (Reno, 1993). These and other progressive policies clearly point away from the selfishness and privileged greed of the 1980s and toward a more even application of national government policy and support of the people.

Nevertheless, minority leaders are asking the current administration to expand its pledge to help remove the racially charged atmosphere of the 1980s. National Urban League president John Jacobs pressed the Clinton administration and the U.S. Congress to establish opportunities for the disadvantaged by making job training and creation for them a priority (Portes, 1994). In addition, the congressional Black and Hispanic Caucuses have urged the administration to abandon any "racist" dimension in its new crime initiatives. Suggesting that job creation remains a top priority of the congressional minority caucuses, the leaders of the country's minorities have expressed their concern that the progressive policies of this administration avoid any obstacles to its overall forward direction.

The legacy of Ronald Reagan and George Bush has left scars that will take a long time to heal. The nation's slide into unparalleled racial, class, and gender polarization has lessened in the relatively more humane and socially conscious climate of the Clinton administration. While the politics of racism and the resulting hatred claimed the offensive in the Reagan–Bush policies, a new day has dawned in U.S. political life. Social justice, civil rights, and equal treatment for all Americans are more possible than at any point since 1980. Indeed, after the Reagan–Bush era, when the principles of democracy and equality in social policy were ruthlessly sacrificed for political and financial gain, the policies of Clinton have a chance of moving the United States forward in a spirit of intergroup cooperation and mutual respect.

Chapter 11

Directions for the Future

Give me your tired, your poor,
Your huddled masses yearning to breathe free . . .
—Emma Lazarus, plaque
on the Statue of Liberty

Residents of Arizona, California, Nevada, and Utah, whose small towns were experiencing considerable growth, were asked in 1994 about the effects of growth on their communities. They talked about the increase in jobs and the benefits of a more diverse population, but their most consistent comments were about how more people meant more *different* people—different values, different religions, different standards, different languages—and how these differences were ultimately *negative*. They attributed to "differences" such consequences as more crime, gangs, violence, drugs, broken homes, child abuse, and a host of other disasters. They also decried the loss of intimacy and familiarity that seemed inevitable with increased community size.

The phenomenon of growth, of communities increasing in size, is seemingly inexorable. Current U.S. population is approximately 260 million. It is projected to grow to 345 million by the year 2020. And most of the growth will come from *groups* of people who are clearly *different* from the majority of Americans. So, not only are our communities growing in size, with decreased intimacy and familiarity, but they are also growing in diversity, increased by people who are different from most Americans.

The face of America continues to change—no matter what the rhetoric from the political and cultural right. Familiar stereotypes about who makes up the majority of citizens in the United States are no longer valid. According to Washington, D.C., demographer Martha Farnsworth Riche, " 'Normal' is no longer everyone being white. The old community—the middle class, leave-it-to-Beaver community—simply isn't going to be there, and rhetoric isn't going to bring it back" (Usdansky, 1992, p. 2A).

The emerging American reality is *increased* diversity: There is the growing economic divide between poor and rich; the suburbs, home to 50 percent of America's population and once the haven of WASP Americans, are now "much more representative of the country as a whole" (p. 2A); the non-Anglo population has risen to an all-time high of 25 percent; and immigration has risen at such rates that it is affecting traditionally untouched states. For example, Georgia's foreign-born population doubled between 1980 and 1990.

How will U.S. society respond when the "typical" citizen fails to fit its cherished WASP stereotype? Given America's dismal record of accommodating differences of nearly any sort—race, ethnicity, gender, and sexual orientation do *not* exhaust the groups who endure prejudice and hostility—we are hard pressed to end this book on a positive note. What we have attempted to highlight is how prejudice and discrimination are entrenched within the value system and virtually all major institutions that make up our culture. We have also shown that the economic and cultural elites will continue their tremendous resistance to any substantive changes in either their piggish amount of power and riches or the underlying ideological value system that justifies such inequality.

The usefulness of this often-depressing litany of abuse and violence is a heightened awareness and vigilance. Americans are historically wedded to the democratic ideals embedded in the Declaration of Independence and the Constitution. But it is important and instructive to realize that Americans are equally wedded to the ethnocentrism and harsh judgments inherent in what we have historically claimed to be America's "manifest destiny": the belief that the United States is not only "special" as a nation but also "better" as a culture.

AMERICA THE MELTING POT: AN ENDURING MYTH OR A GLORIOUS REALITY?

America is God's crucible, the great Melting-Pot where all the races of Europe are melting and reforming! Here you stand . . . in your fifty groups with your fifty languages and histories, and your fifty hatreds and rivalries, but you won't be long like that, brothers, for these are the fires of God. . . . Germans and Frenchmen, Irishmen and Englishmen, Jews and Russians—into the Crucible with you all! God is making the American. . . . The real American has not yet arrived. He is only in the Crucible, I tell you—he will be the fusion of all races, the coming superman. (Zangwill, 1908, p. 37)

Recognizing and admitting that our society is still beset with prejudice and discrimination increases our collective humility—of which we need a healthy dose—and increases our chances of addressing these issues more realistically. Clinging to outdated myths entails enormous risks. Such harmful illusions allow us to ignore painful realities, which we have documented extensively throughout this book. Succumbing to fanciful and comfortable myths also inhibits evolving potential solutions.

For example, we cling to one of our favorite romantic icons, America as melting pot, a phrase coined by Israel Zangwill in a four-act melodrama of the same name that opened in Washington in 1908. While we continue to hold on to this romantic image and proudly proclaim ourselves a nation of immigrants, we are ignorant both of the historical context of Zangwill's metaphor and how the same conditions are being repeated as we near the twenty-first century.

A Nation of Immigrants

America, as any society, is beset with enormous contradictions. For example, we have already described how the "land of
the free" has oppressed sizable segments of its own population:
genocide against Native Americans, past enslavement and current economic oppression of Africans and their descendants, and
imprisonment of thousands of Japanese-Americans in World War
II concentration camps.

Another fundamental contradiction is America's relationship to immigration. It has long been a cliché to refer to the United
States as a nation of immigrants. Most U.S. school textbooks
continue to date the history of North America with Columbus
"discovering" a "New" World (were the various cultures thriving
on the island of Hispañola "lost?"), thus ignoring up to forty
thousand years of Native American history. Plymouth Rock.
Jamestown. These names are synonymous with the "settlement"
of North America and the founding of the United States of America, as if it had been empty prior to the Europeans' arrival. Immigrants all; not a native-born member among the colonists of Massachusetts or Virginia. The contradiction, and irony, is that less
that 5 percent of America's current population is ethnically Native American, so that over 95 percent of the current U.S. population is descended from immigrant stock. Yet there has long existed an ambivalence, and often hostility and violence, toward
immigrant groups and immigration in general by white "natives"
who were also descendants of immigrants.

When Zangwill wrote his play, the United States had just
experienced twenty-five years of unprecedented immigration. It
was unprecedented in terms of sheer numbers, what social scientist Milton Gordon (1964) described as "the largest population
transfer of its kind in the history of the world" (p. 85). But more
important, this growth was unprecedented in terms of the *groups*
who immigrated. From 1880 to 1920, the U.S. population rose
from 50 million to 100 million, and immigration accounted for an
estimated 40 million of the 50 million increase. During this peri-

od, in contrast to earlier, so-called "old" immigration patterns, approximately 75 percent of "new" immigrants came from southern and eastern Europe and Asia, newcomers who were clearly culturally different from the U.S. norm: non-Anglo, non-Protestant, non-English-speaking, and non-middle-class. Their isolation from the mainstream culture was also enhanced by other differences from older immigrant groups. Their illiteracy rates were considerably higher; many were "subject" people unfamiliar with democratic processes; and they tended to live in ethnic colonies within urban centers, rather than in rural farm communities.

Zangwill's metaphor was not a rhapsodic testament to America's love of and acceptance of its newest arrivals. Rather, it symbolized newly arrived groups' attempts to protect themselves, and to legitimize additional immigration, by publicly extolling the value of ethnicity in creating the modern United States.

Social Reaction to "New" Immigration

The United States in which Zangwill lived was in the midst of an attack on immigration and specific immigrant groups that was unheard of and was not to be repeated until the 1990s. Since before the founding of the republic, North America had displayed an enormous amount of cultural diversity, not just between native tribes and Europeans, but between natives themselves. Immigration had always accounted for a significant amount of the nation's population, but the sort of immigrant coming into the United States in the late 1880s was so different that alarms were raised, alarms that sound disturbingly reminiscent of warnings heard today. We did not hear then, nor do we hear now, much about *levels* of immigration, but there was and is a complaint about immigrants' countries and cultures of *origin*.

This masks an obvious and virulent racial and ethnic prejudice and reminds us of the fears and hysteria of one hundred years ago. Americans are not concerned about white immigrants from England or Germany, but our collective prejudices and fears emerge when immigrants are nonwhite, such as those from Cambodia or Haiti. We are afraid of changing the literal face of the United States.

Disturbing Parallels: Social Reaction in the 1990s

The end of the 1800s witnessed America's collective racism in full bloom. Anti-immigration riots erupted against Italians, Jews, Poles, and Irish in major cities and small towns; several striking Italian miners were killed in Pennsylvania in 1874. In 1875 the first limits were put on immigration. In 1882 Chinese immigration was prohibited by the Chinese Exclusion Act, and more immigration restrictions were enacted; California mobs attacked Chinese people in Los Angeles and Sacramento. In 1921 the first immigration quotas by country of origin were passed. This racist ethnocentrism reached a near-frenzy by the early 1900s, and the melting-pot metaphor was forgotten. White Americans no longer had faith that immigrants would be assimilated into the predominant culture; they *demanded* it. And when groups were thought to be unassimilable, they were denied entry to the United States. A group called the Immigration Restriction League used the pseudoscience of eugenics to "prove" that breeding from "inferior stock" would destroy the United States from within. The national celebration of U.S. diversity, called Many Peoples, One Nation, gave way, in 1916, to the fear- and hate-driven campaign renamed America First.

Most Americans considered dark-skinned people inherently inferior, and the Ku Klux Klan openly marched in Washington, D.C. Racism was so prevalent that President Herbert Hoover told an Italian-American, *in writing*, that Italians were "predominantly our murderers and bootleggers . . . foreign spawn [who] do not appreciate this country" (Morganthau, 1993, p. 20). Israel Zangwill, despondent at the reality of racial and ethnic hatred, suffered a nervous breakdown and died in England in 1926.

One hundred years later, this incipient racism and hostility toward immigrant groups is again surfacing, and for many of the same reasons. In 1991, nearly two million immigrants arrived in the United States, the largest single yearly influx of immigrants in U.S. history; the numbers since 1991 remain high. But it is not the sheer numbers that have caused many people to react so strongly; it is the race and ethnicity of most of the groups that is provoking national prejudice and discrimination. For most of the past two decades, the bulk of immigrants have been nonwhite Latin American and Asian, many have been non-Christian, few speak English, and most are poor and unskilled. In a word, they are *different* from the "ideal" typical American.

Newspaper headlines provide a glimpse of the fears currently surrounding immigration: "High Tide of Immigration Overwhelms USA"; "Immigration: Backlash in the Land of Liberty"; "USA Cool to Huddled Masses"; "More Americans Favoring Immigration Cuts, Poll Says"; "Price of Immigration Alienates Taxpayers"; "Refugees Drain Florida Resources"; "U.S. a Charity Ward to Immigrants"; "California is 'Under Siege,' Declares Governor." A 1993 Gallup Poll found that 65 percent of Americans want immigration cut back—the highest such finding since World War II. According to a *Newsweek* poll during the same year, 59 percent felt immigration had been good for the United States *in the past,* but 60 percent felt it was bad for the country *today* (Morganthau, 1993, pp. 16–25).

Over half polled by Gallup felt that racial and ethnic diversity threatened U.S. culture. "My nightmare is an image of the Statue of Liberty dissolving, replaced by an image of the bombed World Trade Center and the association of immigrants with smuggling, drugs and terrorism," said Arthur Helton, immigration expert for the Lawyers Committee for Human Rights (Puente, 1993, pp. 1A, 2A). Perceptions of all immigrant groups have worsened, but a closer look at Americans' attitudes, provided in Figure 11.1, reveals a strong racial prejudice.

Myth versus Reality

Part of the enduring appeal of the melting-pot myth is that immigrant groups have melted into a superior culture. The reality is far different. Most European ethnic groups have successfully

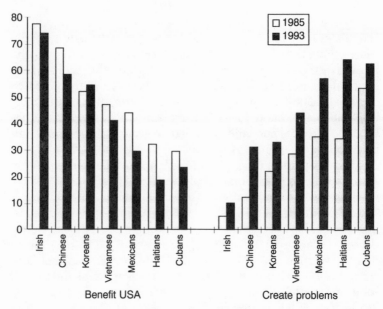

Figure 11.1. A comparison of Americans' attitudes toward immigrant groups, 1985 and 1993. Source: Urban Institute, in Visgaitia (1994), p. 7A.

melted into the U.S. mainstream. Though many were vilified, harassed, discriminated against, and killed when they first arrived, for the most part these groups have melted because they could: They were white (Irish, Jews, Slavs, Italians). However, there remain the "unmeltable" groups: descendants of African slaves, remnants of the once-dominant Native American tribes and cultures, many Latinos and Caribbean Islanders, Asians, and Pacific Islanders.

What do they have in common? Why are they unmeltable? The answer is simple: No matter how many generations they live in the United States, they cannot pass for white. Many immigrant groups of European heritage had to undergo tremendous changes to enter into the mainstream of the Anglo United States: Many changed, or "anglicized," their last names; many refused to speak, or let their children speak, their native language; and many were forced to give up their native language at work, and especially at school. But because of their skin color, most blacks, Latinos, Asians, Native Americans, and other unmeltable groups are *unable* to pass as Anglo by changing their names, learning English, or converting to Christianity.

Continuing Appeal of the American Dream

U.S. history is, in many respects, a history of immigrant groups arriving with hopes and prayers; it is still very apparent that people around the world continue to look to the United States as a potential haven from the political, economic, and social devastation facing them in their native lands. Often, when there has been economic or political upheaval around the globe, another potential group of refugees has looked to American shores for some measure of safety. This is reality. It matters little how shrilly conservative commentators shout about cultural suicide when another wave of nonwhite, non-English-speaking refugees begins to appear.

The process at work is the same metaphor that came out of the popular movie *Field of Dreams:* If you build it, they will come. Make no mistake: Immigrants, legal and illegal, have come and will continue to come to the United States. Even mainstream politicians are beginning to call for drastic measures to halt illegal immigration. In 1994, both Republican California governor Pete Wilson and his main political rival, Democrat Kathleen Brown, advocated deploying the U.S. federal troops to patrol the Mexican border.

But the reality is that U.S. borders cannot be successfully closed to those who are desperate to enter. The border with Mexico is nearly three thousand miles long; most of it is remote, rugged, and nearly impossible to patrol effectively. The Canadian border is more of the same, while our eastern and western borders are open ocean, again very difficult to patrol. To make the point, the federal government is currently spending approximately $5 billion annually, not including state and local expenditures, to close U.S. borders to illegal drugs. The federal government admits to intercepting a mere 5 percent of the total drugs entering the United States, hardly a good return on an enormous investment.

In April 1994, California governor Pete Wilson filed a $2-billion lawsuit to force the federal government to pay for jailing illegal immigrants. Florida governor Lawton Chiles had sued a month earlier, insisting that the federal government also pay for education and emergency health care. Lost in the hysteria and racism is a far more complex picture of the attitudes about and effects of immigration.

There is also contentious debate over how much immigrants pay in taxes to state and local governments compared with what they cost in services. A senior editor of the conservative *National Review* declared immigrants were helping "transform America from a nation into a charity ward" (Johnson, 1993, p. A5). A common prejudice, especially directed at nonwhite immigrants, is that they are more likely than the native-born to be on welfare. However, a study by the Urban Institute showed that working-age immigrants have only *half* the welfare rate of natives: 2 percent of those who have been in the United States less than a decade, as opposed to nearly 4 percent of the native-born (Chavez, 1994). In California, where anti-immigration sentiment is at a fever pitch, only 3 percent of the illegal immigrants granted legal residency in 1986 had ever received welfare benefits, though many were extremely poor.

Focusing on social service costs of illegal immigrants fans anti-immigration attitudes and denies conflicting evidence. Pennsylvania State University researchers found "little support for the notion that immigrants, particularly recent arrivals, pose a substantial burden on public assistance programs." Even more pointedly, a 1990 Massachusetts legislative study concluded, "Immigrants, whether they are legal residents or undocumented, put more into the system in taxes than they take out in services" (Johnson, 1993, p. A5).

Another right-wing stereotype that inflames prejudice is the fear that U.S. culture is threatened by nonwhite groups. Yet evidence exposes this as another unfounded racist fear. A major study of immigrant children in San Diego and South Florida showed that it is the language of their parents that is endangered, not English. According to one of the researchers, "The second generation [of immigrants] is overwhelmingly competent in English. . . . Not only that, but overwhelmingly they *prefer* English. And the preference for American culture is overwhelming as well" ("Study Says Children," 1993, p. A9).

Perhaps what is troubling these reactionaries most is the potential threat that immigrant groups pose to their continued dominance and control of U.S. society. Also according to the Massachusetts study, "Of the 40 finalists in the 1988 Westinghouse high school science competition, 22 were foreign-born or children of foreign-born parents. In San Diego, one out of every four valedictorians and salutatorians has recently been Vietnamese. In Boston, 13 of the 17 public high school valedictorians were foreign-born" (Johnson, 1993, p. A5). These preliminary findings were supported in a larger national survey conducted in 1994, in which foreign-born eighth- and ninth-grade students had higher grade-point averages than native-born students (Friend, 1994, p. 1A).

THE LESSONS OF HISTORY

We have shown the contradictions in U.S. reaction to immigration, both past and present. A good deal of the conflict and violence against immigrant groups is rooted in our cultural ethnocentrism. When faced with large numbers of immigrants who do not share parts of mainstream U.S. culture—race, ethnicity, class, language, religion—dominant groups who *are* superior judge new (and different) groups harshly. Whites often fear their intrusion into the work world, threatening the jobs of white Americans in a period of great economic transition and polarization.

Another reality is that differences create tension and conflict, so we can safely predict *more*, not *less*, tension and conflict around issues of race, immigration, and "cultural survival" in the near future. Conservative and right-wing commentators call the tensions "culture wars." The *National Review* declared "pulling up the ladder may be necessary—if the lifeboat is about to capsize" (Johnson, 1993, p. A5). It is a reality that in less than a generation the "average" American will no longer be white, because of immigration and domestic birthrates, and will no longer be middle class, because of the current trend toward polarization of the middle class, coupled with low skill levels of immigrants. In short, the WASP will go the way of the Piegan and the Bannock, groups that once dominated North America.

Yes, we are pessimistic about the short-term prospects of U.S. society. Combine high immigration levels (mostly unskilled Latinos and Asians) with a job market that already has nearly *20 percent of its fully employed workers below the poverty level*, and what emerges is a clear blueprint for trouble.

This is reality. This is why we are not optimistic. One would have to be exceedingly naive to think otherwise. But there are also signs of accommodation and tolerance toward America's diversity. The number of interracial marriages, against the laws of many states in the early 1960s, has nearly doubled since the mid-1980s and increased at nearly four times the rate of 1970. In 1992 Iranians in Los Angeles produced more than fifteen hours of Persian-language television programming a week. Two twenty-four-hour radio channels cater to an Iranian community numbering close to one million (Heller, 1992, p. A7).

There is also evidence that the tolerance of nonwhite groups is increasing. In social research that has been repeated since the late 1920s, people were asked to rank their feelings about fifty-eight racial and ethnic groups. Unsurprisingly, those groups that immigrated to the United States first, like the British and Protestants, were ranked the highest and those at the bottom were all non-Europeans. However, gains in positive attitudes were made by three groups: Japanese, Chinese, and blacks. Nonetheless, despite the improvement, blacks were still ranked as the lowest group in the poll (Lewin, 1992, p. 12).

SOLUTIONS?

So what is our grand plan, our master strategy, for national recovery? It is very simple: We do not have one. Well, that is not entirely true. If we had the political and moral will, we could institute a widespread redistribution of wealth and jobs throughout our society, aimed at a more equitable balance. We could restructure major social institutions to redress centuries of prejudice and discrimination. Again, this seems quaintly naive, because Americans do *not* have the political or moral will to accomplish it.

What we do advocate, however, is the recognition that seeking equality and justice is a process and *not* a finished product. It is something that needs to be struggled for on a daily basis, dealing with the myriad issues, interactions, and institutions that make up our daily social world. We offer a small example to illustrate our point.

AN EDUCATIONAL EXAMPLE

They chanted, they rapped in two languages, they made impassioned, articulate speeches. Nearly 600 middle and high school students, most of them Hispanic, skipped class Friday to attend a rally at City Hall.

"People don't have the pride to do better in school because we're only learning about people from Europe. That's an insult to us, that we're not important enough to be a part of the curriculum," said Jose Luis Paron, a fifteen-year-old freshman.

The students, who represented every high school in San Francisco and other schools down the San Mateo Peninsula, demanded bilingual education, ethnic studies and more Hispanic teachers. "We want more Hispanic counselors so that when we have problems, our parents can go in and talk to someone who speaks Spanish," said Ursala Loretademola, a 16-year-old senior.

Most of the students who spoke were very clear that they did not want to contribute to tension between ethnic groups. "We've got to stand together. We demand more ethnic studies for la Raza, for African-American students, for Asians . . . " said Solaria Perez, the 16-year-old student body president of Woodrow Wilson High School. ("Students Demand," 1994, p.17A)

We work in an academic setting, so we chose an educational example—college curriculum reform—to highlight both the limits and the possibilities of our approach to confronting U.S. prejudice. Because what is taught in schools legitimizes and perpetuates prevailing ideas and values, school curricula are critical educational vehicles for maintaining the "naturalness" and "moral correctness" of the dominant social groups, values, and norms.

White-Dominated Curriculum

The perpetuation of culture has long been recognized as one of education's primary tasks. Since early in U.S. history, to reproduce U.S. culture—to "Americanize"—has meant to anglicize. What we mean is that education has presented perspectives and experiences that have been primarily or even exclusively those of Anglo-Americans, referred to as an *Anglo-dominated,* or *Anglocentric, perspective.* These curricula have justified the dominance, first of English groups, and later of European groups, throughout U.S. society.

For example, courses on U.S. history often begin with English settlements in Massachusetts and Virginia. Such a biased and limited perspective ignores thousands of years of Native American history, as well as Dutch, French, and Spanish colonies *prior* to English settlements in North America.

The dominant Anglo, middle-class perspective is so deeply ingrained as *the* norm in U.S. culture that it is often possible to see it only when the traditional presentation is altered. Even courses on U.S. art have concentrated on Anglo-American artists and traditional Anglo themes. For example, the Smithsonian recently sponsored an exhibit of traditional (Anglo) art of the U.S. frontier period, "The West as America: Reinterpreting Images of the Frontier, 1820–1920." The exhibit catalog contained commentary highly critical of the romanticization of a period of enormous cultural and environmental devastation. The catalog interpreted the artworks in terms of class conflict, economic and environmental exploitation, and ethnic genocide. The bulk of the fifty-page exhibit guest book contained reactions similar to that of historian Daniel Boorstin, who called it "a perverse . . . destructive exhibit" (*Boulder Daily Camera*, 1991, p. 4B).

Republican politician Pat Buchanan, who challenged incumbent George Bush's reelection in the 1992 primaries, clearly outlined the stakes when he told a cheering crowd, "We cannot raise a white flag in the culture war. . . . Culture is the Ho Chi Minh trail to power. If we surrender that province, we lose America." Buchanan railed against multiculturalism as "an across-the-board assault on our Anglo-American heritage . . . Our civilization is superior to others. And our culture is superior to other cultures" (Kaplan, 1993, p. A5).

Multicultural Curriculum

Since the late 1970s, many U.S. colleges and universities have been involved in a process of often contentious curriculum reevaluations around cultural, ethnic, and gender diversity within the United States, referred to as *multicultural reform*. For example, a few years ago, the University of Colorado reformed its curricular requirements to include courses addressing the "nature and meaning of the categories of women, race, ethnicity, and gender" (Spring Catalog, 1988, p. 4), an institutional attempt to promote cultural diversity.

In a testament to political astuteness, reactionaries have succeeded to a large degree in trivializing these important educational and cultural discussions. Even the casual reader of the popular media is bombarded with weekly accounts of bizarre-sounding academic disputes, reported under the catchphrase, "political correctness." Newspaper and magazine article titles from one six-month period give a small overall flavor of what and how much is available: "Political Correctness: Intolerance by Any Other Name"; "One Nation . . . with Liberty and Diversity for All"; " 'Politically Correct' Peril Is Overstated"; "What Is a Nation? Who Gets to Be One?"; "Are You Politically Correct?"; "Teach Diversity—with a Smile"; "Political Correctness: Art's New Frontier?"; "Educators Weigh How to Respond to 'Politically Correct' Label"; "Those 'Dead, White, European Males' Were Dissenters"; "'PC' Battles: The Tyranny of Public Opinion."

Even though critical economic and social issues are at stake, successfully attaching the "PC" label to any of these issues makes them appear frivolous and easy to dismiss. Thus tightly controlling what information is seen as legitimate and meaningful is one of the ways that those with power maintain their control and prestige.

Attempts are ongoing to open this narrow white-oriented perspective to include voices and perspectives of nonwhite groups, the working class, and women, also referred to as a *pluralist perspective*. However, tampering with college curricula to promote pluralist, multicultural, and democratic ideas and perspectives is inevitably met with enormous resistance.

STRUGGLES AND STAKES

Because knowledge is power, what is presented as knowledge is also power, and those currently holding power positions are rightfully threatened by a new definition of knowledge. Intense struggles erupt in all areas of the educational curriculum. The stakes are enormous and concern the survivability of the American dream—the ideal and hope of democratic equality.

The point is, curriculum reform *should* involve intense disputes and struggles because what is at stake has tremendous educational, political, and social implications. In a multicultural curriculum, the white-American perspective would rightfully be analyzed as the tradition that has defined and directed much of the character of U.S. society but would still be presented as one tradition among many. It is not surprising that many believe that changing the curriculum in such a way also includes "attacking the West and its institutions" (*Chronicle of Higher Education*, 1988, p. A1).

Political implications echo a line from Shakespeare that was borrowed by the women's movement in the 1970s: "That which remains unnamed remains unseen." According to social scientist Milton Gordon (1964), political, economic, and social power emanates from the recognition and respect of the values and beliefs of one's group. Many people who already have considerable social, economic, and political power fear that the dominance of white middle-class culture (and their own influence) would be threatened if school curricula no longer provided a distorted and exaggerated sense of the value and place of this culture in history. In contrast, it has also been pointed out that a curriculum that does not accurately reflect the diverse values and experiences of the *total* U.S. culture will be useless in the economic and social world of the twenty-first century.

For many, the most troubling implications of curriculum reform are social, because they question the integrity and sustainability of U.S. society. Some reactionary critics of a multicultural approach to education claim it is unavoidably divisive, could threaten the fragile fabric that holds U.S. society together, and could even lead to "social and cultural suicide." Advocates of multicultural education argue persuasively not only that maintaining the white dominant perspective distorts and denigrates the past and present realities of nonmajority groups but that maintaining the prejudice and discrimination of the status quo ensures continued institutional discrimination and widespread social unrest.

The Form of the Reform

There are many attempts to make college curricula more inclusive and representative of the huge diversity that has always existed in American society. The struggle is not usually over the need for an expanded curriculum; the fight is over what this new curriculum will look like, how it will be constructed, and just what and how new information will be taught. Conservative critics are desperate to preserve a white-dominated society, and one powerful way is to preserve a white-centered body of knowledge. It is important to remember that *all* knowledge involves choices; that is, there is much more information available than is taught. For ideological reasons and also because of time and other logistical constraints, not all knowledge can be presented; choices are *always* made about just what knowledge is presented and what is ignored. This struggle over curricula is a struggle for equality—equality of knowledge, equality of experience, and equality of the power necessary for any group to have its interpretations and perspectives seen as legitimate and valid.

Limitations

Not surprisingly, the most common form of curriculum reform is what is referred to as the *ethnic* or *cultural additive model*, where nonwhite and other nonmainstream perspectives are "added" to an already-existing body of knowledge. We say "not surprisingly" because this approach provides the least inclusive and least effective multicultural approach.

The danger in this additive approach is that deeply embedded assumptions about the "normal" American experience are never overtly challenged. For example, within the "additive" multicultural curriculum model, a course dealing with the American

Revolution would simply "add" more material and would not alter the underlying substance or perspective of the course. Figure 11.2, borrowed almost exclusively from educators Geneva Gay and James Banks (1975), illustrates a broader, more inclusive, and more exhaustive approach to the same subject matter (Pence, 1993, p. 81).

A more fundamental limitation of any curriculum reform is that it does not directly challenge some of the deeper institutional racist and sexist practices. It is simply asking too much of a school curriculum that altering what is taught will provoke the emergence of a more equal society. Establishing a truly multicultural curriculum will *promote* a more equal society, and it will *hasten* the coming of a more equal society, but by itself, it will not *cause* the fall of U.S. prejudice and discrimination.

We have discussed at length the necessity of recognizing the interplay between personal troubles, such as attempting to establish a more democratic curriculum at some specific college or university, and broader social problems, such as ongoing institutional discrimination within education. C. Wright Mills (1959) anticipated the popular bumper sticker, "Think globally, act locally." It is within this spirit and framework of social activism that we feel prejudice and discrimination can be best attacked. Each of us is faced with daily struggles, many of them opportunities to fight for social justice. Few of them are on the scale of a master strategy, but on a local level, they often provide the most effective arena for realistic social change.

Possibilities

The opportunities for local action promoting equality and justice are endless. For example, the curriculum reforms instituted nearly five years ago by the University of Colorado were criticized for failing to offer a truly multicultural approach to higher education. The university administration, as well as specific departments, ignored suggestions to remedy this continuing discrimination.

KEY QUESTIONS	Black Americans		Native Americans	Anglo Revolutionaries					Anglo Loyalists	British	Continental Europeans
	Slave	Free		Women	Farmers	Wealthy	Poor	Small Business Owners			
Why did they/did they not participate in the Revolution?											
What was their level of participation?											
What were their military roles in the American Revolution?											
What were their economic roles?											
What goals as a group did they have?											
What political effects did the American Revolution have on them?											
What social effects did the Revolution have on them?											
What economic effects did the American Revolution have on them?											
What overall changes did the American Revolution cause in their group status?											

Figure 11.2. Multicultural "data retrieval chart" of the American Revolution. Source: Gay and Banks (1975), p. 463.

In April 1994 the university reaped the results of its continuing ignorance and discrimination. Sparked by three Latino professors charging that their department had a "racially hostile environment," a week-long student hunger strike ended when university president Judith Albino signed a "Declaration of Diversity" (Reinholds, 1994, p. 3). The most substantive actions granted in the declaration were adopting a more multicultural curriculum and establishing an ethnic studies department. If the university had had the moral courage to match its multicultural rhetoric, this truly embarrassing incident could have been avoided. The university could also have been a community leader in celebrating and promoting cultural differences as the basis of a new social cohesion (Pence, 1993).

To a large extent, social cohesion, or social "glue," depends on agreed-upon values and meanings, but what the specific values and meanings are does not matter. The emergence and acceptance of diverse perspectives and voices about the American experience—past and present—can produce a different basis for social cohesion, a different glue, no longer bound by conformity to dominant white values and meanings, but located within an equality of differences.

There is an enormous distinction between divisiveness and differences, a distinction often conspicuously ignored or confused by many who oppose a multicultural curriculum. Simply because we hear from many ignored groups and peoples who have *always* been a part of the American scene does not indicate a lessened social unity. Indeed, including and honoring these often ignored and suppressed voices and traditions only makes more real the American motto *E pluribus unum:* "Out of many, one."

A multicultural curriculum would be more representative of the richness and complexity that has *always* characterized U.S. society. Imagine how much more a student could learn about the American Revolution from a more inclusive and expanded perspective. A student's understanding of such a pivotal event in our nation's history would be tremendously enhanced. A pluralistic

approach would also make the student aware that multiple perspectives and experiences exist in all other elements that make up
the American experience—past, present, and future.

A truly multicultural, pluralistic approach to school curricula would also be more just, more equal, and more democratic. It
not only would allow students to learn more about our nation but
would also subtly promote one of America's most enduring promises: That all people are not only created equal but will also be
treated equally.

Establishing a sincere democratic society is a monumental
task for the citizens of the United States. It needs to be addressed
at multiple levels: cultural, institutional, and individual. Culturally, we need to recognize the blame-the-victim element in U.S.
ideology. U.S. society already has deep-rooted values, such as
fairness and "justice for all," that can be turned against prejudice
and discrimination; these values need to be emphasized and supported. For example, it is critical to move from an ideology that
praises domination and control to one that honors diversity and
pluralism. The struggles at the University of Colorado illustrate
personal involvement in attacking cultural and institutional prejudice and discrimination. The involvement of many white students in the protests and hunger strike demonstrates that they do
not see an expanded awareness of racial and ethnic issues to be
a cultural threat; rather, they view it as a celebration of their
culture's vibrancy.

There need to be continuing struggles to make institutions
responsive to the changing face and the changing needs of the
United States. Individual struggles in Boulder, Colorado, forced a
large and powerful institution to adopt a curriculum that teaches
that diversity has *always* been the American way. Federal and
state governments need to directly address issues of prejudice
and discrimination. For example, in 1994 the Clinton administration promised to double its budget for the homeless. HUD secretary Henry Cisneros's stated goal was a realistic one-third reduction in America's homeless population. It remains to be seen,

as is often the case, if magnificent rhetoric will take the place of concrete action.

We the authors have slowly and at times reluctantly come to the realization that grand programs and master plans for establishing a more just society are important, but that our most effective involvement in this ongoing effort is at the level where we live: in our communities, in our schools, and in our homes. It is an admittedly monumental task, one that will undoubtedly define the United States in the twenty-first century. Dickens opened his *Tale of Two Cities* with the immortal line, "It was the best of times, it was the worst of times," a sentiment that accurately describes the contemporary United States. The opportunity exists to turn the American dream into reality. But does the United States have the courage?

References

Agents break up skinhead plot to spark race war. (1993, July 16). *Salt Lake Tribune*, p. A1.

Amnesty International. (1987). "USA: The Death Penalty." London: AI.

Anderson, T. (1993, October 31). Time to bury the Confederate flag. *The Daily Spectrum*, Iron County, UT, pp. D1, D2.

Angela. (1993, October 12). Personal interview, Cedar City, UT.

Austin, J., and Irwin, J. (1987). "It's About Time." National Council on Crime and Delinquency.

Autman, S. (1993, June 16). Board rejects textbooks that advocate, accept homosexuality. *Salt Lake Tribune*, pp. B1, B2.

Avicolli, T. (1988). He defies you still: The memoirs of a sissy. In P. Rothenberg (Ed.), *Racism and Sexism*, pp. 147–152. New York: St. Martin's Press.

Baca, S. (1994, April 15). 3 Chicano profs: CU sociology department racist. *Denver Post*, p. B3.

Banfield, E. (1970). *The Unheavenly City*. Boston: Little, Brown.

Banks, J. (1984). *Teaching Strategies for Ethnic Studies*. Boston: Allyn & Bacon.

Barazia, V. (1993, March 31). Thousands of American children still at risk, study says. *The Daily Spectrum*, Iron County, UT, p. B1.

Barbie speaks. (1992, September 29). *Boulder Daily Camera*, Boulder, CO, p. A2.

Barrera, M. (1979). *Race and Class in the Southwest*. Notre Dame, IN: University of Notre Dame Press.

Barringer, F. (1992, May 15). After the riots: Census reveals a city of displacement. *New York Times*, Late Edition, p. A16.

Bartocci, B. (1992, November 3). Mom, I'm gay. *Woman's Day*, pp. 77–79.

Bassuk, E. L. (1984). The homelessness problem. *Scientific American*, 251(1), pp. 40–45.

Bassuk, E. L., Rubin, L., and Lauriat, A. (1986). Characteristics of sheltered homeless families. *American Journal of Public Health*, 76(9), pp. 1097–1101.

Bell-Fialkoff, A. (1993, Summer). A brief history of ethnic cleansing. *Foreign Affairs*, 73(3), pp. 110–121.

Bem, S., and Bem, D. (1991). Training women to know their place. In L. Cargan and J. Ballantine (Eds.), *Sociological Footprints*, pp. 50–63. Belmont, CA: Wadsworth.

Benson, E. T. (1987). *To the Mothers in Zion*, The Church of Jesus Christ of Latter Day Saints, Salt Lake City, UT.

Berrill, K. (1992). Anti-gay violence and victimization in the United States: An overview. In Gregory Herek and Kevin Berrill (Eds.), *Hate Crimes: Confronting Violence against Lesbians and Gay Men*, pp. 21–24. Newbury Park, CA: Sage.

Big racial disparity in home ownership. (1993, June 22). AP, in *The Daily Spectrum*, Iron County, UT, p. B5.

Binder, D., and Crossette, B. (1993, Fall). As ethnic wars multiply, U.S. strives for a policy. *New York Times, Themes of the Times*, p. 12.

Blacks make Japanese uneasy, lawmaker says. (1993, March 19). AP, in *Rocky Mountain News*, Denver, CO, p. 36.

Blauner, R. (1972). *Racial Oppression in America*. New York: Harper & Row.

Blum, J. M. (1978). *Pseudoscience and Mental Ability*. New York: Monthly Review Press.

Blumstein, A., Cohen, J., and Nagin, D. (1978). *Deterrence and Incapacitation*. Washington, DC: National Academy of Sciences.

Bogue, D. (1963). *Skid Row in American Cities*. Chicago: University of Chicago Press.

Bohm, R. M. (1986). Crime, criminal, and crime control policy myths. *Justice Quarterly*, 3, pp. 193–214.

Boulder Daily Camera, (1988, October 2). Boulder, CO, p. D3.

Bowles, S., and Gintis, H. (1976). *Schooling in Capitalist America*. New York: Basic Books.

Brantenberg, G. (1985). *Egalia's Daughters: A Satire on the Sexes.* Seattle: Seal Press.

Brenner, C. (1992). Survivor's story: Eight bullets. In G. Hereck and K. Berrill (Eds.), *Hate Crimes,* pp. 11–15. Belmont, CA: Sage.

Brogan, P. (1993, December 19). Despite its own mandate, Congress pays women less than men. Gannett News Service, in *Salt Lake Tribune,* pp. A1, A4–A5.

Broom, L., Bonjean, C., and Broom, D. (1990). *Sociology.* Belmont, CA: Wadsworth.

Brown, J. (1987). Hunger in the U.S. *Scientific American,* 256(2), pp. 37–41.

Brown, R. (1993). "Commerce Secretary Ron Brown Promises Urban Revitalization." News from National Urban League Conference, Washington, DC

Bryjak, G., and Soroka, M. (1994). *Sociology: Cultural Diversity in a Changing World.* Needham Heights, MA: Allyn & Bacon.

Burnham, S. (1985). *Black Intelligence in White Society.* Atlanta: Social Science Press.

Burns, H. (1973). Can a black man get a fair trial in this country? In R. Yin (Ed.), *Race, Creed, Color, or National Origin.* Itasca, IL: F. E. Peacock.

Campos, C. (1993, February 10). Letters to the editor. *The Daily Spectrum,* p. 5.

Carlson, R. (1987). *The Americanization Syndrome: A Quest for Conformity.* New York: St. Martin's Press.

Carter, D. (1985a). Hispanic perception of police performance: An empirical assessment. *Journal of Criminal Justice,* 13, pp. 487–500.

Carter, D. (1985b). Police brutality: A model for definition, perspective, and control. In A. Blumberg and E. Niderhoffer (Eds.), *The Ambivalent Force: Perspectives on the Police,* pp. 321–330. New York: Holt, Rinehart & Winston.

Chambers, J. (1987). The law and black Americans: Retreat from civil rights. In J. Dewart (Ed.), *The State of Black America 1987,* pp. 15–30. New York: National Urban League.

Chapman, S. (1989, March 28). Homeless mentally ill need treatment. *Las Vegas Review-Journal,* p. 7b.

Chavez, L. (1994, May 3). The myth of immigrants and welfare. *USA Today,* p. 11A.

Chesney-Lind, M. (1973). Judicial enforcement of the female: The Family Court and the female delinquent. *Issues in Criminology*, 8, pp. 51–71.

Child killing. (1993, April 23). *USA Today*, p. A3.

Chisholm, S. (1993, July 23). *Salt Lake Tribune*, p. B1.

Christie, S. (1994). Women, work, and the workplace. In L. L. Lindsey, *Gender Roles: A Sociological Perspective*, pp. 234–258. Englewood Cliffs, NJ: Prentice-Hall.

Clark, C. (1991). Sympathy in everyday life. In J. Henslin (Ed.), *Down to Earth Sociology: Introductory Readings*, pp. 193–203. New York: Free Press.

Clinard, M. A., and Yeager, P. (1980). *Corporate Crime*. New York: Free Press.

Cochran, F. (1994). Personal interview. Cedar City, UT.

Combs-Orme, T., and Buyer, B. (1992). America's health care system: The Reagan legacy. *Journal of Sociology & Social Welfare*, pp. 63–89.

Conklin, J. (1986). *Criminology*. New York: Macmillan.

Conservative scholars call for movement to "reform" the Academy. (1988, November 23). *Chronicle of Higher Education*, p. A1.

Coon, C. (1962). *The Origin of Races*. New York: Knopf.

Correctional Populations in the United States. (1988, 1992). Bureau of Justice Statistics. Washington, DC: U.S. Department of Justice.

Cox, O. (1948). *Caste, Class, and Race*. Garden City, NY: Doubleday.

Crime rivals economy as top issue in U.S., poll finds. (1994, January 23). New York Times News Service, in *The Dallas Morning News*, p. A4.

The Daily Spectrum. (1993, March 9). Iron County, UT, p. A1.

Daly, M. (1988, October). Homeless families in America. *Better Homes and Gardens*, pp. 21–24.

Darwin, Charles. (1859). *Origin of Species*. New York: Clarke, Given & Hooper.

Davis, K., and Moore, W. (1945). Some principles of stratification. *American Sociological Review*, 10(2), pp. 242–244.

Death rates for minority infants were underestimated, study says. (1992, January 8). *New York Times*, p. A14.

Dembo, R. (1988). Delinquency among black male youth. In J. Taylor Gibbs (Ed.), *Young, Black, and Male in America: An Endangered Species*. New York: Auburn House.

DeParle, J. (1994, July 13). Big rise in births outside wedlock. *New York Times, Themes of the Times*, pp. 1, 5.

DeParle, J. (1994, October 9). Daring research of "social science pornography"? *New York Times Magazine,* pp. 48–62.

Dobzhansky, T. (1963). Review of C. Coon's book, *The Origin of Races. Scientific American,* 78(3), pp. 117–121.

Does prenatal-care quality vary between races? (1994, January 20). AP, in *Salt Lake Tribune,* p. A3.

Dowie, M. (1977). Pinto madness. *Mother Jones,* 2, pp. 18–32.

Dreeban, R. (1968). *On What Is Learned in School.* Reading, MA: Addison-Wesley.

Drug crimes push prison populations to new levels. (1993, May 10). AP, in *The Daily Spectrum,* Iron County, UT, p. A5.

D'Souza, D. (1991). *Illiberal Education: The Politics of Race and Sex on Campus.* New York: Free Press.

DuBois, W. E. B. (1961). *The Souls of Black Folk.* New York: Fawcett.

Ehrenberg, J. (1993, May 10). Letter to the editor, *Time,* p. 10.

Einbinder, S. D. (1992). A statistical profile of children living in poverty: Children under 3 and children under 6, 1990. Unpublished document from the National Center for Children in Poverty, Columbia University School of Public Health, New York.

Eitzen, D. S. (1982). *In Conflict and Order: Understanding Society.* Boston: Allyn & Bacon.

Elias, M. (1991, September 16). Parents' beliefs can influence kids' studies. *USA Today,* p. A1.

Ellwood, C. (1924). *Sociology and Modern Social Problems.* New York: American Book Company.

FBI *Uniform Crime Reports.* (1994, January 6). *USA Today,* p. A2.

Feagin, J. R., and Feagin, C. (1993). *Racial and Ethnic Relations* (4th ed.). Englewood Cliffs, NJ: Prentice-Hall.

Federal Bureau of Investigation. (1989). *Crime in the United States.* Washington, DC: U.S. Department of Justice.

Fenton, J., and Wilson, A. (1992, August 24). Teacher seeks positive portrayal of American Indians in schools. *Salt Lake Tribune,* pp. B1, B2.

Ferrante, J. (1986). *Sociology: A Global Perspective.* Belmont, CA: Wadsworth.

Finnigan, W. (1986). *Crossing the line: A Year in the Land of Apartheid.* New York: Harper & Row.

First woman pitcher makes a solid debut. (1994, February 16). *Boulder Daily Camera,* Boulder, CO, p. B2.

Flag battle at Georgia Dome. (1994, January 27). *Daily Spectrum*, Cedar City, UT, p. 1A.

Flores, E., Chrvala, C., and Bakemeier, R. (1990). "Breast and Cervical Cancer Screening—Hispanic Women, 1990–1995." Research project funded by National Cancer Institute, Bethesda, MD. Grant CA 52903-0551.

Forty years after *Brown* decision, many schools still segregated. (1994, May 16). AP, in *The Daily Spectrum*, Iron County, UT, p. B4.

Fredrickson, G. M. (1971). Toward a social interpretation of the development of American racism. In N. Huggins, M. Kilson, and D. Fox (Eds.), *Key Issues in the Afro-American Experience*. New York: Harcourt Brace Jovanovich.

Friend, T. (1994, February 22). Immigrant kids tend to make better students. *USA Today*, p. 1A.

Garn, S. M. (1965). *Human Races* (2nd ed.). Springfield, IL: Charles C Thomas.

Gay, J., and Banks, J. (1975). Teaching the American Revolution: A multiethnic approach. *Social Education*, 39(7), pp. 461–465.

Gender bias in the classroom. (1993, Spring). *Summit Magazine*, University of Colorado, p. 22.

Gibbs, J. T. (1988). *Young, Black, and Male in America: An Endangered Species*. New York: Auburn House.

Girls harassed often at school, study says. (1993, March 24). UPI, in *Salt Lake Tribune*, p. A6.

GLB club fire blazes on. (1993, March 11). Letter to the editor. *Thunderbird*, Southern Utah University, Cedar City, UT, p. 3.

Goode, E. (1994). *Deviant Behavior*. Englewood Cliffs, NJ: Prentice-Hall.

Goodman, E. (1994a, February 20). Sexism in schools is subtle but still damaging to girls. *Boulder Daily Camera*, Boulder, CO, p. 6.

Goodman, E. (1994b, February 18). Dieting has become national sport and women's shame. *Boulder Daily Camera*, Boulder, CO, p. 6.

Gordon, M. (1964). *Assimilation in American Life: The Role of Race, Religion, and National Origins*. New York: Oxford University.

Gossett, T. (1963). *Race: The History of an Idea in America*. Dallas: Southern Methodist University.

Gould, S. J. (1981). *The Mismeasure of Man*. New York: Norton.

Graff, S. (1994, January 29). New flag to fly over Dixie. *The Daily Spectrum*, Iron County, UT, pp. A1, A8.

Hacker, A. (1992). *Two Nations: Black and White, Separate, Hostile, Unequal*. New York: Ballantine Books.

Harris, L. (1991, July 19). Presentation to the annual meeting, Education Commission of the States, *Denver Post*, p. 3A.

Hartley, R. (1959). Sex-role pressures and the socialization of the male child. *Psychological Research*, 5, pp. 457–468.

Healy, M. (1994, January 9). Injustice behind the injustice: Bias in radiation experiments. Los Angeles Times, in *Salt Lake Tribune*, pp. A1, A19.

Heller, S. (1992, June 3). Worldwide "Diaspora" of peoples poses new challenges for scholars. *Chronicle of Higher Education*, p. A7.

Henry, T. (1993, December 14). Public schools becoming as segregated as in the 1960s. *USA Today*, p. A1.

Henslin, J. (1993). *Sociology: A Down-to-Earth Approach*. Boston: Allyn & Bacon.

Herek, G., and Berrill, K. (Eds.). (1992). *Hate Crimes*. Newbury Park, CA: Sage.

Herrick, T. (1993, May 2). Schools a battleground in gay-rights debate. *Rocky Mountain News*, Denver, CO, p. 36A.

Herrnstein, R. (1971, September), IQ. *Atlantic.*

Herrnstein, R., and Murray, C. (1994). *The Bell Curve*. New York: The Free Press.

Higham, J. (1988). *Strangers in the Land: Patterns of American Nativism, 1860–1925*. New Brunswick, NJ: Rutgers University.

Historian criticizes Smithsonian images of Old West. (1991, April 21). *Boulder Daily Camera*, Boulder, CO, pp. 1B, 4B.

Hoffman, M. (1975). Assumptions in sex education books. *Educational Review*, 27(3), pp. 229–236.

Hofstadter, R. (1965). *Social Darwinism in American Thought*. Boston: Beacon Press.

Hollinger, R. (1984). Race, occupational status and proactive police arrest for drinking and driving. *Journal of Criminal Justice*, 12, pp. 173–183.

Holmes, S. J. (1936). *Human Genetics and Its Social Import*. New York: McGraw-Hill.

Horowitz, R., and Pottieger, A. (1988). "Gender Bias in Juvenile Justice Handling of Seriously Crime-Involved Youth." Paper presented at the annual meeting of the American Society of Criminology, Chicago, Illinois.

Howlett, D. (1993a, May 26). Gay sailor "deserved" death, killer says. *USA Today,* p. 3A.

Howlett, D. (1993b, February 23). Survey: Anti-gay crimes up 172%. *USA Today,* p. A3.

Hubbard, E. A. (1993). *"Of Course I Fight Back": An Ethnography of Women's Use of Violence in Intimate Relationships.* Unpublished doctoral dissertation, University of Colorado, Boulder.

Huizinga, D., and Elliott, D. (1987). Juvenile offenders: Prevalence, offender incidence, and arrest rates by race. *Crime and Delinquency,* 33, pp. 206–223.

Hull, J. (1994, April 4). Do teachers punish according to race? *Time,* p. 30.

Hungry say relief needed at home, too. (1992, December 10). AP, in *The Daily Spectrum,* Iron County, UT, p. A1.

Infant mortality is higher among minorities. (1992, January 9). AP, in The *Daily Spectrum,* Iron County, UT, p. A1.

Ingrassia, M. (1993, October 25). Abused and confused. *Newsweek,* pp. 57–58.

Jackson, C., and Tolbert, E. (1989). *Race and Culture in America.* Chicago: Bellwether.

Jankowski, M. (1991). *Islands in the Street: Gangs and American Urban Society.* Berkeley, CA: University of California Press.

Jaschik, S. (1986, January 21). Black enrollment rate drops. *Colorado Daily,* University of Colorado, pp. 1, 8.

Jensen, A. (1976). Interview. In R. Evans (Ed.), *The Making of Psychology,* pp. 54–67. New York: Knopf.

Jensen, A. (1981). *Straight Talk about Mental Tests.* New York: Free Press.

Johnson, S. (1983). Race and the decision to detain a suspect. *Yale Law Journal,* 93, pp. 214–258.

Johnson, S. (1993, January 2). U.S. a charity ward? Immigration burden may be exaggerated. Knight-Ridder News Service, in *Salt Lake Tribune,* p. A9.

Johnston, D. (1992, April 24). Survey shows number of rapes far higher than official figures. *New York Times, Themes of the Times,* p. 12.

Jones, B., and Gray, B. (1986). Problems in diagnosing schizophrenia and affective disorders among blacks. *Hospital and Community Psychiatry,* 37(1), pp. 61–65.

Judge lightens sentence because victims gay. (1988, December 12). *Boulder Daily Camera,* Boulder, CO, p. A2.

Jury says victim asked for rape, acquits suspect. (1988, December 16).

Knight-Ridder Newspapers, in *Boulder Daily Camera*, Boulder, CO, p. A3.

Juveniles Taken into Custody: Fiscal Year 1991 Report Draft. Office of Juvenile Justice and Delinquency Prevention. Washington, DC: U.S. Department of Justice.

Kamin, L. (1986, February). Is crime in the genes? The answer may depend on who chooses what evidence. *Scientific American*, pp. 22–27.

Kammeyer, K., Ritzer, G., and Yetmen, N. (1994). *Sociology: Experiencing Changing Societies*. Boston: Allyn & Bacon.

Kaplan, L. F. (1993, September 12). Buchanan to GOP: Don't underestimate Christians. Gannett News Service, in *Salt Lake Tribune*, p. A5.

Karger, H., and Stoesz, D. (1990). *American Social Welfare Policy: A Structural Approach*. New York: Longman.

Katz, J. (1976). *Gay American History*. New York: Crowell.

Keen, J. (1993, April 27). Health-care struggle seen from the front. *USA Today*, pp. A1, A2.

Kelly, D. (1993, June 2). Defining sex harassment in schools. *USA Today*, pp. 1A, 2A.

Kelly, D. (1994, February 28). Minorities' college grad rate lagging. *USA Today*, p. A3.

King gets $3.8 million, goes after officers. (1994, April 20). AP, in *The Daily Spectrum*, Iron County, UT, p. A6.

Kleck, G. (1981). Racial discrimination in criminal sentencing: A critical evaluation of the evidence with additional evidence on the death penalty. *American Sociological Review*, 46, pp. 783–805.

Kluegel, J., and Smith, E. (1986). *Beliefs about Inequality: Americans' Views of What Ought to Be*. New York: Aldine de Gruyter.

Kohn, M. (1969). *Class and Conformity: A Study in Values*. Homewood, IL: Dorsey Press.

Kohn, M., Naoi, A., Schoenbach, C., Schooler, C., and Slomczynski, K. (1990). Position in the class structure and psychological functioning in the United States, Japan, and Poland. *American Journal of Sociology*, 95, pp. 964–1008.

Kokopeli, B., and Lakey, G. (1992). More power than we want: Masculine sexuality and violence. In M. L. Anderson and P. H. Collins (Eds.), *Race, Class, and Gender: An Anthology*, pp. 443–449. Belmont, CA: Wadsworth.

Lacayo, R. (1992, December 4). Jack and Jack and Jill and Jill. *Time*, pp. 52–53.

Lacayo, R. (1993, April 19). Unhealed wounds. *Time*, pp. 26–31.

Lacayo, R. (1994, October 24). For whom the bell curves. *Time*, pp. 66–67.

Law, S. (1993, March 9). Gay club issue heats up at SUU. *The Daily Spectrum*, Iron County, UT, p. 1A.

Lawson, W. B. (1986). Racial and ethnic factors in psychiatric research. *Hospital and Community Psychiatry*, 37(1), pp. 50–53.

Lederman, D. (1993, October 20). Old times not forgotten: A battle over symbols obscures U. of Mississippi's racial changes. *Chronicle of Higher Education*, pp. A51–A52.

Lewin, T. (1992, January 8). Study points to increase in tolerance of ethnicity. *New York Times*, p. A12.

Lewis, M. (1993, April 12). U.S. system of pigeonholing is for the birds, many minorities say. Knight-Ridder News, in *Salt Lake Tribune*, p. A16.

Lewis, O. (1959). *Five Families: The Children of Sanchez*. New York: Random House.

Lewis, O. (1965). *La Vida: A Puerto Rican Family in the Culture of Poverty—San Juan and New York*. New York: Random House.

Lewontin, R. C., Rose, S., and Kamin, L. (1984). *Not in Our Genes: Biology, Ideology, and Human Nature*. New York: Pantheon Books.

Lillard, M. (1993, May 30). When Tailhook comes to public schools. AP, in *Salt Lake Tribune*, pp. A16, A17.

Lindsey, L. L. (1994). *Gender Roles: A Sociological Perspective*. Englewood Cliffs, NJ: Prentice-Hall.

Linton, R. (1936). *The Study of Man*. New York: Appleton-Century-Crofts.

Los Angeles: Is the City of Angels going to hell? (1993, May 10). *Time*, pp. 9–15.

Mandatory Minimum Penalties in the Federal Criminal Justice System. (1991). Washington, DC: U.S. Sentencing Commission.

Manegold, C. (1993, January 13). Abuse trial forces jury to ride tide of minutiae. *New York Times*, p. B1.

Manegold, C. (1994, March 9). Clinton to unveil jobs bill that focuses on retraining. *New York Times*.

Manning, A. (1993, March 24). Schoolgirls sexually harassed. *USA Today*, p. A1.

Maples, P. (1993, June 11). America's women running out of places to hide. Dallas Morning News, in *Salt Lake Tribune*, p. A1.

Marable, M. (1983). *How Capitalism Underdeveloped Black America*. Boston: South End Press.

Marriage and murder. (1990, December 18). *Boulder Daily Camera*, Boulder, CO, p. A2.

Mauro, T. (1993, April 21). Bigotry vs. free speech: Supreme Court's call. *USA Today*, p. 7A.

McCormick, L. H. (1921). *Characterology: The Principles, Rules, and Methods of Scientific Character Reading and Analysis*. Chicago: Rand McNally.

McLemore, S. D. (1991). *Racial and Ethnic Relations in America*. Boston: Allyn & Bacon.

Meddis, S. (1989, December 20). Whites, not blacks, at the core of drug crisis. *USA Today*.

Meighan, R. (1986). *A Sociology of Educating*. London: Holt, Rinehart & Winston.

Meyers, J. (1991, December 16). Stereotypes pit ability vs. intellect. *USA Today*, p. A1, A2.

Mills, C. W. (1959). *The Sociological Imagination*. Oxford: Oxford University Press.

Miner, H. (1956). Body ritual among the Nacirema. *American Anthropologist*, 58(3), pp. 505–506.

Minorities get short end of SBA benefits. (1994, April 11). AP, in *Salt Lake Tribune*, p. 4A.

Mitchell, E. (1990, April 26). Cops burst in, you feel violated. *Detroit News*.

Morganthau, T. (1993, August 9). America: Still a melting pot? *Newsweek*, pp. 16–25.

Moynihan, D. P. (1967). The Negro family. In Lee Rainwater and W. L. Yancey (Eds.), *The Moynihan Report and the Politics of Controversy*. Cambridge: MIT Press.

Multimedia Entertainment, Inc. (1994a, February 7). Teen racism, Part One, Transcript #1414, *Sally Jessy Raphael Show*.

Multimedia Entertainment, Inc. (1994b, February 8). Teen racism, Part Two, Transcript #1415, *Sally Jessy Raphael Show*.

Murdock, G. (1934). *Our Primitive Contemporaries*. New York: Macmillan.

Murray, C., and Herrnstein, R. (1994). Race, genes, and IQ—An apologia. *New Republic*, October 31, 1994, pp. 27–37.

NAACP wants principal accused of bigotry dismissed. (1994, March 9). AP, in *Salt Lake Tribune*, p. A7.

Nasar, S. (1992a, April 21). Fed gives new evidence of 80s gains by richest. *New York Times, Themes of the Times*, p. 10.

Nasar, S. (1992b, May 18). Rich and poor likely to remain so. *New York Times, Themes of the Times*, p. 8.

Nisbet, R. (1966). *The Sociological Tradition*. New York: Basic Books.

Novak, G. (1992). *Genocide against the Indians*. New York: Pathfinder.

Novak, M. (1971). *The Rise of the Unmeltable Ethnics*. New York: Macmillan.

Officer says he was ordered to hit King. (1994, April 22). AP, in *The Daily Spectrum*, Iron County, UT, p. A5.

Ong, P. (1989). *The Widening Divide: Income Inequality and Poverty in Los Angeles*. Los Angeles: UCLA School of Architecture and Urban Planning.

Organizing for equality. (1990, March). *Newsletter of the National Gay and Lesbian Task Force Campus Project*, Washington, DC.

Osborne, D. (1988). *Laboratories of Democracy*. Boston: Harvard Business School Press.

Palmer, D. (1986, February 22). Psychiatrist says treatment needed by many homeless. *Deseret News*, Salt Lake City, UT.

Parade Magazine. (1994, January 9). What Americans say about the homeless, p. 4.

Pence, D. (1992). A women's studies course: Its impact on women's attitudes toward men. *National Women's Studies Association Journal*, 4(3), pp. 321–335.

Pence, D. (1993). *Multiculturalism and Higher Education: The Use of Curriculum Reform to Promote Cultural Diversity*. Unpublished doctoral dissertation, University of Colorado, Boulder.

Perkins, C., and Gilliard, D. (1992). National Corrections Reporting Program, 1988. Bureau of Justice Statistics. Washington, DC: U.S. Department of Justice.

Peterson, K. (1992, December 2). Helping black kids prevail over prejudice. *USA Today*, p. 7D.

Pfohl, S. (1994). *Images of Deviance and Social Control: A Sociological History* (2nd ed.). New York: McGraw-Hill.

Pink Triangles. (1983). Cambridge Documentary Films, Cambridge, MA.

Pizzo, S., Fricker, M., and Muolo, P. (1992). *Inside Job: The Looting of America's Savings and Loans*. New York: McGraw-Hill.

Plummer, W., and Speidel, M. (1991, October 7). Save the children. *People*, pp. 103–106.

Portes, C. (1994). State of the Union and Blacks in America. *Inner City News*, Mobile, AL.

Preston, F., and Smith, R. (1989). *Sociology: A Contemporary Approach*. Boston: Allyn & Bacon.

Preteens developing a fat phobia beyond their years. (1993, March 5). Chicago Tribune, in *Salt Lake Tribune*, p. A15.

PrimeTime Live. (1993, February 11). Interview with Marge Schott.

Puente, M. (1993, July 14). USA cool to huddled masses. *USA Today*, pp. A1, A2.

Quinney, R. (1977). *Class, State, and Crime*. New York: David McKay.

Racism drives massacre. (1993, December 9). AP, in *The Daily Spectrum*, Iron County, UT, p. A5.

Rainwater, L., and Yancy, W. L. (Eds.). (1967). *The Moynihan Report and the Politics of Controversy*. Cambridge: MIT Press.

Redway, J., and Hinman, R. (1898). *Natural School Geography, Part 2*. New York: American Book Company.

Reid, S. T. (1994). *Crime and Criminology* (7th ed.). Fort Worth, TX: Holt, Rinehart, & Winston.

Reinholds, A. (1994, May 3). Chairs support colleague accused of racism. *Colorado Daily*, Boulder, CO, p. 3.

Relief agency to attack hunger in U.S. (1992, November 19). AP, in *Salt Lake Tribune*, p. 12.

Reno. J. (1993). "We Must Invest in Our Children Now or Pay a Higher Price Later, the Nation's Law Tells Urban League." News from National Urban League Conference, Washington, DC.

Riga, P. (1993, January 28). "Ethnic cleansing" as American as apple pie. *USA Today*, p. 13A.

Riis, J. (1890). *How the Other Half Lives*. New York: Scribner's.

Riley, R. (1993). "Secretary of Education Announces 'New Ethic of Learning' at National Urban League Conference." News from National Urban League Conference, Washington, DC.

Robertson, I. (1987). *Sociology*. New York: Wirth.

Rokeach, M. (1968). *Beliefs, Attitudes, and Values*. San Francisco: Jossey-Bass.

Ropers, R. (1985a). The contribution of economic and political policies and trends to the rise of the new urban homeless. In *The Federal Response to the Homeless Crisis*, pp. 833–856. Washington, DC: Government Printing Office.

Ropers, R. (1985b, December). The rise of the new urban homeless. *Public Affairs Report*, 26(5 and 6). Berkeley: University of California, Institute of Governmental Studies.

Ropers, R. (1988). *The Invisible Homeless: A New Urban Ecology*. New York: Human Sciences Press.

Ropers, R. (1991). *Persistent Poverty: The American Dream Turned Nightmare*. New York: Plenum Press.

Rossides, D. (1976). *The American Class System*. Boston: Houghton Mifflin.

Rothenberg, P. (1988). *Racism and Sexism: An Integrated Study*. New York: St. Martin's Press.

Rubin, B., Wright, J., and Devine, J. (1992). Unhousing the urban poor: The Reagan legacy. *Journal of Sociology & Social Welfare*, 19, pp. 111–147.

Sadker, M., and Sadker, D. (1994, February 4–6). Why schools must tell girls: "You're smart, you can do it." *USA Weekend*, pp. 4–6.

Safety Network. (1993). New study shows over 13.5 million Americans have been literally homeless. Vol. 12, no. 6, p. 1.

Samuel, J. (1981). The teacher's viewpoint: Feminism and science teaching. In A. Kelly (Ed.), *The Missing Half: Girls and Science Education*, pp. 246–256. Manchester, England: Manchester University.

Scarlet, P., and Stack, P. F. (1994, October 3). Mormons meet in Salt Lake for fall conference. *Salt Lake Tribune*, pp. A1, A4.

Schott: Racism doesn't exist. (1993, February 12). AP, in *Salt Lake Tribune*, p. D1.

Schott's take on ballplayers: "Only fruits wear earrings." (1994, May 19). *Salt Lake Tribune*, p. C4.

Sege, I. (1994, November 10). The bell curve: The other author; Harvard's Richard J. Herrnstein didn't live to face his final controversy. *The Boston Globe*, Thursday, City Edition, p. 91.

Seifman, D. (1980a, February 29). Nobel scientists are trying to father a "master race." *New York Post*, pp. 1, 13.

Seifman, D. (1980b, February 29). The shocking thoughts of professor Shockley. *New York Post*, p. 13.

Sen, A. (1993, May). The economics of life and death. *Scientific American*, pp. 40–47.

Sexual harassment: Gender gap on Capitol Hill. (1991, November 17). *Parade Magazine*, p. 10.

Sharp, D. (1993a, January 7). Tampa attack is mirror of "how ugly racism is." *USA Today*, p. A6.

Sharp, D. (1993b, June 7). Man set on fire back in Florida for trial of accused. *USA Today*, p. A5.

Shupe, A., et al. (1987). *Violent Men, Violent Couples: The Dynamics of Domestic Violence*. Lexington, MA: Lexington Books.

Silverman, L. K. (1993). Social development, leadership, and gender issues. In L. K. Silverman (Ed.), *Counseling the Gifted and Talented*, pp. 291–327. Denver: Love.

Simon, D., and Eitzen, D. S. (1990). *Elite Deviance* (3rd ed.). Boston: Allyn & Bacon.

Skinner, B. F. (1971). *Beyond Freedom and Dignity*. New York: Knopf.

Smith, T. (1990, December). *Ethnic Images*. General Social Survey Project, Topical Report No. 19. Chicago: National Opinion Research Center.

Smolowe, J. (1994). Lock 'em up and throw away the key. *Time*, v. 143, no. 6, pp. 50–59.

Spring Catalog. (1989). *Degree Requirements for Arts and Sciences Students*. University of Colorado, Boulder, CO.

Stacey, J. (1993, December 15). Uninsured Americans jump in numbers. *USA Today*, p. A4.

Staples, W. (1987). Law and social control in juvenile justice dispositions. *Journal of Research in Crime and Delinquency*, 24, pp. 7–22.

Statistical Abstract of the United States. (1991, 1993). Bureau of the Census. Washington, DC: U.S. Department of Commerce.

Stevenson, R. (1992, May 6). After the riots: Riots inflamed a festering South-Central economy. *New York Times*, Late Edition, p. A23.

Stoesz, D. (1992). The fall of the industrial city: The Reagan legacy for urban policy. *Journal of Sociology & Social Welfare*, 19, pp. 149–167.

Straus, M. A., and Gelles, R. J. (Eds.). (1990). *Physical Violence in American Families: Risk Factors and Adaptations to Violence in 8,145 Families*. New Brunswick, NJ: Transaction.

Students demand ethnic education. (1994, April 23). AP, in *Las Vegas Review Journal*, p. A17.

Study: Racial segregation spreading. (1993, December 13). AP, in *The Daily Spectrum*, Iron County, UT, p. A3.

Study says children of immigrants prefer to speak English. (1993, July 22). Knight-Ridder News Service, in *Salt Lake Tribune*, p. A9.

Sumner, W. (1906). *Folkways: A Study in the Sociological Importance of Usages, Manners, Customs, Mores, and Morals*. New York: Ginn.

Survey: Anti-gay crimes up 172%. (1993, February 15). *USA Today*, p. A3.

Survey: 80% of teens say they have been sexually harassed at school. (1993, June 2). Los Angeles Times, in *Salt Lake Tribune*, p. 1A.

Survey finds some people believe rape acceptable. (1988, May 3). *Boulder Daily Camera*, Boulder, CO, p. 1B.

Tavris, C., and Baumgartner, A. (1983, February). How would your life be different if you'd been born a boy? *Redbook*, pp. 7–10.

Taylor, C. (1982). Folk taxonomy and justice in Dade County, Florida. *Anthropological Research Group Newsletter*, 4(1–2), p. 9.

Terman, L. M. (1916). *The Measurement of Intelligence*. New York: Houghton Mifflin.

Thayer, S. (1988, March). Close encounters. *Psychology Today*, pp. 31–36.

Thomas, L. (1990, December). In my next life, I'll be white. *Ebony*, p. 82.

Thrasher, F. (1927). *The Gang: A Study of 1,313 Gangs in Chicago*. Chicago: University of Chicago Press.

Time to retire the "Stars and Bars." (1993, October 31). (Editorial), *The Daily Spectrum*, Iron County, UT, p. D1.

Tocqueville, A. de (1945). *Democracy in America*, Vol. 2 (P. Bradley, Ed.). New York: Knopf.

Torrey, E. F. (1988). *Nowhere to Go: The Tragic Odyssey of the Homeless Mentally Ill*. New York: Harper & Row.

Toufexis, A. (1993, December 30). A mass murderer's journey toward madness. *Time*, p. 30.

Tourist describes burning. (1993, September 4). AP, in *The Daily Spectrum*, Iron County, UT, p. A3.

Turner, J., Singleton, R., and Musick, D. (1984). *Oppression: A Sociohistory of Black-White Relations in America*. Chicago: Nelson Hall.

Twenty-five percent of children under age 6 live below poverty line. (1990, April 16). *Deseret News*, Salt Lake City, UT, p. 2.

Unemployment rate called worst in 8 years. (1993, January 10). AP, in *The Daily Spectrum*, Iron County, UT, p. A1.

U.S. Attorney and the Attorney General of the United States. (1989). *Drug Trafficking: A Report to the President of the United States*. Washington, DC: U.S. Department of Justice.

U.S. Bureau of the Census. (1991). *Current Population Reports*, Series P-20, No. 449, *The Hispanic Population in the United States: March 1990*. Washington, DC: U.S. Government Printing Office.

U.S. Bureau of the Census. (1992). *Current Population Reports, The Hispanic Population in the United States: March 1990.* Washington, DC: U.S. Government Printing Office.

U.S. Department of Housing and Urban Development. (1984). *A Report to the Secretary on the Homeless.* Washington, DC.

U.S. Department of Justice. (1993, January 4). *FBI Uniform Crime Reporting.* Federal Bureau of Investigation. Washington, DC: U.S. Government Printing Office.

Usdansky, M. (1992, May 29). "Diverse" fits nation better than "normal." *USA Today,* pp. 1A, 2A.

Usdansky, M. (1993, September 16). College doesn't close blacks' pay gap. *USA Today,* p. A3.

Weagel, W. (1984). The use of lethal force by police: The effect of statutory change. *Crime & Delinquency,* 30, pp. 121–140.

Weitzman, L., Eifler, D., Hokada, E., and Ross, C. (1993). Sex-role socialization in picture books for preschool children. In K. Finsterbusch and J. Swartz (Eds.), *Sources,* pp. 51–59. Guilford, CT: Dushkin.

Wheeler, S., Mann, K., and Sarat, A. (1988). *Sitting in Judgment: The Sentencing of White-Collar Criminals.* New Haven, CT: Yale University Press.

White, J. (1993, May 17). Growing up black and white. *Time,* pp. 48–49.

White, W. F. (1919, October). Chicago and its eight reasons. *The Crisis,* pp. 293, 295, 297.

Whites' myths about blacks. (1992, November 9). *US News & World Report,* pp. 41, 43–44.

Why skin color suddenly is a big issue again. (1992, March). *Ebony,* pp. 120–122.

Williams, J., Vernon, J., Williams, M., and Malecha, K. (1993). Sex-role socialization in picture books: An update. In K. Finsterbusch and J. Schwartz (Eds.), *Sources: Notable Selections in Sociology.* Guilford, CT: Dushkin.

Willock, J. (1993, April). On the basis of race . . . State University of New York, Buffalo. The Spectrum, in *National College Magazine,* p. 6.

Willwerth. (1993). A museum of hate. *Time,* vol. 142, no. 21, p. 54.

Wolfgang, M., and Riedel, M. (1973). Race, judicial discretion, and the death penalty. *Annals of the American Academy of Political and Social Science,* 407, pp. 119–133.

Wright, L. (1993, April 30). Homemakers are all work and no pay, and U. economist says that's not OK. *Salt Lake Tribune,* pp. A1, A2.

Yates, D. L. (1984). Correlates of Attitudes toward the Police: A Comparison of Black and White Citizens in Austin, Texas. Unpublished Ph.D. dissertation, University of Texas at Austin, Austin, Texas.

Yates, D., and Pillai, V. (1992). Public policy and black inequality: A critical review of the 1980s. *Indian Journal of American Studies,* 22(1).

Yllo, K. A., and Straus, M. A. (1990). Patriarchy and violence against wives: The impact of structural and normative factors. In M. A. Straus and R. J. Gelles (Eds.), *Physical Violence in American Families: Risk Factors and Adaptations to Violence in 8,145 Families,* pp. 383–399. New Brunswick, NJ: Transaction.

Zangwill, I. (1908). *The Melting-Pot: A Drama in Four Acts.* New York: Macmillan.

Zeman, N., Meyer, M., and Osborn, S. (1992, November 23). No "special rights" for gays. *Newsweek,* p. 32.

Index

Acquired immunodeficiency syndrome (AIDS), 130
African Americans; *see also* Slavery
  Brown v. Board of Education, 31, 50, 125
  civil rights movement, 31
  deterioration of family, 90–92
  Dred Scott decision, 50
  firearm homicides among young males, 106*t*
  Plessy v. Ferguson, 50
  prenatal care, 23
  psychiatric misdiagnosis, 97
  school curriculum, 136–137
  whites' view on, 61–62
AIDS (acquired immunodeficiency syndrome), 130
America First movement, 268
American Dream mythology, 16, 99, 271–273
American Nazi Party, 24
Anthropology, racism of
  behavioral inferences, 74–76
  Paul Broca, 72–74, 73*t*
  character inferences, 74–76
  Carleton Coon, 69–70
  cultural inferiority theory, 68–69
  culture of poverty, 68–69, 87, 90–91

Anthropology, racism of (*cont.*)
  Oscar Lewis, 68–69, 90
  L. Hamilton McCormick, 74–76
  Samuel George Morton, 71–73, 72*t*
  racial inferiority theory
    based on brain size, 70–72
    based on evolution, 69–70
  sexual inferiority theory, 70–74, 73*t*
Anti-Semitism, 21, 23–24, 53–54
Aryan Nations, 24, 25*f*, 250
Aryan Resistance, 61

Banfield, Edward, 87–90, 89*t*
Behavior
  inferences based on lips and skin color, 74–76
  learned: *see* Socialization
Benally, Brenda, interview with, 162–168
Biological determinism: *see* Social Darwinism
Blaming the victim, 3–4
Brain size, studies of, 71–74, 72*t*, 73*t*
Broca, Paul, 72–74, 73*t*
Brown v. Board of Education, 31, 50, 125

305